KIDNAPPED

KIDNAPPED

A DIARY OF MY 373 DAYS
IN CAPTIVITY

LESZLI KÁLLI

Translated by Kristina Cordero

ATRIA BOOKS

New York London Toronto Sydney

ATRIA BOOKS

1230 Avenue of the Americas
New York, NY 10020

Originally published in Spanish in 2000 by Planeta Colombiana
Editorial S.A.

Translation by Kristina Cordero

This work is a memoir. It reflects the author's recollections
of her experiences over a period of years. Certain names and
identifying characteristics have been changed. Some events
have been compressed.

Library of Congress Cataloging-in-Publication Data
Kálli, Leszli, date.
[Secuestrada]
Kidnapped: a diary of my 373 days in captivity / Leszli Kálli ; trans-
lated by Kristina Cordero.—1st. Atria Books trade paperback ed.
p. cm.
Translation of: Secuestrada.
Originally published in Spanish in 2000 by Planeta Colombiana
Editorial.
1. Kálli, Leszli, 1980—Kidnapping, 1999. 2. Kidnapping—
Colombia. 3. Kidnapping victims—Colombia—Diaries. I. Title.
HV6604.C72K3518 2007
986.106'35092—dc22
[B] 2006049298

ISBN-13: 978-0-7432-9131-6
ISBN-10:   0-7432-9131-X

First Atria Books trade paperback edition February 2007

1   3   5   7   9   10   8   6   4   2

For information about special discounts for bulk purchases,
please contact Simon & Schuster Special Sales at
1-800-456-6798 or business@simonandschuster.com.

For my family and the very special people
who live on in my heart

The majority of the drawings in this book are by Leszli Kálli, and are from the original pages of the diary she kept while in captivity, with the exception of those on pages 129 and 252, which are the work of one of the guerrilla soldiers who spent time in captivity with Leszli and her fellow hostages.

KIDNAPPED

THE DIARY OF LESZLI KÁLLI

IN THE MOUNTAINS OF COLOMBIA

Thursday, March 25, 1999

Today, for the first time, I opened the Bible in search of advice. My aunt always does this; she says the Bible sends us messages. This is her method: she opens the Bible, flips to a page, any page, and places her finger on a passage at random and interprets the message contained in the words she reads. This is what I have done today, and this is my "message": *I know thy works. Behold, I have set before thee an open door, and no man can shut it. For thou hast a little strength, and hast kept My word, and hast not denied My name.* (Revelations 6:8–9). With all my heart I hope that the "door" is my trip to Israel. Can this be the message I have been sent? Thank you, God.

Wednesday, April 7, 1999

I haven't written here for a little while, because I was waiting for something to happen, something different. I guess I was hoping for some kind of change because right now my life is so dull, so boring. I get so angry when I look around me and am reminded, yet again, that nothing ever happens to me. Today, however, something has finally changed.

Firstly and most important, I am going to Israel. For how long? I don't know, but all I can say is that I am overjoyed; everything worked

1

out and today I bought my plane ticket from Madrid to Tel Aviv. Today is Wednesday and I am leaving this coming Monday.

Dear friend, please forgive me for not regaling you with all the stupid details of what is going on in my life, but I figured I would only bore you with my stories. Dear God, You and I will always be together, in this life and in any other. You will always be my innermost being, my "self." Even if or when these pages come to an end, You will always be inside of me. The most wonderful thing about having You at my side is that with You all my fears, all my doubts vanish. I know this is true because You are my creation—I have created You, or who knows? Maybe I just allow You to exist. Between us there is no need for goodbyes, and knowing that is a comfort to me. From now on, I will tell You all sorts of new stories about the things going on in my life. The next time I write to You I will be in Israel. Today I will be packing my bag and rest assured, You will be right there at my side. I love You. Leszli.

Wednesday, May 17, 1999

What happened, Leszli? Just when everything was going so well, just when you allowed yourself to feel happy that things were finally coming together, that the doors were finally opening . . . My God, what happened? Why did everything suddenly go black? Why didn't anyone stop to ask me what I thought of all this? I almost can't believe it: I should be in the middle of a kibbutz, telling you what a good time I'm having, telling you how grateful I feel that I have been given the gift of turning my dreams into reality . . . but no. Here I am, writing to you now, still in Colombia, a hostage of the Ejército de Liberación Nacional [ELN, National Liberation Army], in the middle of the jungle, a place that in many ways is much farther from home than Israel.

It all happened so fast that even now, a month later, I still have trouble believing it, and I have to tell myself over and over again:

Leszli, you have been kidnapped.

Dear diary, my one consolation is the knowledge that you are still with me, as always. You can't believe how strange it is for me to write to you from this place. Actually, I have had to start a new notebook, because the rest of you is back with my suitcase, and here I am, starting a new page in a new diary. I couldn't take you with me in my carry-on bag: it was so crammed full of things that there was no way to fit you in, and since the blue suitcase was so huge, they didn't let me bring it on board, and off it went into the baggage compartment. Please forgive me; I imagine they must have read you by now.

You are and will be the only vehicle I have for expressing my feelings. The last time I wrote you I was free, and for a long time I didn't write at all because I figured you were as bored as I was with my empty, monotonous life. And so I swore I wouldn't write again until something worthwhile happened to me.

From this point on I am going to tell you everything. Every last detail I can remember will go down on paper, now that (thank God!) I actually found a piece of paper, and am able to write some kind of summary of my days and nights since April 12.

In brief, this is the story: last year I received a kind of proposal from one of Salvador's friends to visit a kibbutz in Israel. It sounded like an incredible plan—for a long, long time I had been wanting to go on some kind of adventure. I wanted to do something that would allow me to break free from the hellish, boring routine that my life had become.

As you know, every weekend I would get together with my girlfriends to go out to the latest "hot spot," but inside it all made me feel so empty. My life went on like that until the end of December, which is when I got serious about this idea. From that moment on, I put all my energy toward turning it into a reality—I even held raffles to raise money because at home we weren't in the best shape, financially speaking. The one good thing was that at least my flights were free, because my father is an airline pilot, and wherever his airline goes, I can travel for free. The one bad thing, though, was that my father wasn't very keen on the idea of me going to Israel—the thought of me, the apple of his eye, his pretty little girl, all alone at the other end of the earth . . . he hated the whole thing. At first he said no outright—it was a crazy plan, no way would he support it, he said. The best thing I could do, he said, was go to college and forget all about the trip. Every time he said it, though, it only made me want to go more, because that's the way I am. I have always been rebellious that way.

After thinking it over, I told him that all I needed from him was his permission and the plane tickets from Bucaramanga to Bogotá and Bogotá to Madrid. Nothing else. The rest of the trip would be my problem to deal with. Well, mine and my mother's—my mom had promised to help me with everything else; she's always supported me in things like that, in everything.

I pulled everything together, but two weeks before the trip, I started having dark, dark dreams. It's odd, I've always felt that dreams have this strange way of predicting things that might happen . . .

Anyway, though, my bags were packed, my tickets were ready, my dollars saved up, and all I wanted was to get started on my big adventure in Israel. Once I was done with the kibbutz, I planned to spend a few days in Egypt and Greece, two countries I had always dreamed of visiting. People had told me how to swing it so that it wouldn't be too expensive. Then, when it was all over, I would come back to Colombia to do the sensible thing and start college here. What more could I ask of life? Every night I prayed to God, asking him to help me achieve this goal that meant so much to me.

On the night of April 11, I had a long talk with my mother. Among the many things we discussed, a comment slipped out:

"Mommy, I'm scared," I told her.

"Leszli, that's not like you," she said. " I've never seen you scared. Now I'm worried. "

"Oh, no, no, forget it," I said, to calm her down. "I don't know why I said that. It must be the jitters—you know, normal pre-trip jitters."

On the day of my trip, I woke up at 5 A.M., and said goodbye to my older brother Nandor, who was working at a hospital. His shift started at 6 A.M. He hugged me and said, "Take care, honey."

After I showered and got dressed, I sat down and talked for a little while with my mother and my sister Carolina. The plan was that my father would fly with me to Bogotá, where he would put me on the plane that was scheduled to leave for Madrid that same night at 7:05 P.M. Our flight to Bogotá was scheduled for 2 that afternoon.

We were sitting in the living room when the phone rang. It was my father.

"Hi, sweetheart. Listen, we're going to have to leave earlier. The 2:00 flight was canceled. Are you ready?"

"Yes, I'm ready."

"All right, sweetheart. I'm on my way, then."

I said goodbye to my mother and my grandmother, and went downstairs. My sister was coming with us to the airport; she would bring the car back home after we took off. My mother didn't come with us; she and my father were divorced in 1986 and, as you know, they can't stand to be in the same room together.

Once we had picked up my father and we were on our way to the Bucaramanga airport, my father said:

"Sweetheart, you know I think this trip is really a bad idea, everything was arranged so quickly and . . . I don't know . . . I just don't think you should go, there have been so many obstacles along the way, and I can't help but think that it means this just isn't the right thing for you to do."

I laughed out loud at that.

"Oh, come on, Dad! Are you kidding?"

We pulled up at the airport. As we sat around waiting in the cafeteria, he said it again, much more seriously this time.

"Listen, Leszli, there's still time to turn around."

"I'd say you turned around and went crazy, that's what I'd say!"

We checked in, and they gave me my seat assignment: 12F. My father would be next to me in 12C.

I could hardly believe it. There I was, sitting in a Fokker aircraft, on an Avianca flight from Bucaramanga to Bogotá. I had pulled it off after planning the entire thing in record time. Finally my trip was becoming a reality. I gazed out the window, content. The seats next to me were empty. The plane took off and the first thing I did was look out the window and up at the sky, to have a silent conversation with God: *Thank you, God,* I said. *Finally this is truly happening. Thank you so much.*

That day I would leave South America, and the following day I would leave Europe and land in the north of Africa. From there, I would head out to a kibbutz in the Golan Heights in Israel. I was happy, so happy, even though I had had to say goodbye to my mother and my sister Carol. We didn't cry, but they knew how I felt, and anyway, at that moment there was nothing anyone could have done to stop me—no matter how much my father harped on and on about how poorly the trip had been planned, that he had been wracked with nightmares, that he had a bad feeling about the whole thing. He had actually suggested we go to our apartment in Cartagena. There, he said, I could think about it a little more, and at least plan it all a little better—after all, how could it be that just yesterday on the internet I had found the place I would be staying once I arrived in Tel Aviv, just like that? It was all too crazy, he said. And I replied that yes, maybe it was crazy, but there was nothing in the world he could do to make me change my mind. No way, I said, no matter what anyone said. Oh, God, if only I had listened . . .

My father sat down three rows ahead of me to discuss something with someone else who was also going to Bogotá that day, a union organizer who had once been a copilot of his. My father, an aviation commander, wanted to know how the talks were going between the airline and the pilots, and they sat together talking as the plane took off. My father was actually traveling that day for two reasons: one, to take me to Bogotá, to see if on the way he could get me to change my mind about the trip. If he didn't, he would deposit me on the plane bound for Madrid and introduce me to the crew and ask them to help me out if I needed it once we were in Spain. Dressed up in his pilot's uniform, he would help me navigate the labyrinth of El Dorado, the Bogotá airport. The second reason he came with me was that after dropping me off he needed to fly to Cartagena, his base of operations as a pilot. He had to go to the Naval Hospital there to get them to sign some release papers for him. A few months earlier he had fractured his hand in an accident, and he needed the hospital to sign off so that he could get back to work.

As the plane's engines began to whir, I felt a wave of joy come over me, and I looked out onto the runway and the surrounding fields, idly wondering about the Israeli desert and the people at the kibbutz.

What were they like? How would they welcome me? What kind of work would they give me? I sat there, wrapped up in my thoughts for a while, until the sound of the motors and the plane taking off brought me back to reality, and then suddenly we were in the air. Little by little the houses and the trees grew smaller and smaller, and the happiness I felt was complete. Serene and profoundly moved by the experience, I pulled out the in-flight magazine from the seat pocket in front of me, and after a few minutes I emerged from my reverie as I heard the little beep go off, letting us know that the seat belt sign had been turned off and that we could move about the cabin. Instinctively I looked up and saw that, yes, the announcement had been made, and I watched as several people immediately got up from their seats. The first thing I thought was that a fight must have erupted between a couple of passengers, because a man suddenly put on a hood and pointed a pistol at the head of one of the flight attendants. Then, another man a bit further back got up and came over to sit down next to me. He stayed there for the rest of the flight. Right then, at the very same time, three other men opened the overhead luggage bins, removed some black scarves, and placed them over their heads.

I was stunned. The thoughts running through my head were chaotic, disjointed—those scarves were ski masks and, good God . . . first I was stunned and then I felt paralyzed, totally paralyzed as I watched each of them pull out huge silver pistols. One of the men up front went to the cockpit and another one, a stocky man with a husky voice and an accent that I will never forget, straight out of the Colombian mountains, took control of the plane. What is going on? I don't understand . . . am I imagining this? I tried to catch a glimpse of my father, but I couldn't see him from where I was sitting. Right then the man who had commandeered the plane began to speak.

"Attention," he announced to the passengers. "Put your hands on the back of the seat in front of you, keep your heads down, and your eyes on the floor." He paused for a moment, and then continued:

"We are members of the United Self-Defense Forces of Colombia, and we are transferring one of our commanders to one of our regions. Once he disembarks, you will be able to resume your flight to Bogotá. Do what you are told and everything will be fine. I don't want anyone here to try and play hero, because it won't work and we don't want anybody to get hurt."

That was about when I started to panic: I was petrified that my father would get up, to come back to my seat and calm me down, which would make them think he was playing hero, and then they would shoot him on the spot. I looked around me, and the man who had taken control of the plane signaled for me to approach him. The other hijacker, the one who had sat down next to me, said to me, "Honey, they're calling you over."

I stood up and walked five paces, but then the man in control suddenly yelled out, "No! Sit in your seat and keep your head down!"

I spun around and raced back to my seat. The man next to me, who could feel how terrified I was, turned to me and whispered, "Relax, honey, nothing's going to happen to you."

"But it's my father, he's up front, please don't do anything to him. He may get up to come over here," I said. In a gentle tone of voice, my seatmate once again told me not to worry.

"Sir, are you going to take us out of the country?" I asked, taking advantage of the moment to ask him a question. He looked at me as if to say, "Boy have you got an imagination," and then replied, "No, honey, we're going to land and then you're going to keep going."

He rested his hand on the seat in front of him. It was a thin, sweaty, trembling hand.

As I turned to look at the people around me, I could see the anguish in their faces, and I heard whispers, groans, gasps. One woman in my row, on the other side of the aisle, began to cry. At that moment I heard my father's voice calling out to me, telling me to stay calm and not to move, that everything would be fine, and that I didn't have to worry about him; he was fine. In response I yelled out that he didn't have to worry about me—it wasn't me crying. I was all right, I said, and I would stay right where I was. Hearing him speak in such a serene voice calmed me down somewhat, because I had been worried about him, worried that the hijackers would think he was a naval officer, since their uniforms look a lot like pilots' uniforms.

Diary, you know I wear reading glasses, and I was wearing them right then. But I was thinking about the wad of dollars in my bag—it was all the money I had saved up for my trip, and I wanted to get to it before it was too late. So I turned to the man next to me and asked him if I could put away my glasses, because I didn't want them to shatter while we landed: if they broke while I was wearing them, I said, I could end up with glass in my eyes. He said fine. Quickly, I opened my bag, stuck my glasses inside and removed the envelope with all my dollars, and stuffed it in my pocket. That was my one and only reaction at that moment.

Soon enough, the plane's ascent tapered off and we slowly started to lose altitude. Through the window I watched the plane glide over a broad river. Once we reached the far shore, the plane suddenly made a deafening noise and I watched the landing gear come down just as we made our final descent. As we hovered just above the treetops, the plane continued down, down until finally we were on the ground. The landing was surprisingly smooth—"like butter," as they say, though the plane did get splattered with gobs of mud, and as we slowly decelerated, the motors whirred louder and louder and the poor Fokker airplane buried itself deeper and deeper in the muck. At one point the plane almost came to a full stop, and tried to turn around as if to go back in the other direction, but something was stuck and the plane didn't budge an inch after that, no matter how hard the pilot tried: he accelerated as hard as those turbines would let him, but it was completely useless. Shortly after that, the plane came to a halt, accompanied by a thunderous noise as the two engines died down. Immediately the hijackers opened the doors and the man up front, the one who seemed to be a kind of team leader, grabbed the other man in an embrace, and they both began shouting: "We did it! We did it!"

After they finished congratulating one another, they told us that we would have to leave all our things on the plane; all we could take with us were our IDs, which we were to hand over to the person in charge of the hijacking. One by one we got up. My father waited for me to reach him so that we could disembark together, and when I finally made it over to where he was, he asked me, "Are you okay?"

"Yes," I said. "What about you?"

"I'm okay. Let's get out here now, and see what this is all about."

Together we walked toward the exit door, handed over our IDs, and deplaned. The men who had overtaken the plane were still jumping around and cheering the hijacker with the hoarse voice, congratulating him on his triumph. At that moment, I was still unable to feel rage; I was too frightened by the scenario that had suddenly unfolded before my eyes, and everything had happened so quickly that my mind was unable to process the difference between an event that for some was pure happiness, and for others, an exercise in pure humiliation. The one thing I did feel, quite rapidly, was the dramatically different temperature and climate in this part of the country, a suffocating heat and humidity that enveloped me in seconds, disconnecting me entirely from the hijackers' celebration. The heat in Magdalena Medio, the region where we landed, is absolutely insufferable: your clothes cling to your body all day long, and that day in particular the sun was shining with a vengeance.

My father and I got in line behind the other passengers who had gotten off before us and were now walking along the landing strip. As we could now experience firsthand, the plane had been virtually immobilized by the mud in which it had landed—the landing strip was a river of muck that made walking a serious challenge. As you took a step, your entire shoe would sink into the muck, and you had to really work to lift it out again. I was wearing sneakers, thank God; the ladies in high heels and sandals had it much worse than me, and some of them decided to just take their shoes off and walk barefoot. It was much easier for them that way, though it was awful all the same because nobody is used to walking in mud like that, not even the poorest farmworkers. If a bunch of farmworkers had seen us like that, I'm sure they would have felt pretty bad for us, but the people watching over us right then were far from a bunch of farmworkers: they were men and women in uniforms, without insignias or anything distinctive to identify them, and they were all standing at attention along either side of the mud path. It was as if they had come together to create a kind of walk of fame for us: some of them had cameras and were actually filming us as they smiled from ear to ear, proud of the incredible feat that had been pulled off that day. Never in my life have I ever felt as bizarre as I did at that moment, with people recording me as if I were a piece of merchandise to be negotiated at some later point. It was all so strange, and I have to say that it was on this day that I truly learned the meaning of the word "humiliation."

All of a sudden, a shot rang out behind us. We all froze in our tracks and then turned around to see what was happening: one of the men standing near the plane called out an apology, saying he had fired his gun by accident. Nothing to worry about, he said, just keep on walking and don't turn around. I asked my father if he thought they would be able to get the plane out of the mud in time for us to resume the flight, but he said no—they would need special equipment to clear all the mud off the landing strip. Then he told me not to worry about that. We kept on walking. At that point I still believed what they had told us, that they were dropping off one of their commanders and that in a little while we would be continuing on to Bogotá. How naïve I was . . .

"What is all this?" I asked my father.

"Leszli," he said, "this is a kidnapping."

"But Dad, who are these people?"

"They're guerrillas, sweetheart, but I don't know which ones, they aren't wearing any kind of identification." As he said this, he glanced at the people around him within earshot, and from the expression on his face I could see he didn't want me to ask any more questions. Even if he had been able to tell me what guerrilla group they belonged to, I wouldn't have understood anything. Back then, I would have had to ask my father what a guerrilla was, that was how little I knew about this sort of thing. After that we didn't talk anymore. We didn't have to; our faces alone expressed a thousand unspoken, anguish-filled words as we trudged silently down the rest of that miserable, muck-filled track, our ankles aching from the effort and our lack of experience in that terrain. At the end of the long walk one of the men guided us in a decent, if slightly hurried, tone of voice:

"This way, please," he indicated, pointing us toward an immense swamp surrounded by tall grass that looked like sugarcane. In front of us I could see one of the other passengers in jacket and tie, submerged up to his chest in the yellowish marsh water, holding his arms up in an effort to keep at least some part of him dry, even if it was just his shirtsleeves. There was a very disoriented little old woman who had been traveling under the special care of the crew because of her delicate condition and age. As I watched her cross the swamp, accompanied by two of the men in uniform, I could hear her complain about how much Bogotá had changed, and how the El Dorado airport had really deteriorated.

Two big canoes with outboard motors were waiting for us at the edge of a gently rushing river about twenty meters wide. Several uniformed men helped us onto the boats so that we wouldn't lose our balance, guiding us toward the middle of the boat, which was less dangerous than at the edges or over the crossbar. Each canoe could hold about twenty people, if we sat face-to-face with our backs against the sides. The boats were like huge bananas sliced down the middle with all the fruit scooped out. On the floor there was about an inch of dirty water, a mix of mud, gasoline, and black oil. With no other choice, we all sat down in the muck, and I felt terrible for all those nice clothes getting dirty. So many of us wear our nicest outfits when we travel on airplanes, to look nice for the flight and when we arrive at our destination, and now all our pretty clothes would be soiled beyond repair from all that slop and slime, but there was nothing to be done about it.

The river landscape was very flat. Someone pointed out an alligator in the water, but other people said it was just a tree trunk. The strange thing, though, was that this tree trunk, some ten meters away from the boat, didn't move an inch despite the water rushing all around it. Once we were all settled down, the men got to work starting the motor, and they yanked at it at least seven times before it finally took, at which point we began traveling upstream. Eventually, we reached a fork in the river and the boat veered toward the right and started rocking back and forth as it made its way through the spot where the two streams converged. Immediately one of the men called out, "Don't move. Just sit tight, stay calm, and the boat won't turn over." We followed his orders and, just as he said, the boat stabilized. A bit further up we came to another fork, and then another and then another—so many that I began to think we were lost, because it couldn't be very easy to navigate down those intricate waterways. I turned to my father and asked him what river we were on, and he said that it was a tributary of the Magdalena, which, in these parts, splinters off into a kind of delta that eventually catches up with the Magdalena at various points further on.

As we sailed past thickets of trees with trunks growing straight out of the water, we had to lower our heads to avoid getting scratched by the branches. At some point they turned off the motor and the man steering the boat apologized and said that something wasn't working—he should have brought another motor, he said, but he hadn't. Then he pulled out a tool kit and started working on the motor, blowing on it and drying something with his shirt, as the boat began to drift in the current. My father couldn't help laughing, and said, "I can't believe it. Here they are, they just pulled off this incredible stunt, and now this motor's going to conk out and ruin it for them!" We all laughed at that.

I was desperately thirsty after the long walk, the heat, and now these technical difficulties, but my father warned me not to drink the water because it might have amoebas. Try and hang on just a little longer, he told me. He didn't think we were going to stay on the river for much longer, because the motor was so small. After a little while one of the men in uniform handed me a glass bottle of water, but I could see that the yellowish water inside was from the river. I thanked him but declined. Meanwhile, to kill time, the rest of us, the passengers, started talking about our lives, why we were going to Bogotá, things like that. My father, in his pilot's uniform, was clearly the most senior of all the crew members with us, in both age and rank, and the other passengers started asking him what he thought this was all about. Based on his common sense and plane experience, he said he thought it was some kind of hijacking, one that had been planned quite carefully, quite far in advance, and with a fair amount of money, too. None of this came cheap, my father said, and for that reason he could only assume it was a large-scale kidnapping that could end up in one of two ways: either our families would be expected to come up with some kind of ransom money, or else it was an operative directed against the government or the airline, Avianca. I, for one, was still thinking about my trip to the kibbutz—it couldn't go wrong, it just couldn't. . . . But at the same time I couldn't see how on earth it was going to happen now, because there was no telling how long we would be stuck in this situation. So I asked my father how much time he thought all this was going to take.

He stared at me for a few long moments and then said, "Listen, I would be a million times happier if you were on your way to Israel right now, but I think you're going to have to let go of that idea." Given the magnitude of the undertaking, he felt that it looked like we were in for a minimum of six months.

"Dad! Six months? You're crazy, that's impossible. I don't believe it. You've got to be exaggerating. Oh my God, that's a long time. . . ." As I said this, the boat began to approach the shore, where there was a little peasant hut with a thatched roof. Parked next to the house were about four or five Toyota trucks, and more people, all of them wearing army-style uniforms, with rounds of ammunition stuffed into belts that hung over their shoulders and crisscrossed their chests. Grenades and tiny rockets with little wings dangled from their belt loops, and huge machine guns hung from their shoulders. They also carried pistols and knives, and as if that weren't enough, in their hands they each held a huge weapon with a wooden handle and a tripod to make it easier to carry. As my mind absorbed the spectacle before me, I began to panic. My father sensed the anguish that I and all the other passengers felt, and he smiled calmly and said, "Hmm, I guess we'd better be on good behavior around here." We all tittered a little and began to climb off the boat.

Despite everything, I have to say that the people in charge were exceedingly polite to us throughout this part of the ordeal. As we disembarked, we gathered in little groups on one side of a wooden cattle fence—the uniformed men on one side, the rest of us on the other. I suppose we did that instinctively, as a way of giving one another the support we needed right then. The uniformed men offered us crackers, soft drinks, and cigarettes. Some of the women asked to go to the bathroom, and they pointed us toward a kind of latrine: four walls made of wooden planks with four-centimeter spaces between each plank. Anyone who peered into that "bathroom" from the outside could easily see the people inside, but since it was all we had, we just dealt with it. Instinctively, the women gravitated together there, and we organized ourselves into little protective groups: whoever didn't have to go to the bathroom right then guarded the area for those who did, in a gesture of female solidarity. At one point, though, I turned around and remarked to my father that this was awfully uncomfortable for everyone. But he just looked at me and said, "It could be worse."

He was right. It could have been worse: what if we had had to go to the bathroom out on the boat, all of us trapped out on the water? Here, at least, we had the space to walk around and look for a secluded spot off somewhere, where nobody else could see us. And anyway, for the moment, at least, they were showing some respect for our privacy and that was a good sign. Naturally I hoped it would stay this way until our release, but I also knew that their attitude toward us would depend on the trust we managed to establish with them. That was a little advantage we could hold on to.

After that, I walked over to the jeeps, to get good seats for me and my father—somewhere up front, where it would be more comfortable. I went over to him and told him that I had found us good spots, but out of loyalty to the other passengers, or maybe just stupidity, my father said that he had already found a spot in another jeep and that he was going to go over to guard it until they called out his name. According to my father, that was the best strategy. Strategy? I wondered. With his hand in that condition? Well, if he wanted to stay behind with the others in another jeep, more power to him. I climbed into my front-seat spot, looked around, and called out to a woman nearby, "Come up, come up. I was saving you a spot." It was a lie, of course, since I'd really been saving the place for my dad, but the lady very graciously thanked me for the kind gesture, and once we were out on the road, in between lots of moans and groans, she told me that she had been operated on very recently—so recently in fact that the doctors still hadn't removed her stitches. She was afraid that her incision would burst from all the bumps in the road. Poor thing. There I was, thinking about my father's sore hand, and here was this woman who was much, much worse off. In the end, I was glad that my father had gone in the back with the others: thanks to him I was able to give this nice lady a more comfortable seat up front.

Sitting up front with the driver, I could see my father in the back, perched on one of the wooden planks that ran from one side of the jeep to the other. Just as we started moving ahead of the other vehicles, he signaled to me that he was all right. Once out on the road, we went at a pretty reasonable speed given the terrain, and after a while we turned onto another road that was wide and perfectly straight, a well-maintained, flat road as far as I could tell. There, the driver really hit the gas, more and more and more until finally we were going so fast that we begged him to please slow down a little, because all of us were bouncing up and down like crazy, scared to death he was going to kill us. But he just said that he was following orders, that he had been instructed to get down the road as quickly as possible, because if the army sent helicopters out to look for us, they would blast us without a second thought.

"What do you mean 'blast us'?" I asked, to which the driver replied, "It means to open fire with a round of huge machine-gun bullets." Then he said that I was better off not knowing what it meant, because if it actually came to pass we would all end up a bunch of rag dolls. I deduced that "rag dolls" meant we would be killed. I thought about my father again, and cursed myself for not making him ride up front with me.

I asked the driver if the radio was working.

"I don't know," he said.

"Well, let's try it out," I suggested. He said nothing, so I turned the radio on and that was when I heard the news report announcing that an Avianca plane had disappeared en route from Bucaramanga to Bogotá. According to the report, the plane had lost contact with the tower, and had gone missing at 10 A.M. that morning. I glanced down at my watch: it was 12:30 in the afternoon. Instantly I thought of my mother: poor thing, she and my brother and sister must think we're dead.

The driver pulled over to talk to some people standing at the edge of the road. As he did this, I called out to my father, telling him about the news report I'd just heard, and said I would keep him informed.

After two or three minutes, we got back on the road, and as the driver resumed his breakneck speed, we whizzed past several farmhouses where people with sympathetic looks on their faces watched us go by, gazing at us just the way you (or at least I) might gaze at a truck full of cows on the way to the slaughterhouse, staring straight through those bars into their eyes, into those sad faces that seem to perceive the tragedy that awaits them. Did we have the same look in our eyes at that moment?

I noticed that all along the road, someone had placed rags on the welcome signs in every town, just at the part where the town's name appeared. Oh, right: they didn't want us to know wherever the hell we were. Far off in the distance, I could make out the sight of the eastern mountain range, somewhere near the place where we had landed. Suddenly, from behind, the guerrillas yelled to the driver to stop: they had seen a white helicopter flying overhead and they wanted to shoot it down. Instantly I started to panic, terrified that we were going to become victims of the aforementioned blast of machine-gun fire. The truck behind us sped up and pulled over alongside us to find out why we'd stopped, and when the men in our jeep shouted that they were going to bring the helicopter down, my father pointed out that the helicopter was flying at three thousand feet, maybe more, and that they'd never be able to reach it. They would be wasting both time and ammunition if they tried, he told them. In the middle of all this, someone shouted, "Step on it, brother—come on, today!"

At that the driver resumed the intense journey, faster than ever this time, but neither I nor the older woman next to me dared utter a word in protest. On the contrary—we wanted him to drive as fast as he could out of there. We were relieved when they finally decided not to try to shoot down the helicopter, but the entire episode was extremely nerve-wracking all the same, and we just wanted out. Somewhere farther up the road, the driver slowed down to make a left turn onto another road. On that road, we approached a series of gently rolling hills that, up close, turned out to be not so gentle at all, and we had to struggle to make our way up. First, the truck had to cross a perfectly beautiful, crystalline river, and that little stretch turned into a fierce battle between the water, the rocks, and our driver, who pressed hard on the gas, trying to crank every last bit of energy he could from the vehicle's engine. In the middle of all the noise—both from the engine as well as the craggy rocks in the riverbed—the truck went slipping and sliding, ricocheting from one boulder to the other. And us? As we ricocheted violently back and forth, I just clung to the poor woman next to me, who was in excruciating pain from her recent operation.

As we drove up and down those mountains at breakneck speed, in the middle of a road that was barely wide enough for two cars, the driver occasionally pointed out the light green fields on either side of the road.

"Those are coca fields," he would say, before turning back to his diabolical driving. Several times as we careened downhill, the road would turn into a blind curve with a little bridge made of two wooden planks that he would fly over, ignoring our pleas to slow down a little, at least in those dangerous spots. He never once gave in to us. Every so often I saw a uniformed man at the side of the road, observing us as we sped by.

It wasn't until 3 in the afternoon when we finally stopped for a short break on the plateau, where they gave us crackers and bottled juice. The driver had also brought along a pack of cigarettes. Back on the road, we continued on for about another twenty minutes until we reached a series of wooden cabins. We came to a stop and everyone got out, taking advantage of the moment to stretch their legs, and to go to the edge of the road to relieve themselves. There, I walked around, asking if anyone knew who Ana María Gómez was, and a girl around my age said, "Me." I told her that on the radio I had heard her mother, who had said she was extremely worried and that she'd do whatever she was told to do. Other people asked me if I'd heard their names, too, and I said I'd keep listening for them. The uniformed men then announced that we couldn't relieve ourselves there, but it was too late—all of us had already gone to the bathroom. Then they asked us to get back in the trucks, and one of them, a woman, got on with a little dog. Once again we were back on the road, this time for about half an hour more. After driving at light-ning speed down a deep hollow, we finally stopped at a small farm-house with a few wooden huts, some with thatched and others with zinc roofs. There was also a tiny schoolhouse where we went in to rest for a little while.

The schoolhouse had two or three classrooms, a large courtyard, and in the middle there was a big main building with columns and no walls, a cement floor, and a thatched roof. At the far end was a stone fence, and just a little further on I could see a tiny stream. As we slowly recovered from the exhausting journey, some of the passengers started chatting among themselves, and tried to make conversation with the uniformed men. One of "our people"—the passengers, I mean—told us that one of the hijackers had said that they were from the ELN. This meant that they did not have anything to do with the paramilitary group known as the United Self-Defense Forces of Colombia, as they had announced on the airplane, but that they were members of the Ejército de Liberación Nacional [National Liberation Army], also known as the ELN.

In the main house a huge supply of brand-new, thin rubber mat-tresses, still in their original plastic wrappers, awaited us. Outside, they gave us soda, juice, beer, and crackers. At some point in the after-noon I checked my watch, idly wondering if I would ever make it to Bogotá. Right then I realized that my flight to Madrid was about to take off, and that my trip and all my dreams would fly away with it. My father, sensing what was on my mind, came over and said to me, "Yes, sweetie, this is going to be a long haul. There's nothing we can do about it."

That was when I first understood, at least in part, the true mean-ing of the word "impotence."

Later on, our first real meal of the day arrived. How things change, I thought. Looking back, I am sure that if I had written this diary entry that same day instead of today, all I would have said was: "Finally, they gave us food." Without adjectives, for that is what it was: grilled meat, rice, potatoes, spaghetti, and salad. At first I didn't want to eat, but my father came around and said to me: "Do me a favor, please, and eat everything they put on your plate. Who knows whether they're going to feed us this much next time, if they feed us at all. Remember, we've been kidnapped. This isn't a game. You're not at home anymore," he said, in a stern tone of voice, and then walked away.

I wanted to cry, I was so mad. I wasn't hungry, I wasn't hungry at all. The combination of spaghetti and rice was completely revolting to me at that moment, but something in my father's voice told me to do what he said, and he was right. This isn't a game, I told myself, and I sat down to eat. I ate everything. Oh, Leszli, if you had only known that later on they would serve you even more incongruous combinations of food—spaghetti with canned sardines, for one—you would have jumped for joy at that dinner, that marvelous dinner the first day.

After we finished, they gave each of us a bar of soap, a toothbrush, toothpaste, a towel, a flashlight, and mosquito repellent. Oh, those were the days. . . . Nowadays they laugh at us if we ask them for mosquito repellent, and anyway we don't really need it, we're used to the bugs already. Every so often a tired old mosquito will come around and take a bite out of one of us, but that's about it. We're yesterday's news to them at this point.

But anyway, I have to get on with this—if I spend all my time comparing things to the way they were at the beginning, I'll never finish.

A little later on they turned on a small generator, and once it was up and running, they screwed in a little lightbulb at the top of a post, and invited us inside to one of the classrooms—the only room, really—to watch the TV newscasts that were busy reporting our story to the country. On that little television set we watched as the reporters announced that what the authorities had originally assumed was an accident had turned out to be a kidnapping, and though they still weren't sure who was behind it, there was a strong possibility that it was the work of the ELN guerrillas. During the newscast, they broadcast all our names along with individual photographs, and as we watched our faces appear onscreen we all said things like "Oh, my God, there I am," or "Damn, that's me." Oddly enough, five names were not mentioned, and nobody said a word as we all looked around to see the people they had left out. And then, of course, we realized: the kidnappers. Then, when they broadcast some footage of the plane and the place where we landed, it all seemed just too unreal. Never in my life had I imagined that I would end up the main story of an evening newscast! I never used to watch the TV news, and now, watching my name on the screen, in that long list of people . . . it all seemed so strange. After looking at the dark side, I brightened up a little: at least my family—the ones on the "other side," like my mother, Carol, and Nandor—would now know that we weren't dead, that the plane, for better or for worse, had made it to the ground intact.

After the newscast ended, we went back out to the little hut in the patio, where we were told to take a mattress, place it on the floor, and wait as they called us for individual interviews. One of the guerrillas, sitting with a notebook at a little desk, acted as secretary, recording our responses to the questions we were asked by another guerrilla. One by one we went up and gave them our basic information: date and place of birth; home address and telephone number; relatives' names; occupation; company name, address, and telephone number; position; years of service; reason for traveling; health condition. We watched people as they walked away from their interviews, some of them with anguished looks on their faces. Then, finally, our captors told us we could rest and they bid us good night. I didn't hear a single passenger reciprocate with a mutual "good night."

The first person I heard complaining was Juan Manuel Corzo; after his interview he walked over to my father, who was standing around with some crew members and a few other passengers. He said something like, "Man, I got nailed. I really got nailed. I'm a congressman."

Another man piped up and said, "I'm worse off—I'm the manager of Ecogas." Ecogas is an important state-run company. One by one they recounted their woes. Good night? More like Good Anguish.

And it was true. We had all gotten nailed. And we're still hanging.

At 4:45 in the morning, we woke up, rolled off our mattresses, and got dressed and ready. Once again they started questioning us, looking us in the eyes, trying to get to know us. We also heard a snippet of a news report: it seemed that nobody had yet stepped forward to claim responsibility for the kidnapping. It was more or less the same story as the day before. All of us, passengers and crew members alike, gathered together in a big circle, held hands, and prayed. There was nothing left for us to do. Our fate was already sealed.

After a little while they called out to us: "You are going to start walking at 6am. Some of you will travel on mules, others on foot." They turned to me and said, "Leszli, all the mules have been taken. You're going to have to walk."

Right then one of the mules, a wild one, started galloping off like mad, and the man on its back decided he preferred to walk. They offered me his mule, and I accepted. We still hadn't said goodbye to those passengers who, for humanitarian reasons, were being allowed to stay behind—the recently operated woman, the pregnant lady, and the three-month-old baby.

The following hours on the road were long ones: we traveled across rivers, up and down mountains, through valleys, hidden trails, and more places than I am able to remember. The landscape was utterly breathtaking, like something out of a dream.

Finally we reached a little house and went to bed, but we all slept poorly. The next day we all sat around a table and introduced ourselves, in a more official way than we had done before. We talked about where we were from, what we did, the usual introduction stuff.

The food was different this day: this time it was rice and canned ham, with a kind of orangeade, though it was really just water, a lot of water, with the juice of about two oranges and a lot of sugar. But anyway, it tasted something like orangeade.

We settled down into two groups: the women in the best spot and the men everywhere else. That day, while listening to the news on the radio that one of the guerrilla soldiers had brought with him, we saw our first snake: a coral snake, no less. But one of the guerrilla soldiers killed it. That was our second day.

Another day. We woke up early. There was coffee for everyone. We got together and asked the guerrillas if they would please let us wash up, and we went down to a little stream and bathed, the women apart from the men. When we got out we put our clothes on, our skin all wet, and we just had to dry off like that, since we didn't have towels. The soles of my feet were all wrinkled, like they get when you spend a lot of time in the water.

When we reconvened we were given guerrilla boots. They only received one pair in size 38, but we really needed two since Ana María and I are both size 38. I told her to take them, because after all I had my sneakers, and she was wearing sandals. So that's what we did. My sneakers, though, were pretty soaked.

After that we started walking again; it was an exhausting day. I'm not used to walking so much, or riding mules, for that matter, and the terrain was muddy, so the mules kept getting stuck. The people walking had a tough time, too: every time they took a step forward, their boots would sink into the mud, and they would have to grab hold of their legs and yank them out, but their boots would remain trapped in the mud. So then they would have to reach down into the mud with their hands, find their boot, and pull it out. Then they would lose their balance, and bam!, they would fall into the mud and get all dirty. It was a day of sweat, mud, fatigue, and stress, not to mention the thousands of annoying flies buzzing around us all the time. There were so many of them, and they got into everything—our eyes, our mouths, our ears. It was completely unbearable.

Along the way we took breaks: ten minutes to catch our breath, and then back on the path. The guerrillas kept telling us that we had to move fast because we needed to get to a safe place. The Colombian army was already out looking for us, they said, and if they caught up with us there would be a confrontation, which would only make things worse. The entire time we kept asking, "Where are we? Where are we going?" And they just replied, "I don't know, I don't know this area very well." This was very amusing to us, because they always seemed to know exactly where they were going—after all, they were the ones leading the way.

Finally we reached a ramshackle house at the edge of a beautiful river, where we washed off as best we could. By this time we had more or less abandoned the formalities of the previous few days. Ana María Gómez and I became fast friends—we bathed together, ate our meals together, and talked all the time. For better or for worse, I had been kidnapped with my father, but she was all alone and I wanted her to feel that my father and I were there for her, to support her and stick by her.

After listening to the news, we went to sleep. It was incredible: the newscasters had been talking about us and only us for the past 24 hours, since nobody had stepped forward yet to claim responsibility for the hijacking.

In the morning we woke up and ate a breakfast of rice, canned ham, and lemonade, which was more or less like the orangeade they gave us the day before. The guerrillas warned us not to wander around outside very far, because they were worried that a stealth plane might fly overhead and spot us. We all said, "Okay, okay," but after a half hour we were all outside talking again. Because we hadn't followed orders, they rounded us up and made us go up to the mountain, and we had to stay there the entire afternoon. Up there, they brought us our lunch: rice and tuna fish. They hadn't brought any plates or forks, so they served us our food on leaves that they ripped off big trees and bushes, and we had to eat with our hands. Between us, we only had one spoon, and nobody felt much like waiting around for their turn to eat with that one piece of silverware.

After lunch they distributed sweatshirts, T-shirts, socks, and underwear, plus bras for the women. This was a minor thrill for us, because it meant we could finally wash our clothes and put on something clean and dry. In the late afternoon, when it started to get dark, we went down to the river and washed our dirty clothes and put the clean clothes on. Then we got ready for bed and tried to sleep, because by that point we knew what was in store for us with those walks: pure exhaustion.

As ironic as it seems, arguments began to erupt—not with the guerrillas but among the passengers. At one point my father said that if the guerrillas decided to release one group, we ought to pressure them to let the women go first, since everything was so much harder for us. But one of the pilots disagreed, saying that he had the same right as any woman to be released. Most everybody—the women in particular—thought this was pretty obnoxious, because nobody expected a pilot to say something like that.

The next day began at dawn. When we woke up, the men told us that we would be given breakfast only after a three-hour walk. At that point we would get a one-hour break, and then continue on for another five hours until we reached a campsite.

Had we been able to keep up with the pace at which the guerrillas walked, we would have been able to stick to their schedule, but we were a pretty different crowd, and so the first three hours turned into four. Only after we reached our three-hour destination did the guerrillas allow us to rest for an hour. The five hours after that, of course, turned into six, for a total of eleven hours and change. We reached the campsite at around 5:45 or 6 in the afternoon. After they gave us some food we all went to bed, completely exhausted. It was awful.

When we woke up, everything seemed unreal. For a few split seconds we all sat around, dazed and groggy, wondering where on earth we were. Then reality set in: we were kidnapped.

Never in my life did I imagine that this would happen to me. I always thought that people got kidnapped because they had millions and millions of dollars in the bank—this simply wasn't something that I could ever envision happening to me. To me! What irony, what injustice. The nightmare of kidnapping had touched my family, and not through some distant relative: it was happening to me, to me and my father, two people in the very same family. A tragedy, this is a tragedy, I said to myself over and over.

Every day, at every moment I kept asking myself: Why is this happening to me? Why? Why? The more I thought about it, the more furious I became, the more angry I got, because I felt that life had turned its back on me. I always knew the world was filled with injustice, but until then I had never really looked it in the eye. I had never imagined that one day I would have to endure injustice of this magnitude.

The days were long. We talked a lot. Some people drew chessboards in the mud, with 64 little squares, and different-sized leaves in each square. They used the tiniest leaves for the pawns, and different leaves for the knights, rooks, and other pieces. After a little while, they perfected the game by using old batteries, rocks, bits of wood. They did the same thing with Chinese checkers, inventing the board and pieces with whatever was available.

At night we would all gather in the game room or the "dining room," as we called it, to pray. Together we would offer a collective plea for our release, and then we would sing songs of peace.

Because there were 32 of us, we baptized this camp as "Camp 32." On April 25, the guerrillas called a meeting and made an announcement.

"We are going to split you into two groups. The first group is going to head out today to start walking. They are: Francisco López, Juan González, Laureano Caviedes, Uriel Velasco, Ana María Gómez, Gloria Amaya de Alonso, Yezid Gómez, Daniel Hoffmann, Manuel Fernando Torres, Diego González, Fernando Buitrago, Nicolás Pérez, Abner Duarte, Juan Manuel Corzo, Laszlo Kálli, and Leszli Kálli. Get ready. We leave in an hour."

My father went over to the man who delivered the news, and then came over to me and said, "Leszli, the people who are staying are going to be released soon. Tell me if you want to stay."

"Dad, you and I came here together and we're going to leave together. I'll leave, but only with you. I hope you respect my decision," I said.

He didn't like it, but he understood. His primary concern was me, but at that moment, he was everything to me, too.

God only knows why he does these things. In his eyes, everything is valid, comprehensible, possible. But for us humans these realities can be difficult to digest and accept. We said goodbye to the people staying behind and began walking. We had no idea what direction we were going in, since our only means of orientation was the sun, and the thick cover of the jungle blocked it out entirely.

It was a long day. There were sixteen of us, and we managed a little better now, but of course, they squeezed as much energy out of us as they could. We left the camp at 10 A.M. and by around 6pm we reached another abandoned house. Food that night was rice and canned beans, plus the same lemonade as before—or rather, lemon water. After we rested and washed up, I started to feel some sharp pains, because I hadn't been able to go to the bathroom. I think it was all the pressure we were under, the stress, and the idea of going to the bathroom on the side of a mountain. It was hard; I still hadn't adjusted. I told Ana María and Gloria, because they were women, and I felt more comfortable talking to them about it. To my surprise, I wasn't the only one who hadn't been able to make a bowel movement in two weeks; it turned out that they were going through the same thing as me. Afterward, I spoke to my father about it, to see if he could help us out somehow, and I found out that several of the men had the same problem, too. We explained the predicament to the head guerrilla, who told us that he didn't have anything for constipation, but that as soon as he could he would come up with something to solve the problem.

The house we stayed in that night was so tiny that half of us slept in hammocks, and those of us who had mattresses slept underneath. By that point, the ELN had finally admitted that they were behind the hijacking, but still nobody knew whether it was for political or financial gain. I was worried that it was financial, because I am definitely not from a family of millionaires. If it was a political maneuver, the story was different, because then it would just amount to an attempt to pressure the government.

By now, I was a little more knowledgeable about the meaning of words like *guerrilla* and *National Convention,* the negotiation forum that the ELN proposed for carrying out peace talks with the Colombian government. The guerrillas kept telling us that they weren't murderers, and that none of us should even think of doing anything, because for every one of us there were twenty of them willing to risk their lives. Then they said that this would all be resolved in a matter of days. This calmed me down somewhat, because I believed them and I still do. Anyway, what other choice did I have? All we could do was believe what they said and hang on to the hope that this would all be over "in a matter of days."

On April 26 we started walking as the sun rose. It was freezing that dawn, and when we woke up it was drizzling. About halfway down the path, Yezid Gómez got stung by wasps, because the mule he was riding somehow attracted a bunch of them. We were walking in two groups at the time: in the first group, Ana María, Gloria, Yezid, Manuel Fernando Torres, Juan Manuel Corzo, Abner Duarte, Nicolás Pérez, and Daniel Hoffmann. In the other group it was me and the flight crew, which included my father, Commander Kálli.

Yezid's group was about ten minutes ahead of us, but when he got stung he fell behind. Right after it happened he told the guerrillas that he was allergic to wasps and asked them for an Advil, or something similar. When those of us in the second group reached Yezid, he was lying on the ground, drooling, purple, and in convulsions. His tongue was so swollen it looked like a little ball, and eventually he lost consciousness. Fernando Buitrago and I started giving him cardiovascular massages—Fernando showed me how, and when he got tired I continued in his place. It was twenty minutes before Yezid regained consciousness, though to tell the truth I thought he was going to die. I had never seen anything like that in my life.

The guerrilla soldiers who were with us ran off in search of drugs, and to radio their people about what had happened. I felt better afterward, though, because when Yezid finally woke up, he said to me and Fernando: "Thank you. You saved my life."

We told him what had happened, but he couldn't even begin to comprehend what he'd been through. We waited for him to rest, and after a while we started walking again.

The next place we arrived at was a very pretty house where Ana María and I asked the guerrillas if we could make *melcochas*, sweets made with *panela* [brown sugarloaf] and coconut milk. When we finished, we settled down and prepared the "beds" where we would be sleeping that night. Then we went to bathe. Ana María and I were still constipated.

They let us rest for two days at that house. After that, we got back on the trail: our next goal was another abandoned house in the middle of the jungle. This time, though, we didn't have to walk so far. In this next house there were some wooden planks that we moved around, and when we did this two huge scorpions and a tarantula crawled out.

We split up the sheets they had given us. The food that night was rice, bananas, beans, and condensed milk for dessert. To drink they gave us orangeade, much better this time around.

Another day of walking. This time we had to sleep in a shack in the middle of the jungle. We couldn't turn on our flashlights because if we did we would be attacked by the millions of mosquitoes buzzing around everywhere. All of us were sweating buckets, and when we sat down to take off our boots, the smell that wafted out was completely disgusting. That night the guerrillas distributed soft drinks, potato chips, chocolate bars, rice, beef, and boiled potatoes. . . . It was delicious. We slept well that night, thinking that the next day we would be headed to a more comfortable campsite.

The next day we arrived at a campground that was a muddy, mucky mess, and we baptized it "Camp 16" in honor of the sixteen of us that had made it there. There were tents everywhere, the kind they pitch in the middle of a war zone to take care of wounded soldiers. After unloading our things, we went to bathe in a nearby stream, the only lovely thing about that campground, and after that we settled down for the night. The following day we woke up a little later than usual; we didn't have to walk anymore, and so we just sat around talking.

At nighttime, Ana María, Juan González, Juan Manuel Corzo, Francisco, and I sat around talking. Some eyelash-batting and flirting started around then, which was logical, I guess, since Ana María and I were the only girls in the group. Still, we didn't want to get involved with anyone—all we were interested in was friendship, though we knew that sooner or later this would create problems for us.

Around this time I started a collection box to ask for things we wanted, like chocolate bars, gum, lollipops, crackers, and dye for Gloria Amaya de Alonso's hair. Her hair was white, but she dyed it black, and she wanted to get some dye so that when she was released, her husband and her two daughters would find her just as she was when she left them. We spent about a week at this campground, and lots of funny things happened there. On the night of May 4, for example, none of us felt much like sleeping. It was almost 8 P.M., and outside it was raining hard, just as it always rains here, day and night. That night Juan Manuel Corzo suggested we put on a play in the river; he would give each one of us a role to play from *Puss in Boots*, he said. My father said that when he was a child he knew the story by heart but that he'd forgotten it, and asked Juan Manuel to refresh our memories.

Juan Manuel launched into the story: there was a young man, a king, a princess, good and bad princes, a river, and a very smart little cat that ended up eating the bad prince when he turned into a mouse to show that he could, in fact, turn into a mouse, and then in the end the young man turned into a prince, because he married the princess, and the puss in boots ended up a happy millionaire. As Juan Manuel recounted the story I thought about how everything we were going through was like some kind of tragicomedy, much more interesting than any other story I could think of—it was something out of Ripley's Believe It or Not! I mean, here we had a congressman slathered in mud, sitting in a leaky tent on a windy night in some godforsaken place in the middle of the jungle, telling us the story of *Puss in Boots*. The king, Juan Manuel decided, would be played by my father, who thanked him for the compliment and joked that the assignment clearly indicated that Juan Manuel held him in very high esteem. Then Juan Manuel said that Ana María would be the princess, and Abner, the bad prince. As soon as he said this, however, Abner went pale, stood up, and stormed over to his hammock. Immediately we all called out to him, telling him not to get so worked up, that it was just a role in a play, and then my father said that if Abner wanted he could play the king, that it wasn't a big deal. But Abner replied that it wasn't the play that he was upset about, it was Killer. Killer was a rottweiler that belonged to one of the guerrillas, a really crazy guy who we called "the lunatic" because he spent all his time putting together legbreaker land mines with syringes, flashlight batteries, and C4 explosives. He babbled a lot to himself and would spend lots of time pacing around the campground with that dog of his. Abner said he was convinced that the dog was hanging around because he wanted to take a bite out of him. All of us turned toward the entrance and sure enough, there was Killer, sitting quietly, staring at us with a strange expression— not aggressive, but strange all the same. My father then told Abner that the poor dog had come in just to get out of the rain, in search of someplace that was warm and dry—not because he wanted to pounce on Abner. But Abner held his ground, convinced that Killer was after him, that Killer hated him. This, in fact, was true: for some reason the dog despised both Abner and Ana María, and with this idea in his head Abner went back to his hammock. When we turned to look again, the dog was gone, but when we told Abner, he still refused to come back, saying that the dog was just hiding out somewhere waiting to maul him. That's what those dogs are like, he said: they turn on you the first chance they get.

We all went searching for the dog under the beds, and that was when Fernando shouted, "Look at that thing!" It was a huge snake. Thinking it was a harmless country snake, I rushed to its defense, saying, "It's just a *cazadora*, it won't hurt you." But my father wasn't so sure, and quickly said, "Hold on a minute, you don't know anything about snakes. This one might not be harmless at all—in fact it might be very poisonous. They all look alike, these snakes."

That stopped me cold. As the snake slithered toward the light from the flashlights, we all jumped up onto our beds, shining our flashlights on it, shouting as loud as we could, "Guard! Guard!" But nobody heard us: the rain was falling hard outside, plus the guards were pretty far from where we were. In the middle of all the confusion and the screaming and crying, the snake slithered round and round in that little tent, searching for the light.

We remained there like that for a while until finally we got the attention of one of the guerrilla soldiers, Pitufo—everyone called him that because he was so incredibly short, definitely no taller than

4 foot 6, and in his uniform he resembled a little green dwarf. As he entered the tent he snarled at us for causing such a commotion; with all that noise he couldn't sleep. In between yelps and cries we explained that there was a snake running loose under the beds. It was probably just a harmless little country snake, he replied, and quickly bent down and started looking under the beds to trap it so that we would shut up once and for all. But then, after a few seconds, he jumped up so fast and so suddenly that it seemed as if he'd been cat-apulted by a spring. He must have leapt 9 feet straight into the air, and as he did he yelled at us to watch out because it was a bushmaster, which is a very poisonous snake. He warned us not to even try han-dling it because if we got bitten, there was no antidote for it. Then he told us that he was going to go out and come right back with a stick and a machete. As we waited for him we took turns shining our flash-lights on the snake: as she slithered toward one light, someone else would shine another flashlight to get her to go in the other direction, and we just kept on doing that until Pitufo returned, with a machete and a stick that was bigger than he was. First, he circled the tent from the outside and, moving the crisscrossed branches that served as a wall, he created a tiny hole through which he stuck his flashlight. Then he ordered us to turn off all our flashlights, so that he could draw the snake out. Very obediently the snake followed the beam of light from Pitufo's flashlight. Just as the snake's head peeked out from the tent, Pitufo sliced her right down the neck with his machete, and the snake writhed around in a series of tight, fast, circular spins in what appeared to be her final agony. The entire scene was so unbe-lievably frightening, and in the middle of all the rain, the mud, the cries, the screams, and the night, it felt as though we had descended into one of Dante's rings of hell.

Finally, Pitufo removed the dead snake and hung her from a pole outside the tent. Observing her hanging like that, we saw that she eas-ily measured 13 feet on either side. Oddly enough, when she was moving around on the ground, she had raised her head just like cobras do, but without that neck that cobras have. The entire experi-ence left us with the most intense wave of adrenaline running through our bodies, from the terror and total impotence we felt because it was all so frighteningly real, in the middle of all that light and shadow and darkness.

One thing that caught my eye right then was the American who was with us. As all this was happening he lay in his hammock, writing beneath the light of his flashlight. The poor guy didn't have the slightest idea of what was happening, because the rest of us were screaming, jumping up and down, running. I don't know, maybe he just thought we were horsing around because he didn't pay us the least bit of attention until finally my father went in to see him and said, "Look at it, it's right there where we hang our clothes to dry." When the American saw the dead snake he went pale as a ghost and didn't say another word for the rest of the night. None of us slept very well that night, nor did we feel much like resuming our little impromptu performance of *Puss in Boots*.

There was no way to explain to Abner, either, that the dog had actually saved his life, and all our lives for that matter. It wouldn't have mattered to him, though, because Killer kept right on growling at him for the rest of the time he was with us.

Given the circumstances, though, things were going all right, more or less. For me and Ana María, Gloria was like a mother: she gave us advice, bathed with us, kept us company. That week the three of us managed to go to the bathroom, thanks to some pills the guerrillas gave us.

Of course, things must have been just a little too perfect, because on May 7 the guerrillas gathered us together and surprise, surprise: "We're going to split you up into two groups of eight," they said. "The following people are to start walking today: Francisco López, Juan González, Laureano Caviedes, Uriel Velasco, Diego González, Fernando Buitrago, Laszlo Kálli, and Leszli Kálli."

Suddenly I felt as though everything around me had begun to crumble, but I pretended to be strong, and I tried not to cry. I hate goodbyes. Now I was really on my own, the only woman with the group from the plane crew. Leaving Ana María, who was like my sister, and Gloria, who was like my mother, was a terrible blow for me. My father had always said to me, "Leszli, on planes, just like on boats, in the event of an accident or some kind of emergency, the crew are always the last ones to leave." That comment burned in my head now, but all I could do was tell myself, "Leszli, you have to be strong, you have to endure it."

The farewell was awful. Gloria cried; so did Ana María. As for me, I had a giant lump in my throat. I was so scared. We said a prayer. I sat down next to Gloria, but I just couldn't bear it anymore, and finally I broke down in tears, and when they said to us, "All right. Let's go," I was the first one out because I just couldn't bear to feel the pain anymore.

Another day walking. Mud, mosquitoes, sweat, discomfort, fatigue, and stress. After a while we reached another abandoned house, and we all went in to go to sleep.

At first, I got along pretty well with Francisco López. During those first few days, he was very kind to me, but then something began to bubble up, something that I wasn't prepared for and certainly hadn't invited. Somehow, for some reason, our friendship suddenly changed. Before, I felt that he saw me as a friend, but now there was something different in his eyes. We discussed it. I told him how I felt, and he told me not to worry, he understood perfectly if I didn't want to get involved with him. I tried to explain that he just didn't understand, that you can't just fall in love with someone overnight, and I told him that once he thought about it, everything would seem clearer. We resolved to stay friends, but I couldn't help feeling uncomfortable around him after that because it just wasn't the same: I couldn't change my clothes without feeling nervous and I couldn't look at him like a brother anymore, but as someone who felt something for me.

We continued walking. My mood shifted, and I started to feel lonely even though I had my father at my side. There were things—like the run-in with Francisco—that I would have liked to talk to him about, but we didn't have the best relationship, and I didn't feel close enough to him to tell him what was bothering me. I was afraid that the Francisco situation might create problems for me and my father, and under the circumstances, that could have tragic consequences for us. So I told myself that the best thing to do was try to keep the peace among the group and act like nothing had happened, that everything was the same as it had been before, when Francisco still treated me like a sister. And that's what I did.

After several days, on May 12, we finally reached "Camp 8." On the way there we came across a little newborn puppy, which we took with us, baptizing it "Fokker," after the Avianca plane we'd been flying. New ingredients were introduced to our diet: lentils, peas, beans, yucca, potatoes, and *panela*. This new campground was a little more organized than the others, but in the end it was pretty much the same. They assigned us to a big hut with eight beds and they gave us foam mattresses, blankets, and other things: another sweatshirt and T-shirt, another set of underwear, towels, shampoo, toothpaste, soap, radios, flashlights, batteries, notebooks, pencil cases, and sanitary napkins for me. They told me that if I ever felt sick I should tell them because they had drugs for whatever we might need, including a serum for snake bites.

Tuesday, May 18, 1999

My strength is slowly fading. I feel as if I'm sinking little by little, as if there is no way out of the huge hole I have fallen into. I just keep on falling and falling. I think the despair will taper off when I finally surrender to the situation and touch rock bottom. There are so many thoughts running through my head right now, and I want to hold on to all of them, even if only for just a second or two, to organize them, make a list, and decide what I want to keep and what I want to throw away. I wish I could unload all this and cry my eyes out, but I just can't: I've tried to do it and I can't, and that makes me even more furious. I know I have to get rid of all these feelings, that it will do me good to let go of it all. God, if You exist, please help me out of this somehow!

I cannot connect with myself. I cannot seem to banish the sadness and the impotence I feel, not for one single second. I even have trouble breathing here. I dream about being home. Mommy, I miss you so much! I never stop thinking about you, not for a second. How did this happen? When did this happen? All I want to do is run away from here, run and run into your arms and feel that this is nothing but a very bad dream. Oh, Mommy, I love you. It's been a month already, one long and awful month, and I am still here. What happened?

The head guerrilla called us into a meeting to tell us that another guerrilla will be coming to the campsite tomorrow to film us, to send our families proof that we're alive. This is good news, because it means our relatives will be able to see us, even if it's just on a video-tape. The head guerrilla says that we should try to look our best and to be ready when he comes.

Wednesday, May 19, 1999

I feel the same today as I did yesterday: I don't feel like doing anything. And even if I did, there wouldn't be anything to do. Just like they told us, the new guerrilla turned up, he's wearing jeans and a shirt, swamp boots just like the rest of us, and—this is the nasty part—a ski mask. Not once the entire day did he show his face. He's very well spoken and actually brought a professional crew to film us. All of us gathered together in a spot where all you could see was nature— leafy trees, bushes, and mud—and they told us we could talk about whatever we wanted. So that's what we did. I told my mother that I am in good health, that I don't want her to worry about me, that she is going to have to be very patient, and that I love her  with all my heart. I also told her that I feel fine, partly because my dad is here with me, and the guerrilla soldiers have been treating us pretty well—anyway, I told her a bunch of things. The idea, basically, was not to worry her. I wanted to show her that I am happy, even though it's not true.

Today I found a little spot that's a bit removed from the campground, far enough away so that I couldn't hear the guerrilla soldiers' radios, which were blasting *vallenato* [traditional Colombian music]. It is a very quiet little spot, bursting with giant plants and trees of all sizes, and I simply felt overwhelmed by the majesty of these great natural gifts. The trees inspire my deepest awe; they are so imposing, so strong. I gazed up at them, breathless. Up in the treetops I could see enormous black-and-yellow toucans, with their giant curved beaks, and there were woodpeckers, too. I always thought woodpeckers were little blue things, Disney style, but no, surprisingly enough, they are nothing like that. For starters they are huge, reddish in color except on the crest, which is white, and they have massive beaks. I also saw parakeets everywhere and the most angelic butterflies, with sparkling, aquamarine wings. The first time I spotted them, on our second day in captivity, they took my breath away for they are simply spectacular. Up above I can see only the tiniest sliver of sky; the trees are packed so tightly with leaves that you can barely see the stars. The sounds of the birds, crickets, and cicadas, combined with the swaying of the leaves, creates a harmonious melody and the world around me feels calm, serene.

For the first time in captivity I found a perfect place where nature transports me to a state in which I can clear my mind in the most wonderful, satisfying way, where I can revel in this landscape that God has so generously given me. The perfection, of course, was short-lived, because the guerrilla soldiers eventually came around looking for me as I was enjoying all this. Not finding me anywhere on the campground, they probably thought I had tried to escape. For security reasons, they told me, I am not allowed to wander off. I can't come back here, they said. What an awful moment. I felt so miserable, once again reminded of how impotent I am in this situation.

I spend a lot of time thinking about my mother, my sister Carolina and my brother Nandor, about Dany and Mauri. Oh, what I would give to see my nephew Danielito, to hug him and kiss him. . . . I miss him so much. With all my heart I truly regret not having spent more time with all the people I love so dearly, not having shared so many moments that we had and never really appreciated. I wish I could turn back the clock to tell them how I feel about them, and I regret not having expressed my feelings in the moment. I never said anything—maybe out of fear, or maybe because I just figured there would always be time later on, sometime in the future, to say those things. Only now do I truly understand that saying that goes, "Never put off for tomorrow what you can do today."

I swear that if I make it back, I will express all these things: who I am, what I feel, my fears and my truths, my joy and my sadness. The problem, though, is that I don't know—none of us here knows—if tomorrow even exists. Here, the only real thing we have is the present moment. The past is made up of many presents that come and go, and the future is only a projection of the present. Everything is now. And I hope that this "now," this present moment, will become part of the past very, very quickly. Because if it doesn't, I don't want a future, or a present, or anything at all.

Things are bad right now. Really, really bad.

Thursday, May 20, 1999

It rained hard. Last night I stayed up talking to Francisco for a long time. He told me that his feelings for me are very powerful, and that he thanks God that I am in the same group as him, because it makes everything so much more bearable. I was speechless, I really had no idea what to say. On one hand, it's nice to have someone say those things to you; it makes you feel useful to someone else. But on the other hand, it's terrible: I have absolutely no desire to get involved with anyone here, least of all him.

I am somehow going to have to figure out a way to explain this to him. I hope he'll understand. He seems like a nice person, and he really has been terrific with me. And I don't want anything to change between us, aside from the trust that he already sort of violated with me.

Friday, May 21, 1999

I feel worse than ever today, all because of Francisco. I confronted him about the things he said to me, and he told me not to worry, that the last thing he wants is for me to feel uncomfortable around him. I wish I could believe him. Why is this happening to him? Why can't he just see me as a friend? This is such a drag.

Saturday, May 22, 1999

I think I'm better off leaving this problem alone. I wish I could escape, but there's no way out of here.

Tuesday, June 1, 1999

Today has been the saddest day of all; the sky was slate gray when we woke up. I haven't taken a bath for two days; the last time I went down to the river I tried to escape. I went down, my body filled with adrenaline, and I started running and running. I ran for ten minutes

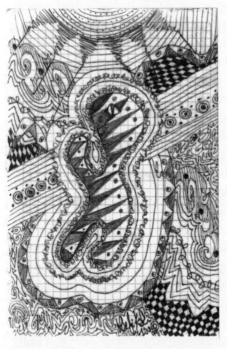

straight until I reached a huge boulder, and then I stopped and finally I started to cry. After a while, I calmed down and went back up to the campsite. It was really dumb, doing that. But I was thinking about my mother, and how badly I want to see her—I can't believe it's been more than a month, and I'm still here, completely powerless. Sometimes I think the solution is in my hands, like I thought when I tried to escape, and then I lose all hope. That's why I tried to escape: I thought that if I ran downriver, I would reach a bigger river, and that from there I could just keep walking until I reached some farmer's house. Then someone could show me the way to the nearest road, and from there I could figure out how to get home. Well, I can dream, can't I? That's what I thought. Anyway, when I stopped at the boulder, I started to think about my father—how the hell could I leave him like that, all worried, not telling him where I went? In the end, my mother is safe and sound, but my father's in the same boat as I am. So I turned around and went back, but right now I feel so filled with anguish, all I want to do is get out of here, even if only in spirit, however I can.

Francisco, as I could have predicted, has changed completely. He doesn't talk to me like he did before—God, I'm lucky if he says hi to me now, which is too bad because I really enjoyed those conversations we had. Aside from my father, I don't really talk much to the others. All they talk about is planes, all day and even part of the night sometimes, though I guess that makes sense since they're all either pilots or flight attendants.

I'm uncomfortable sleeping in this hut. Today I talked to the head guerrilla to see if they could set up a separate hut just for me. I feel funny changing my clothes with all these men around—to say nothing of Francisco, who looks at me with pure hatred in his eyes all the time. That's the way it feels, at least.

On the news today we heard about another kidnapping—over a hundred people are being held captive in the Church of the Virgin Mary in Cali, by the same group that has us, the ELN. I wonder what's going to happen, if this is going to make things better or worse for us. I feel bad for those poor people, because I really know what they're in for. I bet they're all wondering, asking themselves over and over, "Why me? Why is this happening to me?"

It's an ugly, sad thing to have to go through this. I think I'm getting worse every day. Everything makes me uncomfortable, especially the comments from the group. Wouldn't I love to tell them what I think of them. They are such idiots.

Wednesday, June 9, 1999

It is twenty minutes to eleven. I'm sitting in the new hut they built for me, and I have been here for 9 days now. Today we received some very sad news: Carlos Gonzáles, one of the captives in the other group, died. It was something with his heart. I'm trying to find out more about it on the radio, but all they talk about is soccer. All of us are very shaken by the news. He was a very quiet, very nice man. God, why is this happening? It isn't fair, to be dying while you are waiting and hoping for your freedom. His family must be taking it very hard. To think, they will never see him again. Our family, too, must be thinking that at any moment we might come back home in a black plastic bag. God, all I ask of you is to take care of us so that this doesn't happen to us, not for us, because the dead at least get to rest, but for our families.

The head guerrilla told us that he felt really sorry about what happened, and that he didn't want us to think that if one of us got seriously ill that they would keep us here. This would not happen again, he said. I wish I could believe him, because it would bring me some measure of relief from all my fear and anxiety, but it's not easy, especially after this.

God, please take care of Carlos, and send peace to his family.

Right now I am writing beneath the light of the flashlight, listening to La Mega, a radio station, which is playing the song "*Yo rezo por ti*" ["I Pray for You"].

Yesterday I saw my mother on the TV news. They reported that the families met with President Andrés Pastrana in Bucaramanga and that the meeting went well.

A few days ago, my father asked the men to get him some *aguardiente*. Today he got drunk. I know it was because of what happened to Carlos. My father was very upset by his death, it was a real blow for him. . . .

Just now we were talking about the cockroach issue, and my dad told me I had to get over my fear—how is it possible, he asked me, that I'm not afraid of a thirteen-foot-long bushmaster, a venomous snake as thick as my arm, and yet I'm frightened of a little cockroach? It's completely illogical, he said.

My batteries are wearing out, and it's starting to rain.

My ulcer is flaring up. It's gotten really bad lately; in Bucaramanga it used to flare up occasionally, but it never hurt this much. . . . Oh, it's unbearable. And the food here only makes it worse, since they cook everything with so much oil. I told the head guerrilla before talking to my father about it, because I didn't want him to worry—he wouldn't be able to do anything about it and it would only make him feel worse.

It's 11:30 at night, and I'm not tired at all. I'm looking out at the eyes I drew on the tent (I draw a lot, and I always draw eyes), and the Last Eye is looking over me, looking after me, taking care of me.

Thursday, June 10, 1999

It's a quarter to two in the morning. There's a snake in my hut and it's really pretty, with little swirls of yellow, black, tan, and deep copper. Very, very beautiful.

I went out to see the guard today, but I didn't mention the snake, because he would have killed it. I just asked him for a candle, but he didn't have any; my batteries are running out. By the time I came back, the snake was gone.

I just put new batteries in my flashlight. What joy!

Finally I heard my mother on the radio. She told me that she is staying calm, that she loves me very much, that the people at the kibbutz are saving my place, and that I got a very good score on the ICFES, my college entrance exams. Then she told me that my ex-boyfriend Diego is planning to come back to Colombia in September, and that he wrote me two letters. She also told me about Abelardo, who asked me and my dad to stop smoking.

I'm a little spacey from the two Normatons they gave me for my anxiety. It's 3:20 A.M. At 10:30 last night, the guerrillas gave me two Tramals for my ulcer, which doesn't hurt at all anymore, but I definitely feel kind of weird. They also gave me injections of ranitidine and Lisalgil to take the edge off the pain.

I vomited blood, how gross.

Today I went down to the stream and I had kind of a nasty run-in with Uriel. This is what happened: since I am the only woman in the group, I like to bathe by myself; I usually take about twenty minutes. But getting down to the stream is tricky because you have to go down a very steep hill, and then when you're through, you have to climb all the way back up, and you end up all sweaty again. It's a giant drag. Anyway, when I got down to the stream, Uriel was already there, in his sweatpants. When he saw me, in a very cold voice, he told me to go back up because he hadn't finished washing up—even though he'd been down there since 8 A.M. and it was already 11. I asked him when I could come back down and he said ten minutes. Obviously I didn't go back up, I just moved a little bit away to sit out the ten minutes. That way, as soon as I saw him go, I could take my bath. So, for starters, he took twenty minutes, not ten. I was really sweaty and on top of it I was in a rush, because back at the camp, on TV, they were broadcasting the release of the first group of passengers. And so I went over to him and said, "Uriel, are you done yet? It's been twenty minutes already."

"No, you're going to have to wait some more."

Like a jerk I sat around waiting another half hour. He was doing it on purpose, I knew it, and so I went back up to the camp to tell my dad, who told me not to do anything about it. When I went back down to the water—this time with my dad—Uriel trotted right off. Then, as I was telling my father what I really think of Uriel, what a resentful idiot I think he is, I realized that he was hiding out, listening to our conversation. And so he said to me, "Listen, do me a favor and don't call me an idiot, because I'm not an idiot. And if I took a long time, that's just tough luck for you. I'll take as long as I please."

I fired back at him with the very same words he'd used on me. I bet he thought I'd just keep my mouth shut but no way am I going to let anyone here push me around. In the end he just turned around and walked off, and I said to my dad, in a loud voice, "So on top of being a resentful jerk he's got a big mouth, too."

My father told me I had to calm down, and said that maybe Uriel was at fault, but so was I for saying what I thought of him. Then he told me that when these things happened, the best thing to do was shut my mouth and count to ten, because sometimes the best response is no response at all. Of course my father was right, but come on, how am I supposed to sit there and take that kind of crap? Plus, I was actually kind of hurt that my father had kept his mouth shut, that he didn't say anything to Uriel, when he knew perfectly well that the whole thing was his fault.

Anyway, I finally took my bath and when I finished I went back up to watch TV, to watch the release of the other passengers: Gerardo Santos, the mayor Juan (a guy who was the mayor of a small town near the Venezuelan border), Tatiana Gutiérrez, William Óscar Bolaños, Néstor Saavedra, Julia Sarmiento, Rehace Murillo. They must be so happy now, but the bummer about this is that I'm sure our family is thinking that we're going to be released with them. How awful it will be when they realize we're not with that group.

On the news they broadcast a photo of me with Mauri, Danielito was in my arms, and with Carol looking pretty in a green shirt, and then one of my mother walking through the Hotel Dann in Bucaramanga. Oh, how I wish I was with them right now.

I'm so happy for the people who got released, but what about us? When are they going to let us go?

Friday, June 18, 1999

Today I saw my mother on TV again. On the news reports they've started talking about the release of the other group, but they don't seem to have their stories straight. I don't know what to think anymore.

Wednesday, June 23, 1999

I just can't understand it: how can these people disrupt our lives like this, how can they destroy our dreams, our families, so easily? I always used to say that nothing and nobody would ever come between me and my life, much less put an end to it all. Today I realize how wrong I was. This is the worst kind of agony, no matter how you look at it. Sometimes I think that these guerrillas regard us like animals, like creatures that don't think, or have feelings or rational thoughts, sort of the way adults sometimes listen to children without really paying attention. Something is really wrong with them. They are so very wrong.

I am so stressed!

Thursday, June 24, 1999

I think I am beginning to adapt to all this nothingness. Maybe I'm not making any sense at all, but I'm just writing all the things that go through my mind. I think something's wrong with me, or else I've just gone crazy. I'm not kidding, this is serious. In a way I feel as if I'm just getting to know my real self. I feel like another Leszli altogether, a strange Leszli, with lots and lots of personalities, someone who adapts and acts differently in every situation. This Leszli is very tough on the outside, and she has held herself together, but I keep asking myself how long this is going to go on, and I wonder if we are really the same person, me and all these different personalities. I have no idea where I am getting my strength from, but to tell the truth I don't think we even care anymore, me and this other Leszli. It's like we aren't afraid of anything anymore, not even death. . . . To tell the truth, I was always like that but still, there are some things I think I ought to be afraid of, and it makes me mad that I'm not. I want to touch everything, and that's not good. But this head of mine can't seem to wrap itself around that idea.

In some ways, I wish I could be like everyone else; I wish I could act like them a little bit at least. But then on the other hand I don't want to be like everyone else; I don't want to be one of them. I have my own personality, and I always will. Anyway, when I really get to thinking, I know that it's much worse to go through this experience with fear. I'm okay the way I am. But I really feel as if I'm in a constant battle with myself. I know that sometimes the other people can't stand me, but they know that I can't stand them, either. . . .

Anyway, I guess I'll write more later, because if I don't stop now I'll just end up angry at myself, and that will only make things worse. I miss Pablo, my cat.

Saturday, June 26, 1999

My father and I aren't talking. He's mad at me because I supposedly called him an idiot. I tried to explain, but he doesn't believe what I say. What happened is, I told him I was very angry because I, trying to be the good daughter, went over to him to give him a couple of pillows and in the process I turned my flashlight on his face. Like a brute, he sent the flashlight crashing down on the floor, and so I picked it up off the floor, furious, and stomped off. I had walked about five steps outside the hut when I said to myself, "That's what you get for being an idiot." Since I was the one who was supposed to be annoyed with him, I stopped talking to him after that. I was waiting for him to say sorry to me, but he didn't and so finally I asked him why on earth *he* was mad at *me*, since I was the one who was supposed to be mad at him, not the other way around. And he said it was because I'd called him an idiot. I explained what I had really said but he didn't care, he just said that I needed to know that calling him an idiot had its consequences. After a while, he cooled off, I think because he realized I was right. If not, well, what do I care? I know I'm right. Anyway, I pretty much just dropped the subject. And I think I have an idea of the "consequences" he was referring to: my trip.

Juan Carlos García, the DJ from La Mega, is on the air, and suddenly I think back to the day I met him and chuckle to myself. One day the radio signal with Bogotá got messed up, and they weren't able to air the program all over the country, just from Bucaramanga. This was during a period when I was really bored with my life at home and I turned my schedule around so that I slept during the day and stayed up all night. Late at night, I would tune in to La Mega and listen to all the people who called in to offer their opinions on whatever subject they were talking about. When I heard that they were airing the show from Bucaramanga, I got inspired and I called in with some comment about the topic they were discussing—I don't even remember what it was anymore. After I said my piece, Juan Carlos asked me not to hang up, because he didn't have any other phone calls coming in and he said he was about to fall asleep on the job. At first I gave him a fake name, but then, once we got to talking off the air, I started to tell him about my life. It was weird, because I'd only just met him, but I felt like I'd known him forever. We must have talked until 5 A.M., and then he asked me for my phone number. From that point on, he would call me to talk about his life, his problems, and I'd do the same. We kept saying that we had to meet in person, but we never did. I like him a lot. It's so nice to listen to someone you know—if I can say that I actually know him—on the radio.

Sunday, June 27, 1999

It's twenty to six in the afternoon and I am sitting here staring at an eagle. She's perched at the top of a tree in front of the communal hut. She's beautiful, huge, a brilliant shade of chocolate brown. Now, that's an animal that inspires respect, complete and total respect. The men fired at her, trying to kill her, but thank God they are terrible shots and all they did was scare her. She is so pretty.

Last night I had a terrible dream: I was talking to my mother in the living room and she was leaning against the wall. Suddenly I saw a face, a perfect face, forming on the wall. My mother turned around to look at this thing that I was looking at, and she got scared. The two of us then ran out to the bedroom and started praying with Carolina. Then, a little bit later, I went out to see if the face was still there and it was. Then I started to cry, and in fact I woke up crying, I was so scared. It was 4:30 in the morning, and when I got up, you know what I saw? That awful face I drew on the side of my mosquito net—it was so creepy that I had to go outside after that, and I just sat around waiting for the sun to rise. Only then did I feel safe enough to go back inside.

My mood is slowly beginning to improve. I'm going to do what Dad said: enjoy this to the fullest, try to kill time by reading, writing, painting, or simply studying everyone else's personalities. My father says that I am in the best place in the world to ponder the issues in my life, to think about what my life has been like so far and where it will go once I'm out of here. The important thing is to kill time in some kind of productive way, not in a boring way, he says. So that's what I'm going to do, because if I don't, I'm either going to end up crazy or dead. And I'm really going to try hard to not let this affect me so much: I have to keep my mind positive, and push away all the bad energy that comes my way.

Today I did abdominals: 120. Tomorrow I'm going to do more, to use my time productively. Maybe I'll feel differently tomorrow, but today I feel really good and that's what matters. After all, tomorrow is another day.

Monday, June 28, 1999

Big surprise. The head commander of the group told us to get our things—that is, the foam mattresses we sleep on, the sheets, our clothes, our toiletries, and our mosquito nets, because we're going to another campground. We asked them why and they said, "Well, we've been at this one for a while, and in the guerrilla world we never stay in one place for too long, for security. There's nothing to worry about, though, this is normal."

On the news today they announced—or rather, they spread the rumor—that people are going to get released soon, but our commander reiterated that we were just moving to another camp, that's all.

Fernando Buitrago asked us to place bets on what we thought was going to happen. Everyone had to say what they thought. Some people said, "They're going to release the other group of passengers," while others said, "Four from here, four from the other group," and reeled off the names.

Then someone else said, "I think it's going to be the women from the other group, and Leszli from ours."

Someone else said, "Six from there, and two from here."

We kept on talking like that for a little while—it wasn't anything, really, just another way to kill time. Everything was going perfectly fine until they got to my dad.

"Me, Leszli, and two others get released," he said.

That was when Uriel spun around like mad.

"You know what, man? I'm sick of you and your comments. What's the deal, does Leszli have some kind of pull, or something?"

Nobody knew what to say after that. It was so stupid, because we were just playing a game, but he really seemed to be looking for a fight. My father, quite admirably once again, said to him: "Listen, Uriel. First off, Leszli is my daughter, and secondly, they were asking me, not you. You already had your turn and you said what you wanted. So I did, too." And then he laughed it off.

Uriel looked like he was about ready to punch my father out, but my father is not the kind of man who gets into fights. He is the calmest man in the world, a person who uses his brain, not that animal instinct the rest of us use. The head guerrilla peeked into the group hut, to see what was going on, and told Uriel to control himself, to stop acting like a child.

As we started walking, everyone asked my father how he had managed to stay so cool throughout that scene. They actually seemed scared by how calm he had remained.

Tuesday, June 29, 1999

We finally made it, exhausted. We walked for an hour and a half through the thickest jungle paths. Uphill, downhill . . . a hundred times before we finally made it here.

This campground is almost flat, with bushes and mud everywhere. All we've got are four huts. Four huts for all of us. Now we have to sleep in twos: Uriel with Juan, Laureano with Francisco, Diego with Fernando, and me with my father, obviously. The guerrillas are going to have to build the other huts from scratch, and that means the kitchen hut, the TV hut, then another one for the head guerrilla's office, which they set up with four pitchforks and some wooden planks, and then there are the other shacks they need to put up for the other soldiers, plus one for storing the food, which is usually *panela*, rice, beans, peas, and yucca when they have it. They're using a chain saw to chop down trees; that's how they'll get the wood to put these huts together. In addition to that, though, they also have to forge a path through the woods and down to the nearby stream, which is really more like a small river. God, when I think back to the other campground and how I complained because the stream was so far away . . . this one is twice as far.

We're all in a terrible mood. It's all so depressing, the way we have to live: we don't have a kitchen hut yet, which is where they usually do the cooking by piling up the mud from the stream, which gets hard and becomes a kind of clay oven. Instead they have to cook with an open fire, which takes much longer to get started. This is awful! What a disaster. There are no bathrooms here, either. We have to make our way through the bushes and plants and do our business there.

The head guerrilla just called us into a meeting and promised that in a month's time this whole area will be dried out. Then he said that they're going to clear the way for a soccer field. A soccer field? Are they serious? There isn't room here for another tree, the forest is so dense. I'll believe it when I see it.

Wednesday, June 30, 1999

On the news today they announced that the hostages in the Cali church have just completed a month in captivity.

The mood among the group has changed—for the better, actually, although my father did get into an argument with Uriel on Sunday.

Yesterday I heard my mother on the radio. She seemed very sad; her voice sounded awfully strange. I can tell she's having a rough time. Carolina also spoke for a bit.

Among other things, Francisco is now talking to me a little more, or at least he's trying. Why? I have no idea. I don't care if he talks to me or not, it makes no difference to me at all.

I miss my mother, my house, and everyone. How are they?

Friday, July 2, 1999

It's 8:40 A.M., and I woke up in a bad mood today, because of my mother. She just sounded so sad. I wish I could tell her that I'm really fine, that the only bad thing is that I'm so bored here, because all I do is smoke, bathe, and eat, because here you can't talk to anyone—I

mean, we've exhausted every last topic of conversation already. And I feel awful, so awful that I can't tell her how I am, because I know she must be thinking I'm in really bad shape. If for whatever reason something happens to me, I want her to know that she is the best mother in the whole universe, and that I thank God for giving me her for a mother, and for letting me share so many things with her. Whenever I feel sad, she is always the one who gives me strength, she's the one who spoils me, gives me whatever I want. Her arms were always the ones that embraced me and doted on me. I have always had the best, the very best family anyone could ask for.

I want my mother to know that I am not angry or resentful about anything, and that she is always with me in my heart. Both of us know that the body is the prison of the soul, and for that reason if I die, and if there is life after death, which is the way it should be, I will be waiting for her at the other side to tell her how much I love her. I want her to take care of herself and search for true happiness, because I could never be happy or at peace if she didn't do that for herself. It goes without saying that I am grateful to her for everything, and that I adore her. I hope she knows that I will always be with her, and that love never dies, because love is something you carry in your heart and not in your body.

Monday, July 5, 1999

Oh, I hope this ends soon! God, don't they realize? I am Leszli Kálli López, I have a family, a mother who loves me and misses me, a sister who is waiting for me at home, and a brother whom I talk to and who loves me. I have a nephew who has probably forgotten who I am by now, and a cat that I love: Pablo.

I really do miss that cat. At home, whenever I feel sad, I grab him and cuddle him for a little while. He's very conceited: he only lets you cuddle him when he feels like it, not when you feel like it. The best thing about Pablo, though, is the way he looks at you. I swear it's like he's talking to me when he gazes up at me. Sometimes it seems as though he doesn't care about anything, but the truth is, he is very aware of the things going on around him. At home we always sleep together because we have the same schedule: both of us stay awake at night and sleep during the day, and since my room is always dark, he is always happy with me, and I am happy with him.

This situation is so bad, so ugly, so boring, so frustrating: a slow death, that's what it is. I'm really getting worse; this is so hard for me ... God, please let this end soon, we've been here a long time now. I have a trip to take and a life that's waiting for me on the outside. Don't You care at all? Whatever I needed to learn, I learned. I understand now. The things I needed to learn to appreciate, I appreciate now, very much. Why is this taking so long? It's not fair. Help me, help me, I beg You! Help me.

I want to climb up high, very high
To the very tips of the branches
So that the altitude no longer frightens me.
I want to make friends
To share adventures.
I want to learn from you
So that I may feel safe and secure every step of the way.
I want to love, because it would be a bore to travel down this
*   path alone.*
I want to build a nest, just like the one that you, one day long
*   ago*
Tried to make for my family.
And when I get up there, way up there ...

I want you there with me,
Because if I am ever able to fly, it will all be thanks to you.

Gloria gave me this poem that her daughter dedicated to her so that I could dedicate it to my mother.

Thursday, July 8, 1999

Today I heard my mother and brother on the radio, such an amazing gift. Nandor told me that he's gone bald from scratching his head so much, thinking about us and worrying about us, that Danielito is already 15 months old and talking; apparently he says two words that don't have much to do with anything: *"gol"* and *"bomba."* Nandor also said that their first thought every day when they wake up in the morning is for us, and that he hopes this will be over soon. My mother said that she was sad because they haven't heard any new news since June 1. The best thing, though, was that at the end of the program they dedicated a really pretty song to me: *"Es mi niña bonita"* ["She's My Pretty Girl"]. I'll never forget that song, or that moment; they will stay with me for the rest of my life.

Today I made a vow to let my eyelashes grow. Ever since 1989 I have been pulling my eyelashes out; it's this nervous habit I have. My mother always tries to coax me into letting my eyelashes grow by telling me she'll give me this or that if I actually do it.

"Give me that gift, Leszli," she always says to me. "I don't want to die without seeing you with your eyelashes." I am going to give her that gift. I promise.

Friday, July 9, 1999

Today I started to warm up to the group a little, but I don't know . . . it's hard for me. I do it for my father, so that he doesn't see me so isolated and alone all the time. I know it worries him. The only person I talk to, aside from him, is Laureano. We're good friends. He's such a nice, calm person. With him, everything's okay, he never disagrees with anyone—he just says what he thinks, and he never goes around telling other people that they're wrong about this or that.

A few days ago Uriel decided to go on a hunger strike as a way of pressuring the guerrillas. My father did not agree with this tactic; he said that if we go on a hunger strike we'll all get sick, which will only make things harder on us. In this type of situation, he said, the best thing we can do is stay calm, and show our captors that we are ready and willing to do whatever they tell us, to avoid problems. To tell the truth, I was about ready to join Uriel on the hunger strike, but then when I heard Dad's argument, I realized he was right and so I said no. Laureano said, "I will help however I can, but if I start getting really hungry you're going to have to count me out, because I don't want to risk anything happening to me. Laszlo's right."

I had to laugh at his response—it was a very ingenious way of, basically, saying no.

I guess I began to distance myself from all of them for a couple of reasons, most importantly because they're all men and I'm the only woman in the group. Fernando and Diego are occasionally nice to me, but they can also be a little two-faced sometimes. For example, one of the guerrillas brought us Parcheesi for six people, to break the monotony, to give us something to do. Well, I was the one who wanted to play the most; my father and Uriel didn't really care so much. When I saw Fernando and Diego walk past my tent with the game, I asked them if they were planning on playing, and they said yes.

"Oh, great, I'll be right down," I said.

I got up quickly, put my socks and boots on, and went over to where they were. But Fernando, when he saw me, suddenly said: "Oh, no . . . we already told one of the guerrillas that we'd play with him."

"Oh, right," I said, and just left it at that. Then I walked over to a fallen tree trunk off to the side of the playing field, where nobody could see me, and I started to cry.

I felt really rotten after that. Obviously Fernando and Diego didn't want to play with me. Why? I still have no idea. There's never been anything between us, good or bad. The only thing I can think of is that maybe they just don't like me, because I don't recite the rosary every night with them. But the truth is, I think it's completely ridiculous to recite the rosary if your mind wanders all over the place like mine does. Repeating words just to repeat words makes no sense to me. You get to a point where you don't even know what all those words mean. Really, it's so ridiculous. Fernando, especially, he's always hitting himself on the chest and praying all day long to every last saint you can think of, but in general he really acts like a jerk. So then what's the point of all that praying if your thoughts are still black as anything? It's like that song that says Jesus is a verb, not a noun.

The head guerrilla caught me crying by the tree trunk and came over to talk to me. He told me not to pay any attention to them and not to feel so bad. Then he told me that whenever I wanted to play to let him know, that if he wasn't too busy he'd play with me.

I thanked him for that. It was so nice that someone other than my father actually cared about how I felt. A little later on the guerrillas gathered us around to call a meeting for tomorrow. What for? No idea. I hope for something good.

Saturday, July 10, 1999

The commander spoke to us today.

"All right, people, I want to tell you that I've been talking to one of the men from the COCE [the central command of the ELN], and he told me that they are in conversations with the Santodomingo Group. They've had two meetings already and they are doing everything they can to get you out of here. I know that this has been dragging on, but the COCE men asked me to extend their apologies for having told you that you would be out of here very fast. We don't want you to think that we don't keep our word."

They also told us that they didn't know how long we'd be in captivity, but that we'd better prepare ourselves for a couple more months in the jungle. In other words, five months in total. He said he understood how difficult this was for us, and that he knew what this was like from all of his friends who'd been in jail, but that it was all for a good cause, and we had to understand that. Then he told us that he admired our patience, though mentally I said to myself, it's not patience, it's resignation. Finally, he asked us how we were, and I replied, "We're pretty bored."

That, in short, is the news of the day.

As of today, we've been here for three months, and though you'd think I'd be out of my mind by now, I'm not. I had a very good talk with God, and asked Him to send me a lot of serenity, and to help me fulfill my goals. And that's what I've done.

I asked my grandmother Gisella to help me, too. And I also asked my other grandparents, plus Carlos González and Gonzalo Rodríguez. I still can't fully believe that he died just a week before I was kidnapped. He was such a happy person, such a special man . . . and now what will happen to his children, and his wife Leíto? I had so much fun with them on December 28, 1997. I'm very good friends with them, especially Sergio, their older son. He was in awful shape the week Gonzalo died, and I just didn't know what to say to him. His death really shook me up—in fact, I'm still pretty shaken up by it. That's why I decided to ask him to help me get out of here in the next fifteen days, after saying seven Our Fathers, seven Hail Marys, and reciting the creed seven times. I promised to do this for the next seven days. I started yesterday. At night I started talking to Carlos González. I told him that he, more than anyone, knows what all this is like, and I told him that if he helped me out of here, I would go to his grave to thank him for it, and when I was sitting at his graveside, we would remember the night of July 11, when I asked this favor of him, and of everyone else, the Virgin Mary, and God.

Friday, July 16, 1999

Last night we felt a rumble beneath us, and the earth began to shake. All the toiletries on our little table began to tremble, and we heard something loud, strong, but it wasn't our things: it was the sound of the earth. It lasted about 35 or 40 seconds, and it began with a thunderous boom and a massive jolt. After a while it subsided, little by little, but then, all of a sudden, everything started to move again, even more violently than before, and then finally it really did end. I was very worried that something had happened in Bucaramanga, where there's a fault line, the kind that causes earthquakes, and since my family lives in a top-floor apartment, I got very scared. On the radio they mentioned the tremor, and also some good news: they started talking about us on Caracol, one of the radio stations. I feel certain that it's because of the promise I made to God. If this is true, then I should be home by August 10. Both me and "the other Leszli" are very, very happy. Ahh!

Saturday, July 17, 1999

Around 9:05 in the morning, the earth shook again, much more violently than last night, and it actually woke me up. Again I started thinking: what if something happened in Bucaramanga? Since we're stuck here, we have no way of finding out anything beyond what they report on the radio.

Today I cleaned up the hut a little, made the beds, and swept. It looks a lot better now.

I've been thinking a lot about Laura Díaz, a neighbor of ours who was on the plane that crashed into the mountainside after taking off from Cúcuta a couple of years ago. Last night I dreamt about her. I was looking out the window in our apartment and I was very small. Laura was inside a big antique, dark wood armoire with dark and light green upholstery. At some point it seemed as if a lot of time had gone by, and from my window I was suddenly looking out at the same old furniture sitting on an ugly little patio, and I felt sad, so sad, as I watched time go by. Then I saw a big coffee-colored spider crawling on top of the furniture. It was so awful I woke up in the middle of the dream.

Sunday, July 18, 1999

Very early this morning I heard my mother and Carolina on the radio show "Despertar en América" (Awake in America). Over the airwaves I heard my mother say that she loved me very much, she hoped I wasn't getting sick, and that she knew I was a brave girl just like her. She also told me to try to treat all of this like an extended vacation, and then she asked me to take good care of my father. Today, she said, they were expecting the arrival of the German diplomats who would be interceding in the negotiations with the ELN, and she finished off by saying that she was keeping my room pretty and that everyone was thinking of us. After her, I heard Carol's voice asking me and my father to never forget that we are in her heart, and that her first and last thoughts every day are of us.

After that I got up and went to eat breakfast. Then I heard shouts: it was Laureano, Francisco, and Juan killing a snake, a brown-and-white coral snake. It was so sad! Then one of the guerrillas came by carrying a pigeon with a broken wing. Together with my dad, we made her a little nest, and with little bits of the foam mattresses we sleep on, we made her a tiny pillow. Then we gave her water and food and I gave her a drop of medicine to ease her pain. She's very pretty and quite big, though not as big as a carrier pigeon. She's a reddish, red-wine color with black flecks. When I lay her out in the sun the little flecks sparkle. She really is so lovely and sweet. Maybe she thinks I'm going to hurt her, but really, all I want to do is help her get better so that she can fly again, be free again. I ache inside when I see her like that. God, please help her, don't let her die. She must have little babies and a family somewhere, and it would be so sad if she never flew again.

My father just brought me some figs, *mmm.* . . .

Monday, July 19, 1999

It's 8 A.M. and the pigeon already ate breakfast. My father gave her a bit of rice, water, and Tramal, and he also gave her a little sling to immobilize her wing. The group leader gathered our letters. On the news we heard that John F. Kennedy Jr. died in a plane accident. They still haven't found his body.

Yesterday I completed my promise of saying all those prayers.

Fernando is once again acting the way he did before. I thought that he'd changed after that last incident, but no, of course not. Today he organized a game of Parcheesi very quickly, so that I wouldn't join in, and everyone else just acted like nothing odd was going on. This time I am really going to try and not let all these things affect me so much. Last night a cicada crawled into the hut where Laureano and Francisco sleep, and since they're such chickens when it comes to all these little insects, they came running to me to help them get rid of it.

I hope the letters I sent today reach my mother fast—she hasn't heard from me since June 1. Apparently the other letters I sent her never arrived.

Three years ago today, in 1996, I was on a plane headed for Colombia after spending my summer vacation in Atlanta, where they held the Olympics.

Tuesday, July 20, 1999

This morning Francisco asked me if I wanted to play Battleship, but I said no. I think my father talked to him about including me in their games, but it makes me uncomfortable to think that he did that—they all must think I spend all my time complaining about him. That's why I said no.

The day has been long and boring. Right now I am listening to the mother of a little girl named Silvia Yesenia, on the Colombian national radio station. She hasn't seen her daughter in three years. Silvia must be fourteen by now; she was kidnapped when she was eleven.

Fernando acts very differently with me now: he's unbelievably annoying, and he's always trying to make me look dumb in front of everyone else, giving me stupid nicknames, whatever idiotic thing comes into his head. I don't know why he does that—before, he was perfectly normal with me; we were on pretty decent terms. I never gave him nicknames, so I have no idea why he's doing it to me now. My father tells me to just act like he and Diego don't exist, and that's exactly what I'm doing. The truth is, I can't stand them, either.

At 9:05 P.M., when I returned to the tent, my father told me that the little pigeon died. I just took a look at her, she's stiff as a board. It hurts so much to see her like that, though I know God did the right thing, because she was in such great pain, that little bird. Still, if I had known she was going to die, I never would have left her cooped up in that cage—I would have left her out on a tree so that she could die free. This is so hard for me; I was so fond of that little bird. I had secretly hoped I could take her back with me to Bucaramanga, where they could put her wing in a cast so that she could recover and fly again. But it's too late for that now.

I hate it when things like this happen, especially to a defenseless little animal that doesn't have words to tell you what hurts. She must have suffered a great deal. If I could have made some kind of sacrifice—any kind, a big one even, to help that little bird get better, I would have done it gladly. Now, however, I have made a decision: I am going to stop eating meat for all the little animals that are unjustly killed.

I spent an entire morning and an entire afternoon thinking about the day of my release, and how I would manage to carry the pigeon home with me without harming her. Then I thought about all the walks we'd take together . . . all that and now this! And then I have to ask myself why such a tiny animal should have to endure such terrible suffering. Why didn't it happen to me? I can talk, I can complain, I am able to say what hurts and where. . . . The day I die, if I can talk to God, among other things I would like to know is this: Why don't people care about animals? Why do some people kill animals? Will some form of justice punish them? I hope so, with all my heart: those people should pay for what they do.

Today I stayed with the dead pigeon for a long time, looking after her. Yesterday I told her about all the things I had dreamed of doing for her: I told her that I would free her, I told her how much I loved her. I hope she understood everything I said; I'm really glad I did it, because I was speaking to her from the heart. I know she is at rest, and that my words and my affection are with her now.

I hope there is a heaven up there for animals, and I hope that it is much bigger than the paradise where human beings dwell, because animals are the creatures that bring joy to life on Earth, they are the ones who make this life a little easier to bear.

I pray that God is with you, and that you are happy at this moment, my beautiful pigeon. . . . Wherever you are, I love you very much.

Wednesday, July 21, 1999

Today I played Battleship with Francisco and I let him win—that poor guy always loses when he plays with me. I had a happy afternoon because I received a letter from my mother, Mauri, Carol, and Nandor, and they filled me in on lots of things. They also sent us medicine and some other things. I'm so happy: every time I read and reread what they say, I can hardly believe it. I want to be with them as soon as possible. Today they gave me a black Gef T-shirt and socks. Nandor told me that he bought me some white Gap shirts and my mother bought me a pair of sandals.

My mother also told me that she has been traveling a lot, that she actually went to see the politician Horacio Serpa at his house. Apparently, he spoke with Juan Gabriel Uribe, the peace negotiator, to see if he could get her a meeting at the jail in Itagüí, so that she could talk to the ELN commanders there, but he said no. Then she told me that she's planning to go to the south of Bolivar, which is where the ELN landed our plane, to help get me out of here, but I really think it'll just be a waste of time. Then my mom told me that María Helena, Diego's mother, who is very religious, was fasting for me, and that Diego Rafael Luna and Luz Stella—I have no idea who she is—wrote to me in *La Vanguardia*.

It's five to nine and I just saw my mother on the TV news, at the San Pedro church. She said she was planning to go to Germany to talk with the COCE people if nothing happened on Friday. She was wearing a very pretty white blouse. Today we cut some wooden planks and used them for the beds and the two tables. They look really nice.

An airplane flew overhead at 10:25 P.M.

Uriel had a talk with me and my father. I'm really glad he did that; I think we'll all be a lot better off if me and my dad can reintegrate with the group. Diego also came over to talk to us, and that made me even happier: he asked me if I was angry with him, and I told him no, and we started talking about the letters, and how emotional it was for us to receive them, and we also talked about how much we wanted to see our families, to be free again. Juan has never been unpleasant with me, but he never really talks to me much, either. Today he did, though, to tell me I should write to my mother to ask her to bring me back some things from her trip to Germany.

Oh, Mommy, I adore you, I miss you so much! I always stick up for you here with my father, I never let him say anything bad about you, because as far as I'm concerned you are the best mother in the world. Today I can truly say that I value everything so very much and that makes me feel good: to value both the good and the bad things.

It's 10 P.M. and I just heard Carolina and my mother on Caracol, telling us about their two new cats. My mother loves to pick up stray cats from the street and bring them home with her. Just listening to them makes me so, so happy. That message from them was the most perfect ending to my day—my best day yet in this place. Today I received letters from my mother, from Carol, from Nandor, and from Maru, and I also heard about Diego, Jairo, Lito, Líela, Lina, Andrea, Diego's cousin, María Helena, Carla Carrillo, and Sergio.

There are two more cats at home now, plus Pablo is still alive. I do cherish my cat, along with all the cats and all the other animals in the world.

I am crying right now as I write this. I'm just so overwhelmed by all the emotions I feel. Thank you, God, thank you.

Friday, July 23, 1999

Last night Carolina and Nandor spoke. Nandor said, "*Aló, papi, mami!*" Kind of silly, but anyway. Carol told me that Kike Acuña arrived.

Today the guerrilla soldiers more or less finished building the playing field, just like they promised. This place doesn't look anything at all like it did before, when we got here, all full of weeds and things. Now it looks like a real country estate: we now have a clear path down to the river; the mud has finally dried up. It's really like a deluxe ranch, with chairs all over the campsite, and the soldiers also built a bunch of huts for themselves. With power saws, they chopped down a lot of the trees in the area so that they could make that playing field. Once they felled the trees they cut them in long planks that they'll use as firewood. Then, with shovels and hoes, they dug holes around each tree, lifted out the roots, and hacked away at them with axes to level off the ground. Then they covered up the holes and stomped around to make everything flat. They did that over and over again, and when they were through, I'd say they must have gotten rid of some forty trees and lots of underbrush.

The campsite looks so pretty. Fokker, our little dog, is now huge, plus he understands everything we say, and eats everything we give him. I love to spoil him. A few weeks ago they brought us eight little hens, which soon became big hens and now we have even more little chickens. Every so often one of the guerrillas goes out and makes the rounds, to places only they know about, and comes back with chickens and hens. We've got about fifty of them, in all shapes and sizes, running around the campsite.

Today I dressed in black from head to toe, and played Parcheesi. My father tells me that I look really thin, but I know he's lying: I'm fat as a pig. That's the way I see myself, at least, and it only makes me sadder, more frustrated, and more depressed than ever.

Yesterday I made a list of all the words that I need to work on. I'll do the same thing today, because in one of his letters Nandor told me that I really have to work on my spelling.

I hope time passes quickly, because the mood here is getting worse and worse, and the guy in charge here never gives us a straight answer for anything. They're not even talking about us on the news anymore, and I just look out onto the horizon and ask myself over and over again: When are we going to get out of here? Why is it so hard for me to imagine that I might actually be freed someday? Why? Lately I have started to get the feeling that I am going to die here, that I will never see the people I love ever again. What did I do to deserve this fate? God, I feel that I am losing my strength.

After watching the news, I walked past the two chairs where Diego and Fernando were sitting, and I just kept on walking. I went down to see the supply lady and the Nice Old Man, her husband, and I asked them for some toilet paper. Then I went a little bit further down and got ready to "make my hole," which is the term we use here for going to the bathroom. In the middle of this, Diego yelled out to me, "Leszli, Leszli!"

"I'm coming, I'm coming," I yelled. "I'm making my hole."

When I was done I washed my hands and headed back to the supply tent to get some soda crackers and mayonnaise, and when I was done I walked back up with the supply lady, and gave her a lighter. Then I went back to Diego and Fernando, and explained why I couldn't answer them before, and they told me that Carolina and Juan Carlos García had been talking on La Mega, the radio station, and that Carolina spoke in this very cutesy little voice. Then, apparently, Juan Carlos said something about La Mega's little rich girl, and asked my sister how old I was, and who my favorite singers were. When she told them I was 18, and that my favorite singers were Laura Pausini and Ricardo Arjona, they dedicated a song to me, *"Emergencia de amor"* by Laura Pausini. How stupid that I missed it all because I was going to the bathroom!

After I finished writing about everything that happened last week, I went over to the tree trunk and Francisco came by.

"Leszli," he said, "is it true that you got into a fight with Fernando over who was going to make my birthday cake?"

I explained to him that it didn't happen exactly that way, that it hadn't been because of the cake, but that we had gotten into a fight because Fernando wanted to make it and since I had already started it, if I let him start over I wasn't going to be able to eat the figs and the raisins that I had put in. Anyway, I tried to make him understand what had really happened but I don't know if he bought the story. I don't really give a damn what he thinks, though—right here, right now, in the situation we're in, I could care less what that slob thinks.

It's 8:15 and I'm not tired at all. My conscience is bothering me about the 25 crackers I ate with half a jar of mayonnaise. Why do I do these things? I go all day without eating a thing, and then when I finally do eat, I gulp everything down like there's no tomorrow....

I don't feel so bad anymore, because I just vomited everything and I feel good. Now I'm going to try and sleep with some of those pills Nandor sent me, although I don't think they work at all—they haven't done a thing so far.

God, please take care of me so that I don't waste my time thinking about such stupid things.

It's 10:20 at night and we've been playing Parcheesi since 9. It's really a big drag, because there are six of us and we still haven't finished. I just got out of "jail" and I'm tired. I don't know how much longer this is going to take but I wish they would win already.

We just heard some awful news on Caracol—it sent a chill down my spine, and my eyes filled up with tears. The commander of the ABC column of the ELN said he is going to demand ransom money for the hostages from the airplane and the church, as well as the ones in Barranquilla. The commander's name is Mario and they say he despises people with money.

"Just like the government levies taxes during war, so do we, and if the people don't pay them, they'll pay with their lives."

The journalist responded, "When will they be freed?"

"When they've paid up."

I feel so horribly impotent right now. Life has been so unfair to us, it feels like a curse to have been born on this goddamn rotten earth—to think that they have put a price on my life as if it were something you could buy and sell!

God, if I am not going to get out of here anytime soon, please let me die soon. Day by day, minute by minute, this is hell.

Until tomorrow, my dear, beloved diary.

Saturday, July 24, 1999

How much longer are we going to have to put up with this torture, this agony? I want to die. I knew something like this was going to happen and I have this terrible feeling that release is far, far away. I don't want to believe that I am going to die here, but if that is how it's going to be . . . oh, it is so frustrating to think that there is nothing I can do about it. I guess we will just have to wait to hear what they say on the news; maybe they will say it wasn't true.

I just saw my mother on the 7 o'clock news. She was wearing the blue dress I love, the one with the white flowers; she looked so pretty. She said she would pay whatever she had to pay, that the freedom of a child is priceless.

Sunday, July 25, 1999

The lady in the supply tent is definitely a hypocrite: sometimes she's as sweet as honey, and then other times, like today, she doesn't want to hear from me. What an idiot!

Monday, July 26, 1999

Today I woke up very early. I can't take it anymore: nobody here listens to anything I say. These people don't care what I think, what I feel. It's all so frustrating! If I could only figure out some way to get out of here . . . I'll write more later on. . . .

Today when I went to take a bath I found a pair of scissors; I think they belong to one of the guerrillas. I asked him to cut my hair but he said no; he said that women were supposed to have long hair. I insisted and insisted but he still refused, so I took the scissors myself and chopped off a big hunk of my hair. When he saw my hair all lopsided, he said to me, "Hey, Leszli, what's the matter with you? You're doing that to get me to cut it, right?"

I said yes, and he said, "All right, come on, I'll even it out for you."

Once he was done, I told him to cut off a little more. He said no, that it would look really bad, plus they might punish him for cutting off so much.

"Fine," I said to him. "Thanks very much, now lend me those scissors."

"I'll give them to you, but if you cut off any more of your hair, I'm warning you, it's going to stay like that, because I'm not going to even it out for you again."

"Fine."

He handed me the shears and it was all over in a matter of seconds: this time the scissors touched my scalp and I just kept on cutting and cutting until it was as short as it would go. When I was through, I grabbed a razor and began to shave off what little hair was left. Watching my hair fall away and drift down the rushing river was a singular, extraordinary feeling. Total release.

It was definitely a fit of rage, but I don't feel bad about it. On the contrary, I feel good without a single hair on my head. I always wanted to do it, but I just never felt the motivation to really go through with it. I can hardly believe I really did it. My father is really angry with me, but he just doesn't understand what I was going through—on the inside, it felt as if something was killing me. I hope he can accept what I did; in reality it was just my way of breaking free from this unbearable monotony. I'm pretty weird, though, I know: I mean, there are times when I can barely figure myself out, so how can

I expect him to understand me? I don't care if I look ugly or pretty: I didn't shave my head thinking about looking better or worse, I did it because I felt the need to effect some kind of change in this life of mine that is so unbearably difficult. Now, with this new hair, I am going to try to be another person: with my new hair, a new Leszli will be born. . . . I don't know why but every time I want to make a change in my life the first thing I do is change something about my hair.

My father has taken it very hard, my being bald and everything. If I had known this was going to happen I wouldn't have done it. Now everyone thinks I have some serious mental problem, and to make matters worse, I agree with them. I just don't know how to help myself. The only thing I care about right now is my father, though. I want him to be okay, and I know he's not. Seeing him this way only makes me feel worse, and I don't know what to do about it. I will change, but I don't know how to do it.

Today I made a vow: I am going to eat three meals a day. Before, I only ate one or two, depending on how I felt, and then I would run out to throw it all up because I would feel so guilty when I saw how much I ate and ate, without ever doing the least bit of exercise. I am not going to throw up my food. That, I think, may be what's bothering me so much. And I am going to integrate better with the guerrillas, I will be attentive and courteous with everyone, I will make sure my father doesn't worry about me, I will try not to blurt out all the stupid thoughts that run through my mind, I will be more organized, more in control, so that people will think I'm all right. . . . Once I get back to Bucaramanga I am going to talk to Nandor about this vomiting thing, to figure out the best way to get over it. I can't go on like this. I know I'm hurting myself and, even worse, I'm hurting my father with everything I'm doing.

I feel so awful. Everything is a big mess and I feel so guilty for everything that's happened. I mean, my father is here, kidnapped, because of me, because of my trip. The only one who should be here is me. And I want to tell him how I feel but I just can't find the way to do it: I want to tell him what I am feeling, what I am thinking, but I'm scared that I will only make things harder on him. I want to tell him how awful I feel but I can't, I just cannot do it. Plus, he doesn't even want to see me; he already told me to leave him alone. Oh, God, what agony I am in!

Father, when I see you in that bed, supposedly asleep, I know you are suffering for me. It may seem hard to believe, but I don't know what I am doing or why, I don't know what I think or why I think the things I think. All I know is that I have a lot on my mind that I cannot explain. I wish I could just let go of all the things that fill me with rage and pain, all those things that keep me from living in peace, but I can't. I know that what I'm doing is bad, I know that I am a mess and a problem. I wish I knew how to get out of this, but I feel that this is something that's been building inside of me for a long, long time. Ever since I was a little girl I have been different, complicated, incapable, maladjusted. These things have only grown worse with time, and the bigger they get, the more obvious my problems are to everyone else. I always try to search for a situation, a place, and a person to blame, but deep down I know it's me—the only guilty party here is me. I am just a problem for the people I love. Daddy, I know that when you look at me all you see is a giant problem. You don't know what's going to become of me, of my life, and you think nobody will ever put up with me. In some sense, that is what really troubles you about me.

My problems, insignificant as they may be, have a way of becoming these massive walls that I just seem incapable of tearing down. Everything is such hard work! I don't know what to do; maybe that's why I keep coming up with these dumb ideas—I guess because I sometimes feel that the only way out is by thinking this way. But there are other times when I do feel that I can topple those walls and I gather all the strength I have and race toward them, but most times I only end up hurting myself. I turn around, leave the problems half-solved, and keep on going until I find another problem, and then when I realize that I have this new problem plus the other ones I left unresolved, it goes on and on and seems more and more insurmountable. . . .

Daddy, I'm not going to ask you to understand me. All I ask is that you forgive me. I never meant to hurt you. I adore you. I'm even angrier at myself now because I know I'm the one who's gotten you so upset. I never, never meant for you to suffer, and I never want anything bad to happen to you. You and I never used to spend much time together, and for that very reason I now give thanks to God for making this happen to us, for bringing us together here in this situation. I hope and pray that I feel this way forever, and I hope to always have you with me. It hurts me to think of how I didn't really spend my childhood with you, but I know that you were always there in some way. For once and forever, I ask you to forgive me for being the way I am, but I also want you to know that I love you with all my heart and soul.

Tuesday, July 27, 1999

Carolina and Nandor spoke on the radio today. I could tell from their voices that they weren't feeling very optimistic, even though they tried to sound positive. Nandor said he doesn't know what to do anymore, and Carol told me to keep eating well, to keep my defenses up. She also told me that Diego called on Thursday and that Kike and Jairo said hello.

Today the Nice Old Man and I had a long chat that was pure and total psychology. But I'm still the same as ever. As for my father—forget it, he doesn't even want to look at me, and since I don't know what to do, I just stay out of his way and don't get involved. He asked me not to talk to him, so I guess that's the least I can do.

I started reading one of the books Toto and Cony, Lucía's relatives, sent me. They're so nice. I thank God for having this book here at this moment: *Don Simeón Torrente ha dejado de deber*, which says that any situation, no matter how bad, can always get worse. I hope to God this one doesn't.

Wednesday, July 28, 1999

We got some news on TV today: Pastrana said that the ELN has just named the spokespeople who will be talking to the government to negotiate the release of the hostages from the Avianca Fokker plane (us), the Church of the Virgin Mary, and Barranquilla. I hope they do it soon.

Last night I had the most incredible dream: I was on my way to Argentina and I saw a white, five-story building with the most beautiful balconies, overlooking a cliff. Behind it I could see a crystal-clear ocean, with a huge sheet of glass in the middle through which I could see all sorts of things: a humongous, and I mean humongous white whale with the most beautiful smile, and there were also dolphins and millions of little fish, and I could see all the underwater plant life and the coral reefs, too. . . . I was going up in an elevator, which was really scary because the elevator floor was also made of glass and I could see all the way down. There were lots of pools in the building, some were surrounded by gardens and planters, like Jacuzzis, and then there was another pool on top with a waterfall.

What a dream! That's the best one I've had yet.

Thursday, July 29, 1999

Last night I had a dream about the gym at the San Pedrito Claver school. It seemed much smaller than it really is: it was all very, very tiny and there was a room, like a kind of theater, very cute, tidy, pretty, but I felt so sad as I watched the time go by. An older man told me not to worry and then he asked me if I wanted to go back to school there. I said yes, and then suddenly I was a little girl again. And everything was instantly so simple. . . .

It's 9:30 in the morning. I'm waiting for some kind of news, for them to come by and tell me: "All right, get ready, because you're leaving tomorrow," or that at least tomorrow we're going to start the 20-day walk back to freedom. I want to hear something, anything that will allow me to hang on to the hope I felt yesterday when I saw the news. I pray it's true, because I just don't think I can take another disappointment.

Later on this evening, my mother spoke on UIS, the radio station run by Santander Industrial University. She told me to hold on and stay strong, because in ten days I'd be back home. I got so excited when I heard her say that, I thought I might explode. But then when I got to thinking, I wondered why she said such a thing. I really have no idea. The day I'm released I'm going to wear a bandanna to hide my bald head, because I know that she, and everyone else for that matter, are going to flip out when they see me. When she was finished talking I played Parcheesi with Laureano, Uriel, and Daniel (one of the guerrillas). Uriel won first, and then I won, because I cheated.

I've been thinking about Diego a lot lately. When I get out of here I am going to tell him how I feel. He can do what he wants—he can take it or he can leave it. If he takes it, great. And if not, well, I don't care anymore. It's time we finished this chapter in our lives once and for all; we've being going round and round for four years already. It's time for someone to come into my life; and to stay there forever, someone who loves me and who I love back. No matter what, though, I want to stay good friends with Diego. Oh, God, enough with this already, I'm like a broken record. . . . I really miss those conversations we used to have with Jairo, I miss them so much!

It's just me now, just me: my doubts and my certainties, my life and my hopes, my questions without answers. . . . Sometimes I feel that I go through life trying not to leave my mark anywhere, so that nobody remembers me. I live in a world . . . no, a world lives inside of me. I enjoy my solitude and the world enjoys its pleasures without me. I just look up toward the heavens and wish I could be up there.

Friday, July 30, 1999

My thoughts on kidnapping
For whomever is interested

I AM NOT A SHIELD!

I reject kidnapping. I reject the notion that these people can take my life and use it as a shield, whether for political or economic gain. I, gentlemen, just like you, am a human being, and as such, my freedom deserves respect. My political beliefs and the social or economic class to which I belong are irrelevant: above and beyond those things, I am a human being. And I was granted the right to my freedom the very moment I came into this world.

Let us not attack one another, let us not hurt our fellow

man, or place obstacles on the path to our dreams, and please let us not erect prison bars that prevent us from living our lives.

I, like millions of other human beings, am sad because I see how kidnapping affects the father, the mother, the brother, the neighbor, the friend, the acquaintance, the son, on a day-to-day basis. It is a reality that is tormenting the Colombian people.

People suffer a great deal in captivity, far more than they should. We are consumed by feelings of impotence and often we feel our faith fail us, as loneliness takes over. . . . A minute becomes an hour, and an hour becomes a day. Time passes by very slowly and our strength fades.

It is so unfair to have to watch the days go by knowing that you are far from those you love, knowing that you are alive when in fact you actually feel quite dead, given that you no longer participate in the ordinary activities of everyday life, and it is so unfair to never know what on earth is going on beyond that wall that has been erected in front of you.

I am telling you, *no more*. I am simply pleading with you, from the bottom of my heart, to be aware of your actions. And, well . . . yes, I tell you *no more*. Enough with this. That is the dream of all Colombia.

Yours sincerely,
Leszli Kálli López

Saturday, July 31, 1999

I am so glad to see another month come to an end. I try to think about how it's one month less, not one month more. Yesterday I wrote a letter that I hope to publish once we're out of here. It's all about the idea of no more kidnappings. On the other hand, I'm pretty happy because today my father and I made up. Plus, we remodeled the hut.

Today I talked to the painter guerrilla in the TV shack. It was nice. I think I am getting fat but I vow not to vomit my food.

I hope that God is listening carefully to the things I say to him. I have faith that before August 10, I will be out of this. The promise regarding my eyelashes still stands: as of today I have gone twenty-three days without touching them, and I am very proud of myself. I never thought I'd ever be able to keep that promise, and I know that God has a lot to do with it. The best thing about all this, however, will be the look on my mother's face when she sees me with eyelashes. I may be bald but I have my eyelashes. By the time we're released, though, hopefully my hair will have grown back a little.

Oh, I feel so full, I can't take it. I'm going to vomit. . . .

11:40 P.M.: the last few minutes of this Saturday and of this month. My dad and I are staying up until 12:30, to listen to *Amanecer en América,* to see if anyone sends us a message of some sort.

I can't sleep. I'm too wired, thinking about the day we'll be released, and about Diego, too. How is he? I wonder. I know he's thinking of me, too, right now. There are so many questions running through my mind, I don't know how I am going to answer them all.

The oddest thing happens here: every Saturday it rains, like clockwork. Incredible but true. Now, as I say goodbye to these last few minutes of July, and to the entire first half of the year, I affirm my belief that in the second half of the year we will finally be released.

Sunday, August 1, 1999

There were no messages for me on the radio last night, except for one from Esperanza Duque, but I was so sleepy that I didn't hear it. Today, though, there was good news on the radio: they reported that Gabriel García Márquez, Horacio Serpa, and Yamid Amat told the Colombian government that they would be wise to talk with the guerrillas first and then get them to release us, rather than doing it the other way around—waiting for them to free us and then starting the talks. They are waiting for an answer from the ELN.

Today Laureano said to me: "You know what, Leszli? I think they're going to free you first, because you don't have anything to do with all this, plus you're the only woman in the group. Your mother really seems to be moving things, and that's a big help to you."

Today I ate tuna and salad for lunch. I ate very little so that I wouldn't feel so full and then have to vomit. Laureano and I have struck up the nicest friendship. I really like him, and I know he likes me, too, but I don't want to get involved with anyone here. Anyway, he's very shy and never says anything—but that's perfectly fine with me.

According to my mother, I've got eight days left here. If that's true, this will be my last Sunday here. I want to believe what she says, but something tells me that I shouldn't be quite so naïve.

My hut has an entrance and a rope for my clothing, and also a *velero,* which is a pole with a little candle, a table made of three wooden planks that my father built. Then there are our two beds.

As of today we have been here 112 days: me, my father, Francisco, Juan, Laureano, Diego, Fernando, and Uriel Velasco.

The captivity is beginning to take its toll on Laureano: he seems totally dazed and wanders around as if he were drunk. What a strange reaction. The poor guy—he's even quieter than I am, much less expressive than me, too.

Last night something kind of unpleasant happened with the guerrilla who was so nice to me before: when he said good night, he insinuated that he kind of liked me. I don't know why—I never did anything to try to seduce him into feeling anything for me. Of all the guerrillas, he was one of my favorites. I'm not going to say anything to anyone about it; anyway, he's gone, and it's over.

I haven't seen the head guerrilla in a while.

I think I'm starting to isolate myself from the group again.

Monday, August 2, 1999

President Andrés Pastrana is in Bucaramanga, talking about us. He says that he will initiate a dialogue with the ELN only after we've been released, that he gives his word. But I know that's just the same old, same old: nothing! As for me, I'm still bald, and I've still got those eyelashes, but now I have a tiny sty on my left eyelid. What a drag.

Diego González is not doing well at all. Last night I talked to him and Fernando. Diego told me that every day he asks God to let him die. I tried to cheer him up and told him to look at it in another light, as a life lesson that we had to face up to with a great deal of strength and resolve. What nobody knows, of course, is that I feel exactly the way he does—I just don't show it because that would only make things worse. I have to show them that I am strong, even when I feel the opposite.

We've been in captivity for 113 days now. Francisco and Juan set up the net to play volleyball.

Things have gotten a little better, I guess, partly because there's a new guerrilla here, a health aide who arrived yesterday. She told Francisco and Laureano that they ought to do some exercise to prepare for the walk back, which will definitely be a long one. Francisco, who was kind of playing, but kind of serious, said to her, "Right, since we're going to be leaving in seven days . . ."

And she replied, "I don't think it'll be that long." But who knows if she was joking.

The head guerrilla just told my father to wash the pants of his pilot's uniform, to have them ready, and then gave him a fresh pair. Lately we've gotten a lot of indications like that. I pray the rumors are true. The hours this week are going to be endless, I know it, but I am so thrilled to think about the day we'll be released. Tomorrow we'll get more messages. I hope my mother writes to tell me something— anything—to confirm all this.

Thank you, God, for this.

I have to sign off now because I am going to ruin my eyes if I keep on writing in the candlelight.

Until tomorrow.

Me.

Tuesday, August 3, 1999

My dream last night was very weird. It was around 5 P.M. and I was in the ocean in Miami, in the canal we always went to with my dad. I took a dip in the water and with my hand in the sand I took off the silver necklace and bracelet that my mother gave me, and I was totally frightened. Then I was with Diego, right there in the same place, and I felt something dragging us over to the other side, and people were screaming at us, asking us if it was a shark, and I said no. We were moving very fast, and then suddenly a huge wave rose above our heads and Diego and I hugged each other tight. The wave crashed down and then another image appeared in the dream: it was night-time, and I was in a boat on the open sea. Instead of Diego, my mother was with me now, stroking my back. Then another image: I saw myself alone in a cemetery, at night, with a flashlight that I shone onto one of the gravestones, which had the name of two children who had died that same day, a century earlier. The inscription said something about a great-great-grandfather whose name began with an O. . . . And then I woke up.

There was nothing on the news at 12. But I am convinced that all those offhand comments can't mean nothing. Last night, at around midnight, I got up and talked to my father.

Today is day 114 here. Today is the day we get the messages on UIS. I hope I get lots.

Lunch today was rice and beans, which I ate without any hunger at all. I ate to eat, just to kill the boredom.

I always love it when the sun goes down because it makes me think of how another day is over, and that maybe tomorrow we'll get a nice surprise. But then, when I wake up I always feel sad and depressed, because the sun begins to shine down on the hard reality of yet another day here. I really do love the night; it is so wonderful. I only wish it could be dark 24 hours a day, because it's so peaceful. In the dark you can think, you can gaze into your soul and, most importantly, you can dream.

Thursday, August 5, 1999

Thank you, God, for the gift you gave me, letting me hear my mother, Nandor, and Jairo. My mother said that yesterday she went to Bogotá to knock on some doors. Nandor and Jairo told me that everyone is thinking of me, which gave me a big boost. Diego, Lito, and Andrés Castro also said hello.

Thank you, God. Help me get out of here soon, please. Remember that I have to be home by the tenth, that's what we said. Today I wrote some letters, which the head guerrilla came by to pick up but I hope that it is your will to get me home first, so I can tell them in person all the things I said in those letters.

Last night I sat up late talking to Francisco. That guy is so stupid, he's always making up stories, just to see the look on my face.

Saturday, August 7, 1999

Here is a letter I have written to myself:

All right, Leszli:
You must always look up, and always think of the present. Don't allow yourself to be consumed by agony: you are great and powerful; you can and will move ahead. You are the most important person in this world. If only you knew how much I love you, you would keep on going without a second thought. As hard as this road may be, and though you may not find answers and you think you are all alone on this rocky path that stretches out before you, I want you to know that I am always with you: when you laugh, when you cry, and even more when you feel sad and filled with despair. You are precious: never let anyone humiliate you or look down on you. And if they don't love you, don't blame yourself: the mistake is theirs, not yours. Just give thanks to God for letting these things happen, because while other people may think that they are dragging you down, what they are really doing is asking you to look at yourself. And when you do this, you have to realize that you are not like everyone else, because of the simple fact that you are a step ahead of all of them. It is useless to try and explain this to them because they are ignorant and they will never under-stand—and even if they did they'd never accept it, because that would mean accepting that they are inferior to you. So feel better: you are the best! I will always be right here at your side to give you strength and to help you move ahead, because in the end you and I are one. . . .
    Leszli Kálli

Today the supply lady fixed my black pants and made me a blue scarf. She also fixed my dad's brown-and-blue pants and got rid of the extra material in his boots.

Right now my father is making a little door at the back of our hut so that I can pop out at night to go to the bathroom without having to walk all the way around.

Yesterday I was very obnoxious to Francisco, so I'm going to apologize today. I went too far, I just didn't realize.

I just finished eating. We had rice (of course), beans, and rice pudding, and I ate and ate and ate until I thought I would pop. Then I threw it all up, because that was the point of it all: to eat until I felt like vomiting, because lately I feel that I am getting very fat. I know I have to control myself, and this is the only diet that works for me around here. The meals here are so poor—all we eat is rice—and I obviously can't decide what I'm going to eat. And if I try and follow some other diet—like, eating every three or four days—the others will realize and start hounding me about it.

It's 6:10 in the evening. In Bucaramanga my friends must be getting ready to go out, figuring out the plan for the night. And me? Here I am in a black sweatshirt, faded green T-shirt, and dirty sneakers. I look so awful! Oh, and I forgot: I've got a plan, too—that is, to go out and watch television. What a drag. At night, at around 12:30, they air the messages on *Amanecer en América,* the radio show for kidnapping victims. And so basically, that's my plan for the night. Wow, some plan.

The crickets are making an incredible racket, and my hand is trembling. My head hurts and I just smoked a cigarette. Luis Miguel, the singer, is crooning something about a nightmare.

Today I saw the TV show *Padres e hijos* and Elga, Laura Díaz's sister, was on.

We've been here now for 120 days and the truth is I don't feel like doing anything, not even taking a bath. Yesterday President Andrés Pastrana spoke. He said that the ELN had expressed a willingness to dialogue with him or an envoy, that Gabino is in Europe, and that we, the hostages, are all fine. My father is convinced that we will get out of here soon; he thinks that by August we'll be out. He was sitting in the chair that he made when he said it to me:

"Leszli, you know when I think it through, the truth is I've got twenty years left, maybe less even. And when I put it in those terms, I think: why do I need to get out of here in such a rush? This is like my farewell to the natural world."

If my dad is right, well, then I thank God for letting him say his goodbye to nature, and with me by his side. Then I said something to him that I meant as a joke, but it came out awfully serious:

"Well, if that's the way it goes, let me just ask you this: if you can do anything for me from up there, if you can help me to be happy, and do the things I want to do, whatever you can, do it . . . and don't forget!"

"Of course, sweetie, of course, don't worry," he said.

The whole thing sounded terrible. I hope I die before he does, before my mom and Nandor and Carol die, too, because I couldn't bear it if any of them died.

When I am as old as my father is right now, forty-eight . . . or, well, rounding off to fifty, he will be eighty, because he is exactly thirty years older than me: he was born in the 1950s, and I was born in the 1980s.

Tuesday, August 10, 1999

Today is the one-month anniversary of our little meeting with the head guerrilla. According to him, we had one month to go here. Tomorrow we will have been here 122 days. When I get out I think it will be just like a dream, or like waking up from a long dream.

Speaking of dreams, last night I dreamt that Carol died and everyone was crying, but I told them not to be sad because her body was dead but her spirit, her soul, was still with us, and there was no reason for us to be crying. Everyone calmed down after that, realizing that what I said was true, they saw it.

For a minute, just as I was waking up I thought that I was at home, but then I realized that no, I was here, in this horrible reality I just can't escape from. . . .

These are the questions I plan on asking when I get back: What time did they find out we had been kidnapped? What did they think when the news reports said there might have been an accident? Where were they when they heard the news? Who called them to tell them what had happened? Who waited around? What did they say?

When Francisco came back from taking his bath, he looked at me and, seeing me with my diary, said, "Dear Diary!" What an idiot.

As far as God is concerned, I have just told him that I am not going to speak to him until I get out of here. I am really angry with God right now, because he has not looked after me. I have begged him and promised him things, many things, like praying for seven days straight, and I even threw in an extra day because I felt like it. I have given him a lot of time to fix all this, but it was all for nothing—nothing. I don't know what is wrong with him, but if he's busier with other things that are more important than me, well then, me, too. That is why tonight, as I gazed up at the stars, I yelled and yelled at him, telling him all those things and more. You see, I get to thinking about my life and all of a sudden I realize that everything has come out wrong: at school, ever since I was little, I have always been the "different" one. At home, my parents were separated. And then of course there's Diego. When I broke up with him I asked God to bring us back together, because I was so upset, and as always, the answer was no. Then with Cristhian, my second boyfriend, it turned out he didn't love me. . . . Oh, what a headache with that guy! Everything I went through . . . I held back my urge to tell him to shove off, all because I didn't want be alone. Then I got back with Diego, and now, just when I was finally feeling a little bit free from all that anger, just when I was ready to fly away to see the world, thrilled because I had worked so hard to put my trip together, I had to come here and live with this excruciating boredom, just like I did when I was at home.

God really has it in for me, but come on, this is too much already! In that book, *Don Simeón,* it says there is no evil that can last a hundred years, nor a human being capable of enduring it. But there are evils that last eighteen years, and let me tell you, there are humans that can last that long—I know from experience. It also says that "every situation, no matter how bad, can always get worse." I tell you, Murphy's Law is a hundred percent true with me: I always seem to win the lottery of bad luck. This situation is proof of that. It's simple: there are forty million people in Colombia, and 1,500 of us are victims of kidnapping. This means, then, that one out of every 26,666 Colombians gets kidnapped. So I am paying for those 26,665. Then, of course, there's my father: that makes 53,332 . . . I mean, come on! Oh, I better just try and go to sleep, maybe that will help me get rid of all the anger I feel.

Changing topics, Nandor spoke on UIS today and told me that if they ever give me the chance to get out without my father that I should stay. He said he knew it was a difficult decision, but that they would all feel better knowing I was here with him. He didn't need to tell me that—after all, the reason I didn't leave that first week was because I felt I had to stay with my father. Why would I do it now? I would never leave him.

I have talked to God many times now and asked him to help me get out of the situation with Diego when I get back to Bucaramanga. I want to close the chapter with him, finish that whole story. I'm tired of it all. I've thought a lot about it here, and the truth is that Diego may be a wonderful person and everything, but so am I and I need someone who can truly love me. I just can't go through it with Diego anymore. I just want to be friends. I've been banging my head against a wall for too long already, all for nothing. So many opportunities have passed me by, and I didn't take advantage of a single one of them. I don't necessarily think that was a mistake, but it does hurt. I mean, I don't regret anything, because you do learn something from every negative experience, and from this one, boy did I learn a lot: I learned that it is no good to get worked up over something for such a long time. If he agrees, fine. But if not, I'll just have to turn around and say goodbye to God. As far as friends go, I haven't got many. I can count them on one hand.

From now on, I am not going to let life laugh at me: I am going to laugh at life.

Wednesday, August 11, 1999

9:05 P.M. I'm outside, sitting in the chair my father made, with a little candle so that I can write. I just saw the news on TV, and then the soap opera *Marido y mujer* [Husband and Wife].

The ELN just sent a communiqué saying that instead of releasing the seven hostages, they will only release one, to carry a message. Why do we have to wait so long? I have no idea.

Even though I have my father with me, I feel alone. I wish someone would come over to me and ask me how I feel, what I think—I wish I could share all the things in my head and just talk; I wish I could let go of all these thoughts and feelings. I don't tell anyone about what I'm going through, but if I really think about it, I guess I never did—I've always just swallowed everything. Only here have I finally opened up and let go. I know that advice can be very helpful, and I also know that friendship and companionship are nice and everything. So why, why is it so hard for me to open up to other people?

Thursday, August 12, 1999

It's been four months now, 123 days. We just saw the news on Caracol because that was what Juan wanted to see, and it was his turn. They reported on our situation for about a second, and then nothing. When they were through talking about us, Uriel, my father, a guerrilla, and I asked if we could switch to another program during the commercials on Caracol, but Francisco and that 33-year-old man who acts as if he's 17 said no, they didn't feel like it. What idiots. They do it on purpose—nobody ever sends them messages on UIS, and none of their relatives ever go to Bucaramanga to find out what's happening, and so they just don't care. They know that nobody's going to turn up on the news talking about them. I feel bad for them. One of them is married, but his wife seems to be a lot more worried about her education than him, and frankly I can see why. Just talking to that guy is completely impossible. And the one who's 33 only gets messages from his girlfriend and his mother, and only on Saturdays. As men, those two are completely repugnant. What bad luck that I had to end up in this situation with those two guys who have no personality whatsoever, and yet they think they are the best thing on earth and that everything they do is totally amazing.

Friday, August 13, 1999

Today, at 5:45 in the morning, Jaime Garzón was killed in Bogotá. How sad, and how unfair. The ELN issued a statement saying they felt very badly about his death, because at some point Garzón had been a member of the ELN. The paramilitary claims they didn't kill him. I hope to God they find whoever was behind his murder.

On August 11, at 11:50 P.M., I got bitten by a scorpion for the second time, and I got pretty sick: my arm went numb, I had an awful headache, and I couldn't fall asleep. When I walked out of the hut at around 4:45 I almost fell over. They took my pulse, which was 60/70, gave me some drops of medicine, and after a little while I felt better. All night I was freezing cold but I perspired like crazy; it was dreadful. The first scorpion bit me when we were at the other campsite, but this time it was much worse, because the thing was huge. It was waiting for me under the mattress, and when I stuck my hand in to pull out the flap of my mosquito net, *bam!* The damn scorpion jumped up and got me.

Over the radio Carolina told me not to count the days; she said that counting only makes it worse, and I think she's right.

Sunday, August 15, 1999

Today, at 1:45 A.M., I went out to go to the bathroom. It was raining and next to the nurse's hut I saw a snake that was about five feet long—a bushmaster, a poisonous snake. I practically stepped on it but I caught myself just in the nick of time, and called out to my father. Everyone came running out. It turned out that the thing was dead already—the guard had killed it earlier in the evening, but still, it was a pretty big scare. On top of that, I had stomach pains all night thanks to the 10 *cancharinas* I ate—they're these fried pancakes made with wheat flour. I felt a lot better by the time I woke up.

Seven years ago today I received my first communion, and eight years ago today my father's son Laszlito died.

Two new guerrillas arrived today. It's 10:45 and I think I'm going to take a bath. The water is probably pretty murky since it rained last night, but I don't care.

Lately I have been very thirsty all the time, and my lips and tongue are all dried out. When I get up I often feel dizzy, and as I walk to the dining hut I feel as if I'm about to fall over, and I have to grab on to something or else sit down. Today we received the August 12 edition of *La Vanguardia,* with photos of the 16 of us who are still in captivity.

5:40 P.M. Time is going by slowly, very, very slowly. . . . Every minute is an eternity. Today I played Parcheesi, took a bath, ate, and puked because Fernando and Diego told me I am really fat. I just ran out of cigarettes, and now I'm wearing my black shirt and jeans, my blue scarf, and the shoes that used to be boots that my dad fixed for me. I am trying hard not to think about the time so that it passes by a little faster, but I can't help thinking that today is day 126, and I can hardly believe it. I pray that I will be out of here by my birthday, which is December 11. No way on earth do I want to spend my nineteenth birthday in this place.

Monday (holiday), August 16, 1999

Last night I dreamt about San Pedrito Claver, my old school. I was little, and I was getting in line with the other girls in second grade. The teacher was at the head of the line and was handing out some kind of diplomas. There was a very strong wind blowing, so hard it almost blew us away. Then I remembered another dream I had back at home, a dream of me on a plane, and then on a bus traveling past the Ardila Lulle hospital.

Dreams are really so amazing. They are simply incredible: they come out of our bodies, transport us to the most unbelievable places, moments, landscapes; they introduce us to people who seem so familiar, people we hug and kiss, and then when we wake up we realize we've never seen them before. Dreams are so endlessly fascinating, they are such a mystery. The mind is such a marvelous thing. . . . Sometimes I think that dreams must be trying to tell us things, warn us in some way. . . . For example, take the dreams I had before I left on this trip. Very strange. In one of them, I was about to get married, and I was riding in a horse-drawn carriage, and suddenly I looked out and saw a dead man lying on the street, all bloody and mangled. Then, as I was traveling down a cobblestone street, I suddenly caught a glimpse of the church, and I began to cry and cry because I didn't want to get married after all. The other dream took place in a ravine filled with beautiful plants and trees, and it was very cold. I jumped down a corridor, and suddenly when I looked down I realized that the dining room floor was surrounded by a very deep abyss, and I was very scared. That felt like an omen.

Today, for a change, they gave us beans with little bits of pasta. I didn't eat lunch, though, because I am trying to eat just one meal a day.

Today I looked up at the sky and felt the most incredible sense of peace. For a few minutes there, I felt as if I had floated up to another world, and for that brief time I didn't feel any of the pressure I usually feel here. It was such a tremendous, amazing feeling. I only wish that all my time here I could feel like I did at that moment.

Tuesday, August 17, 1999

Last night I dreamt that I was buying lingerie in a department store because I was going to marry Diego. A very strange dream, no doubt. I also saw a woman covered in blood, and then I saw myself packing my bags at home, talking to Juan Manuel Manrique about my trip to Israel.

Today I asked Francisco what they said on the news and he told me that Piedad Córdoba asked the government to let the men at the Itagüí jail have their radio phones back. Then, a little later on, at 7:45, Nandor dedicated the song "Wind of Change" by the Scorpions to me.

Carol's message tonight left me trembling: she described what they all went through when they received the news that our plane had disappeared. First, she said, they all began to cry, and Nandor said that he had feared the worst because whenever a plane disappears it always means there's been a crash, and people rarely survive plane crashes. That sent chills down my spine. When I heard that I wanted to cry, and Nandor's song made me teary, too, as did my mother's pained voice, asking for proof that we are all still alive. Nandor said that sometimes he thinks I'm in the house, and he pictures me holed up in my room, or smoking in the living room, and when he gets up in the morning sometimes he thinks he just had a bad dream, but then he realizes that no, this is the horrible reality we're all living through. Then he said that he doesn't mind if we're in here for a long time, as long as we're okay.

Dear God, where am I? Why do I feel that I have lost my strength, my faith? Why so many *whys*? Right now I have trouble breathing, I feel as if I can't quite fill my lungs, and that little by little, my heart will soon stop beating.

"Let us not look back in anger, nor forward in fear, but around in awareness." That is the sentence I keep repeating to myself, over and over, right now. But how can I do that? How can I not feel anger when I look back and see all this, and how can I not be wracked with fear when I think of tomorrow given where I am right now, not knowing if tomorrow will be another day just like every other day, like today, filled with so many whys, so much anguish, agony, uncertainty, and the desperate need to cry? Oh, Leszli, where is that little girl who had such deep faith? Where are those conversations that we always had, when we supported and counseled each other about confronting the present and accepting the past, those conversations that were such a source of peace and calm, that allowed me to think about the mark I am leaving on life? What happened to those chats that gave us the strength to carry on, to build a future by always remembering that the future is shaped by the arrival of a new present that instantly becomes part of the past? Where, Leszli, where are the infinitesimal moments of joy that must exist somewhere in the middle of this massive, dark hole? What would you say, little Leszli, if we reminded ourselves that people love you, they wait for you, and worry about you? Why are you so selfish, wanting only to reach the end of the tunnel of the waiting room of the eternal universe? Stay strong, Leszli, hold on and have faith. Life is beautiful and it is waiting for us to live. . . . I love you for who you are, and you love me for who I am.

Wednesday, August 18, 1999

Last night was awful. My ulcer flared up at 3 in the morning and it felt so awful that I had to get up. First I vomited, and then I went to the bathroom, but nothing. I woke up the health aide but she just gave me a pill and told me to go back to bed. I took it and sat up, waiting and waiting, but I didn't feel any better. At 4 A.M., I took out one of the vials of Lisalgil that Nandor sent me and went back to the health aide.

"Listen, I hate to do it but if you don't give me this I'm going to die."

She gave it to me. I went back to the hut, waited, and after 15 minutes the pain subsided and I was finally able to fall asleep.

The latest news appears to be promising: on Friday the guerrillas and the government are going to talk at Itagüí. I assume something will come of it, but we'll have to wait until Friday.

Today I took two baths: once in the morning and then again just a little while ago. It's 4:35 and I can hear a song by Franco de Vita, either *"Un buen perdedor"* ["A Good Loser"] or *"Claro que sé perder"* ["Of Course I Know How to Lose"].

Thursday, August 19, 1999

Today the head guerrilla met with us in the dining/TV shack and asked us how we liked the food they've been serving us, how we're doing as a group, and he also let us know that a doctor would be coming by tomorrow to give us checkups. Today there was a problem with the supply lady—my father said he didn't like the way she's been playing favorites with some people (meaning Francisco and Juan) and not with others. The problem involved a leftover *arepa*. The topic was brought up with the head guerrilla, but now the health aide has started getting nasty with us. My father and I could care less what she thinks or says about us—the truth is, we really don't give a damn what anyone else thinks.

Last night I dreamt that I was playing with a sweet little cat that had a lovely, smooth black coat. Then I dreamt I was talking to Carol, but I woke up.

It's 7:10 P.M., and I'm listening to the song "Imagine," by John Lennon, on Mega. My father is translating it for me. It's his favorite song, and tonight he asked me to play it when he dies. He said he hoped I would think of him and this moment whenever I hear the song.

The nighttime is so wonderful, but the daytime is so unbelievably awful here, I really despise it. I love the week and hate the weekend because on Friday, Saturday, Sunday, and even Monday I don't hear from anyone on the radio, and that makes me feel lonelier than ever. But I love Tuesdays, which is the day we get messages. By Wednesday I already start feeling blue because all I've got left is Thursday, and I hate this time of day, because I just want Tuesday to come already, and that's not possible. But everything will come with time.

Just now I was sitting outside the tent, because my father told me to blow out the candle, and I decided to come out here. Then Uriel called out to me about the messages being broadcast, and I went running. What joy! Just when I was thinking about them, about the day I'll see them again, I find out that they miss me as much as I miss them.

Today my father and I talked about the day we will be reunited with our family, and what that will be like. I told him that for them it will probably be a lot like seeing a dead person, because at one point they actually did think we were dead. Anyway I know we will all be so, so happy. We agreed that had we in fact died, Nandor and Carol would have taken it the worst. I think my mother would have, too, but I didn't say anything to my father about that.

I think that if we had died we probably would have thought the same things we did when we realized the plane was being hijacked: my mind went blank for a second, and then a parade of images raced through my mind, of those last few hours with my mom, Carol, Nandor, and Daniel. I remembered how Carol and I talked about nothing in particular at a little table in the airport; how Nandor actually came to my bedside to say goodbye; and I remember my mother and how she put the chain with the little red star around my neck. . . . On the plane, though, all these images sped through my mind very, very quickly. Then I thought of other days, much more distant in my memory, months and years old. . . . It all happened so fast! Then I thought of my father's life and prayed that they wouldn't kill him, because I was afraid he would get up to come sit next to me, and that when he got up—*bam!*, they'd get him. I really feared the worst, and I lost control; I remember I started crying. Then one of the hijackers told me to calm down, and I did. I explained to him that my father was a little further up front and asked them to please not do anything to him—they could kill me but please, I begged, not him. I told him that I loved my father very much and didn't want anything to happen to him. A little bit after that, I think the guy actually started laughing, and then I did, too. Right then, though, the truth is that I thought of everything, I even thought that maybe it was all a dream, a bad dream, and I scratched myself, and . . . shit! It was all real, realer than ever, a cold, hard reality.

I do thank God, though, that nothing worse happened that day. Now I just have to put up with the boredom, and the sadness I feel at not being able to be with the people I love. In the end, though, it is a tremendous experience that will stay with me for the rest of my life. Maybe right now I don't quite realize how important it is, but I know that later on I will draw some very good things from this experience—like they say, every cloud has a silver lining, and something incredibly good will have to come out of such a bad, bad thing as this. And so I tell myself: "Keep going, Leszli!"

Friday, August 20, 1999

Last night I got up to eat at midnight, because my ulcer was killing me. After about an hour I was finally able to fall back asleep but I was still in a great deal of pain. This morning, at around 6 A.M., I asked the health aide to give me an injection of Ranitidine, and after she administered the injection the pain subsided.

Last night I dreamt of Carol, Danielito, and my mother. I dreamt that I was inhabiting another person's body, and that I was walking down a flight of stairs, and I just stood there looking at them, and they looked back at me, and my mother and Carol hugged me. Danielito was really big, and even spoke pretty well, in this very sweet little voice. I grabbed him and hugged him as hard as I could, because I was just so happy to see that little doll. Then, in another scene, I saw myself walking down a street choked with mud, just like the muddy track where the plane landed. I was with Ana María Gómez and a few other people I knew, and then I saw Gloria and yelled out to her. Then another image appeared in my mind: it was an image of me with Laureano and Francisco in a pool filled with garbage. I also saw Diana and Tila, too. Then another image flashed through my mind right after that, of me on the road. Laureano was crying and I was telling him to stay calm, that everything would be all right. Another image: we were arriving at Bucaramanga, and everyone was waiting for us in an empty lot. As I hugged my mother, people snapped photos of us. I was happy.

Thank you, my God, for letting me dream that, and for letting me remember the dream.

Today, the head guerrilla brought my father a pack of Belmont cigarettes. I am waiting around until 12:30, to see what they say on the news about the situation at the Itagüí jail, since today they are supposed to hold a meeting there. I hope that some good news for us comes out of it. The head guerrilla told us that the doctor finally arrived.

Last night, just as I finished writing, the most awful feeling came over me for a few seconds. It was this overwhelming sense of emptiness—as if I had fallen into a deep, deep hole. I began to feel panicky, and it took me a long time to fall asleep after that.

Later on I kept on writing. . . .

The doctor gave me a pretty quick checkup. His accent sounded Peruvian, and he was definitely a real doctor. He told me I had to take care of myself, and then he gave me some Omeprazole. When he asked me how I felt, I lied and told him I was fine, because if I told them that I wasn't well they would probably free me and I don't want to leave here without my father. When all is said and done, the two of us arrived here together and we're going to leave here together. I hope the doctor believed me.

Saturday, August 21, 1999

The doctor left today. While he was here with us, he paced around a lot, or he would stand up and then sit back down, and then finally he pulled out a book and started reading. I asked him if he was Peruvian and he said no, and then he flashed me a look as if to say, "And don't ask me any more questions." Everyone involved in the guerrilla operation is very wary; they never tell you anything. Whenever I start asking questions, the head guerrilla always just laughs and says, "Listen, Leszli, the law around here is: the less you know, the better. Less problems."

The truth is, he's right. I'm so dumb, asking all those questions about everything, always so curious. I would definitely be very bad guerrilla material. But to think, that poor doctor was absolutely beside himself with frustration and boredom and he was barely even here for a day.

Today I tried working on my spelling exercises again. I got through a lot of the day doing that stuff. At the very least I learned that all words ending in *bla, ble, bli, blo, blu* are written with "b" and not "v" and that the word *necesidad* [necessity] has a "c" first and then an "s." That word really annoys me—I've never been able to spell it properly—but today, after giving it some thought, I came up with a rule: the letter "c" comes before "s" in the alphabet, and this word is spelled exactly the same way: first "c" and then "s."

It's 5:30 P.M. now. For the first time in 132 days, I have eaten an orange. I was so moved by this that I ate it little by little, savoring every drop of it. I took off the rind and gave it to my father—the poor guy was even more choked up than I was; he actually ate all the rind. Incredible! I talked to him for a while about the universe and the world—you know, earth, life, what comes after life. Then we discussed our personal theories regarding the topic. He thinks that a person comes to earth an infinite number of times, and that sometimes you come as a cockroach, a tree, a rope, a snake, another person, until you have incarnated into all the different creatures that make up the endless array of living beings....

Sunday, August 22, 1999

My theory regarding life is that one's being comes down to earth as every life-form imaginable, and every time you come to inhabit the earth, your spirit evolves until it finally understands that you should never harm another being, and that the world should be a much better place than it is. From there, you move on to another world inhabited by superior beings, and this cycle repeats itself on and on throughout infinity. I don't believe time exists in other worlds: what death is to us may very well be life in some other world. And so, within a certain amount of time we will manage to become perfect, and as we are born over and over again, we continue evolving. The way I think, act, and live in this world, I don't understand how people can spend their lives trying to harm others. And I think that people who lead that very misguided sort of life must be people who are still on their first few journeys through existence. Yes, they will keep on doing what they do until they pass through life a few more times, and only then will they finally realize that they shouldn't commit evil acts. The way my mind works, I am convinced that I see beyond what other people are able to understand. I really do believe I'm a little bit ahead of some people, and that's why I feel that this is the waiting room, the antechamber to the rest of the universe.

I don't think this world will ever change, just because this is the way it is. If it changed, it wouldn't be possible to go to other worlds and try to be better. And so in this world, we get an idea of what is good and what is bad, until finally we reach a more advanced stage of thinking. People aren't simply born into that advanced state. I must have been really awful in my previous lives, and I must have felt pain, and rage, and lots of other things to have ended up the way I am today.

My father told me that he saw my mom on the RCN news, asking for proof that we are still alive. She was wearing a white T-shirt with a photo of me on the front.

Today is a long, boring Sunday. 133 days and counting. Eight days from tomorrow, the month—another month!—will be over and it will be September. What a bore. I hope we finally get out, but the way things are going I bet we'll be here until Christmas. Incredible. It would be so very absurd, though not at all improbable, if we celebrated the year 2000 here.

Last night I dreamt that Diego gave me a kiss on the arm, behind my elbow . . . very funny. He told me that he had to go because his girlfriend was getting very annoyed at him. Does he have a girlfriend now? I wonder. I thought about that for a while. . . . It wouldn't seem so strange, after all. . . . Anyway, I also dreamt I had very long hair and that I looked ugly as hell. I dreamt I was brushing and drying my hair in the bathroom with Carolina, and the two of us were primping and preening.

Monday, August 23, 1999

Today the head guerrilla had a meeting with Fernando, Diego, Laureano, and Francisco, at their request. He told them that he thought we might be released in September because, according to conversations he'd had with other guerrilla leaders, the negotiations were moving ahead quite well, and if they didn't get stuck again, if things kept on going the way they were going, we'd be out in September. I hope it's true, because my father and I were already figuring on spending Christmas here.

Now I'm going to write a little letter to my mom.

Wonderful Tuesday, August 24, 1999

Today the health aide started me on some pills to help with my depression, and I feel a little better. They also brought us some things: I got a sweatshirt, a T-shirt, a pencil, a pencil sharpener, a towel, and a brown scarf with white flowers. I think what they're saying is true, that we'll be out of here in September. I don't know why, I just have a feeling. I hope I'm not wrong. Last night I dreamt I was kissing Diego and that I went to the residential complex where he lives to ask Jairo something, and everyone was there and Diego hugged me and said he was happy that I was there. Jairo said the same thing, and everyone else did, too.

Wednesday, August 25, 1999

Last night we heard Nandor and my mom on the radio. They both sounded pretty desperate and hysterical. My mother was extremely critical of President Andrés Pastrana, and Nandor trashed the president of the congress, but to make a long story short, they also said how much they loved me, and that they are feeling down because they haven't heard from me. My mother told me to tell myself: "I am a rock and nothing can happen to me, nothing can affect me." And she said that the best gift I can give myself is my health.

Right now a little plane is flying overhead, the one that flies very low in the sky. This always alarms us because if those planes realize we're here, or if they spot a guerrilla campsite, they could drop bombs or open fire on us. That's what the guerrillas say, anyway. For security reasons, they may have to move us to another campsite, and boy, will it be a major drag to have to do everything over again: the playing field, the path to the river, the kitchen, the huts, the TV shack, then that chain saw hacking away at all hours of the morning with that infernal noise, chopping down trees here, there, and everywhere, the mud, the boots, the filth, the discomfort, another latrine, not to mention the hike to a new campsite. Oh, I can't even think about it. We've already gotten used to this place.

My father and Laureano told me that my mom had been on the radio saying that she sent a letter to the president asking him to give the radio-phones back to Francisco Galán and Felipe Torres, the men at the Itagüí jail.

Full moon. My father and I gazed up at it with our binoculars. It came out at 6 P.M.

"Don't worry, be happy." That's what the song on La Mega is telling us.

Thursday, August 26, 1999

Today I went to the bathroom and a blood clot came out. Scary. I'm kind of worried because I have no idea what it could be. I told Ricardo and my father about it, and Ricardo told me that these irregularities happen when someone hasn't had sexual relations. My father told me to be very careful. I think I'll focus on what Ricardo said and try not to worry.

Friday, August 27, 1999

Things are the same with me: I'm bored and despondent. I just don't know what to do to pass the time. I think I'm about to go crazy—if I'm not already crazy, that is! My eyelashes are long, but not that long. I thought they'd come out the way they were when I was a little girl, but they didn't. What do I care, though? The important thing is that I have them.

Saturday, August 28, 1999

The chain saw is a major annoyance. All these people do is chop down trees. Last night I dreamt that I was in Israel and that all the women had heads just like mine, with the same haircut and everything. Last night I saw *Midnight Express,* not so different from what we're going through. I am going out of my mind!

Today the head guerrilla came over to talk to me, and asked me how I felt about things. I told him I was fine. Then he spent a little time telling me about the ELN: he told me, for example, that they are a group of people united by a common cause; that they are fighting for the Colombian people; that people in this government don't give you the time of day unless you come at them with an assault rifle. That, he said, is the reason they feel obligated to use force, and he admitted that it is very sad to have to use weapons to get people to listen to you, but that's what they have to do. According to him, the guerrilla wants the war to end more than anyone else—after all, he said, carrying a rifle everywhere you go, wandering through the mountains, hiding out far away from the people you love, is not an easy thing to live with. These kidnappings are rough on them, too, he said, but they have to finance the war somehow, since the ELN doesn't receive money from the drug cartels. The ELN is against all that because the drug trade is even worse than the kidnapping business, since drugs destroy people for life, whereas kidnappings last for a finite period of time. . . .

"And though you may not believe it, Leszli, after getting released from captivity, you'll be a better person for it, because you will truly understand the value of life."

The head guy also said to me, "Listen, Leszli, I'm not asking you to believe what we believe. You were raised differently. In one way or another, you had everything; we didn't. And I'm not just talking about us, I'm talking about more than half of Colombia, believe me. That's what we're fighting for. I'm not asking you not to hate us, either. You have every right to hate us if you want. We are keeping you far away from your family, your life, your world. You are being subjugated by us and it is logical that you should hate us. But I'm telling you all this because you seem like a pretty sharp girl. Just listen and analyze. . . . You don't have to say anything to me. . . . And have patience."

Then he told me I ought to try and mix with the group a little more. The same old story.

The truth is, I don't hate them. I agree with a lot of what they say, and part of me admires them because the rest of us just sit around judging everything and never lift a finger to actually do anything. We always just hang around, waiting for someone else to come around and solve the problem. Still, there is no justification whatsoever for kidnapping. Sure, maybe they do make an effort to understand what the experience of kidnapping is like, but it's one thing to be a spectator and another thing to be a protagonist in the story.

I started reading *Red and Black,* the ELN book. It talks about all the fronts on which the ELN operates, where they operate, how they started their military movement, and it also explains their ideology. . . . It is a long, thick book. Manuel Pérez Martínez, the Spanish priest who founded the ELN, is on the cover. It's like the Bible to them. I'm on Chapter 11.

Sunday, August 29, 1999

Day 140. Today they brought us biscuits, chocolate bars, potato chips, talcum powder for me, lotion for the men, nail clippers, crackers. . . . What joy! My father and I distributed the things among the group.

Last night I saw *Braveheart.* What a lovely movie. I got my period.

Monday, August 30, 1999

I ate chocolate bars all day. I feel happy, so I decided not to take the medicine for my nerves. But I think I'll go back on it in about a week or so.

My father just told me that there was good news on the radio, that the two sides finally reached an agreement. He called out to me to come and eat, but I told him I'd go later on. And so he yelled at me, "No, now!"

And I repeated what I said before: "No, later!" And finally he went.

Francisco, just to be more of a pain in the ass, said, "Yeah, Laszlo, let's go already."

I hate feeling pressured, it's so irritating. At home nobody ever says anything if I don't want to eat. I hate feeling that they're watching me, looking over my shoulder. I like to feel free, to go about my life without having to tell anyone about what I'm doing or what I'm thinking—unless, that is, I happen to feel like telling them.

I want this nightmare to end already. I can't take it anymore.

Today on the Caracol news they reported that some of the hostages in the Church of the Virgin Mary in Cali might be released. I hope this is true, I really do hope they free those people, even if they get out before we do, and then I hope they free us. I will find strength where I have none.

"Let us take the things that bring us together, and leave behind the things that drive us apart." That's a quote from the priest Manuel Pérez, in the ELN book. Great quote.

Tuesday, August 31, 1999

Today I went back on the pills for my depression. I'm now on Chapter 23 of *Red and Black,* which is entitled: "Che: the tender side of the revolution." There are 88 chapters in all. I am going to try to read them very slowly, just to have something to do.

Before I forget, I want to mention that today the entire country is going on strike, so there are no messages on UIS. A giant pain in the butt, and I mean giant.

Today they released two of the Cali hostages. You know, despite all the things we do, the days here are just so unbearably boring, it's always the same place, same people. The only thing that changes the routine here, even if only momentarily, is when something new happens. For example, it's always a big day when books arrive: the ones I like the best are the ones by Ernesto Sábato, also the *Vademécum,* which the health aide keeps on hand for reference, and a *Pequeño Larousse* dictionary, which I use to learn the words I don't know—

those odd, difficult words—and to brush up on my punctuation. All of this, of course, is just another way to kill time, to make it go by as fast as possible, as we inch closer and closer to the day of our freedom, the freedom we daydream about and that seems so far away, so impossible, so unattainable. The lack of freedom often creates friction among us: for example, there are times when the others feel all right but I'm not feeling so hot, and vice versa—it is a rare day when all of us are feeling "all right"—that is, if it is at all possible to feel "all right" in these circumstances.

We all experience wild mood swings—something as simple as an egg or an *arepa* can cause a serious explosion of jealousy. Inevitably, whenever this happens, someone complains to my father, who looks into the issue, gets to the bottom of it, and then goes to the head guerrilla and asks him to get the other guerrillas to stop playing favorites. My dad always ends up in the worst position of all as a result, because both the people playing favorites and the ones enjoying their favors end up resenting him. But he just quotes the book by Manuel Pérez, also known as the famous Father Pérez, the Spanish priest who came here and joined the guerrilla movement. The people really grew to love Pérez and when he died he left behind a legacy of commitment to the revolutionary cause, and he served, and continues to serve, as an example for all the guerrillas. Somewhere in his book, he talks about how he eats the same food as everyone else, never pulling rank in any way, since all people are equal and worthy of equal respect. And whenever my father sees what goes on, most of all in the kitchen, the way the people in there really cross the line playing favorites, he starts quoting Father Pérez in front of the head guerrilla, who finally puts an end to the whole thing.

Sometimes the guerrillas say the scariest things, too. One night, while we were watching television, all of a sudden, a grenade exploded a few yards from where we were sitting. Immediately the guerrillas screamed, "Fokker people, hit the ground. Guerrillas, take your positions!"

When this happened I was sitting with Martín, a painter and guerrilla commander who was visiting the campsite. He had arrived a few days earlier with a guy we called his "bodyguard," plus another guy, a very tall, strong man who Martín said was a guerrilla instructor. As soon as I heard the explosion I raced over to my father, shaking like a leaf, but my dad just said, "Don't worry, everything's all right. Just look at Martín. See, he's not scared. Look, he didn't even get up from his chair. This isn't anything serious. They must be testing their people with some kind of simulation, that's all."

After a little while the people who went out to investigate the explosion came back and said that a tree branch must have fallen onto a legbreaker land mine, or maybe a snake activated it.

Who knows. But one thing is for sure: after that day everything changed, everyone's mood changed. Now, the guerrillas are all on very high alert, much more nervous in general. At the main hut, one of them told us that whenever *la plaga* ("the plague," their nickname for the army) or the paramilitaries launch an attack they always start by tossing a grenade and then they close in with machine guns, opening fire on the people who are still flustered and disoriented by the grenade. For this reason, they tell us, whenever we hear an explosion we need to listen very carefully for any kind of gunfire afterward, because if they start firing we'll all be dead ducks. And if there is no way out, they will unfortunately have to kill us—of course, they say, they will do this in the most humane way possible. According to our captors, if the army or the paramilitaries were to get us in an attack like that they would kill us all with chain saws and then blame it on the ELN.

After listening to this, my father went straight over to Martín and said that if that was how things were, then at the very least we had to figure out some kind of escape plan. Martín and Yadira, two of the head guerrillas, agreed and between them they mapped out a plan. In the event of an emergency evacuation, my father and I were to go to point "A" if the attack came from the area between the huts and the river, and point "B" if it came from the area between our hut and the group hut. At either of those spots, depending on the situation, my father and I were to look for Candilejas and Lola, who would then take us to some location deeper within the security rings of the campsite. My father thought the plan sounded good, and we decided to stick with it. The other hostages also mapped out a plan with other guerrillas and other meeting points, within the larger escape plan that had been designed for the entire campsite.

Even so, the whole thing about having to kill us in the event of an attack had a terrible effect on everyone, despite that bit about doing it in a humanitarian way. Yadira, one of the head guerrillas, said it was all a bunch of lies, and that we should trust her and not bother listening to those other guys. She said they just go around telling stories to scare us. It was at that point, though, that we all began to regard the guerrillas as potential executioners, and the feeling of injustice is indescribable: all they have to do is let us go. They have the power to end our suffering. What have we ever done to them? I have this image in my mind of my father running alongside me, and then the guerrillas opening fire on him, me, and everyone else. I try to stop picturing this scene but I can't, because if what they say is true, it could happen at any moment. And so I just ask God that if this happens, to make sure it happens as they claim it will: in a "humanitarian" way, a "humanitarian" death, a "humanitarian" murder . . . How on earth can they put those two words together? Humanitarian murder . . . yeah, right.

Anyway, the sum total of everything is that we just have to resign ourselves to the fact of living here, with this possibility hanging over our heads. God, we're like laboratory rats that they sacrifice at will, just to prove their little theories, and the worst thing of all is that I bet the government will just write it off as a "political" issue.

Five days after the bomb, my father pulled me and Laureano aside and told us that he had a plan and an escape route figured out. He warned us that it was very risky but said that if we were going to die, we might as well die while trying to escape. Of course, this was only if anything unusual or unexpected happened. He had two plans. In the event of a surprise attack, he said, the first few moments would be chaos, nothing but a lot of noise and gunshots. Now, if we could get ourselves used to that idea, we would have a window of opportunity during which we could take rapid advantage of the chaos. The idea, he said, was to run off and hide, because at first everyone would be very distracted, too busy thinking about saving their own lives because everyone, absolutely everyone, is terrified of dying. In the event of an invasion, my dad said, the best thing would be to get over to Fernando and Diego's hut; behind it there was a hill we could slide down, using one of the long hanging vines. The guerrillas know the terrain around there, he said, and they would never imagine that we would throw ourselves down that massive ditch. Once we got down there, he said, we would just sit tight and wait patiently under all the foliage for everything to blow over, listening for sounds. This was the plan in case the attack hit while we were in our huts, but if they caught us by surprise in the river, or somewhere else, we would have to just drop to the ground and drag ourselves to a safe spot, away from the gunfire, and hope for the best. In that case, he said, there wasn't really any other option.

The second plan went like this: if at any moment we overheard the guerrillas talking carelessly about having received orders to kill us, we were to get up right then and there, without taking anything, and go straight down to the river, not via the usual path but by the slope behind our hut, until we reached the bottom of the valley between the two mountains. From there, my dad said, we were to keep on walking until we reached a fork, then bear left and keep walking until we reached a really huge tree, like the kind you see in the river, in front of the dam, the kind with trunks so thick you could blast through them and make a tunnel big enough for a minivan to pass through. That was the spot from which we were to walk down to the river, and we were to walk upstream until we reached an area full of huge rocks some two yards high. At that point, he said, we were to bear right and walk to the top of the hill. From there we would be able to see a little cabin and a tiny bridge over a little stream. Up there we would also see a big fallen tree, and there where the roots were, he had left two giant logs in a "V" formation. Right at the tip of the "V" we were to dig into the earth, and we would find a plastic sack full of provisions, enough for three days—cans of tuna, rice, matches, candles, medicine like Cipro for infections, Maxitrol for the eyes and ears, Band-Aids, and a big black plastic sheet which would serve as a sleeping bag and a mat for making the fire at night. He had also buried a small frying pan, a spork, beans, rice, salt, and two hunks of *panela*, as well as a little map which he had drawn up by copying a map that Francisco had lent him. He told us to hold it with the sun he'd drawn at the top, toward where the sun rises. Once we had the map in position, we'd be able to figure out where we were with respect to the village of Remedios. The airport in Remedios, for those who don't know, is a very important aerial coordinate, a reference point in Colombian aviation. My dad had managed to figure all this out by watching the airplane patterns overhead from the little soccer field at night. He'd actually been able to see the reflection of the lights from the village in the sky, and while he did all this, the guerrillas just sat around laughing at him, figuring he was some kind of nut who was into stargazing. Anyway, he said that once we got there, we would be fine because the map included the most essential information: distances, which he had put in degrees. Every degree represented sixty minutes, and every minute represented 1.851 meters. He said we were to get up to walk very early in the dawn, and only until 6:45, because that's the time of day when the guerrillas leave their sites. At night, he said, we could only start walking after six, because the guerrillas generally return to camp at five in the afternoon, but taking into account the possibility that some guerrilla might be running behind schedule, he said it was better to head out only after six, when the sun goes down. And that was it: if we kept up with that (relatively slow) daily pace, we would cover some two or three kilometers per day, which would mean that we'd reach Remedios, which was no further than ten kilometers away, in about three days. We would have enough food to eat, and even if after three days we ran out of food and still hadn't found Remedios, we could surely hold on for a couple of days without food. We would make it, he said.

He also told us that a guerrilla who had once worked in a sawmill showed him how to tear off the bark of a tree in a long strip. After sanding it down, he had covered it with plastic and used it inside the tent as a kind of door. Then he told my dad how the nylon rope we use as a clothesline inside the tent, along with the little rods we use to hang our things in the closet, make a decent bow and arrow. As far as the arrows, he said, all we had to do was affix pages from any old notebook on it, like you would affix feathers to an arrow, so that the arrow would fly in a straight line.

My father finished by telling us that it was better to die in an attempt to achieve freedom than to stay put and not do anything to fight or defend ourselves. He also told me that if for whatever reason he didn't make it, we should go on by ourselves, even if it was just to make *melcochas* with that *panela* he buried.

Wednesday, September 1, 1999

Yesterday there were no messages because the people at UIS are on strike. And they freed seven, not two, of the hostages in the church in Cali.

I got up late today, 10:30. Uriel got down to the river to take a bath before me, so I have to wait until he comes back up before I can go down.

Last night I dreamt I was hugging Jairo J. and Diego, too, but I wanted to leave. It was as if I just didn't care about them anymore. I also dreamt about a little innocent cat that I killed for no good reason. I cried and cried and cried over that all night.

Right now I am happy because it is finally September and I hope that I finally get home this month. Today is day 143 in captivity and on the twelfth of this month we will have been here five months.

On the news all they talk about is the national strike. Who would have ever guessed that even we would be affected by that strike? They also mention the murder of Juan Manuel Corzo's cousin.

It's 4:10 in the afternoon right now and it's raining. I feel such an overwhelming urge to cry and cry and cry until I have finally been able to get rid of this horrible feeling—it's like I'm drowning, little by little. I am trying to avoid writing about how I feel because I know it's just so repetitive, but I can't help it, it's inevitable: I think it, and I do it. I don't know where I am finding the strength to go on, it's just pure survival. How long will it last? I have no idea. I actually hope I run out of energy at some point, just to see what happens. That's the problem, though: around here nothing ever happens, everything is always the same, always boring, always frustrating. Every day we sink a bit lower; who knows where we will end up? When will we reach the beginning of the end? I can only answer with what I feel and what I know, a giant question mark:

"I only know that I don't know."

Thursday, September 2, 1999

Tonight there were no messages for me, which made me sad, and I went out to the little chair that my father built and started to cry. I was feeling so lonely, so sad, and so depressed that my father came out and hugged me and tried to make me feel better, telling me not to worry, to try and be strong. The simple act of coming out to hug me was so wonderful. Really, it was the best thing he could have done. After a while the bad feelings subsided and I felt a lot better, more certain of everything. And I felt so glad that God had given me that moment with my father, because I know he loves me very much even though he never shows it. He's pretty reserved, and so today was a big exception for him—the kind of moment he very rarely indulges in, and when he does it's usually because he's been drinking. But today, without a single drink, he came over and gave me a big hug. We also talked about my grandmother Gisella and about how much Hungarian he speaks. He told me a bunch of words but I forgot some of them. He has a very good grasp of the language.

Nagyon jó: Very tasty.

Viszont látásra: Good night.

Leszlika: little Leszli, kind of like the way they say it in Colombia.

Laszlika: little Laszlo.

Friday, September 3, 1999

145 days. I woke up in a slightly better mood today. Or maybe it's just that I'm more resigned now. I've been practicing my Hungarian with my father. I've been working on this letter I keep meaning to finish and send to my mother, but I don't know what else to say to her ... that I'm fine, I guess. Of course it will just be a lie.

Saturday, September 4, 1999

Today I got up very early to take a bath in the river. I brought the sheets with me and washed them. Then I climbed back up and as I

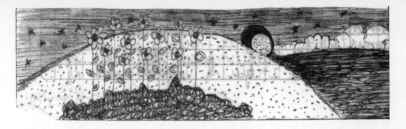

started to tidy up the hut a little, I realized that it's been a very long time since I spoke to God. I'm in a very strange state of mind lately—it's as though I feel out of joint, out of place somehow. Sometimes I feel okay but it usually doesn't last for long; most of the time I feel overwhelmed by everything.

Yesterday we got some very, very good news. Apparently the government gave back those radio-phones that the ELN commanders at the Itagüí jail were asking for. They said it was only for humanitarian reasons, but still. Does this mean that we might be released soon? My father and I have been looking up at the stars at night, and he's been telling me about the constellations, how you can see the figures of the zodiac in the night sky. I really like that. . . . God, I really hope the government doesn't take away those radio-phones again from the men in the jail, because that could have some very serious consequences for us. There would be hell to pay, I just know it.

My father has been virtually glued to the radio, all the time, trying to hear whatever he can. Today he took a little break and we talked about my trip to Israel; he said he doesn't want me to go so far away, that it scares him, but that he'll ultimately let me because he knows how important it is to me.

Sunday, September 5, 1999

They freed four more of the Cali hostages. It's 6:00 and I just ate. It was awful: rice, spam, yucca, mayonnaise, and sugar water. What revolting food! Today they killed two chickens but my father and I didn't want to eat them. God, I feel so fat. I don't know what to do: it makes me so sad. Here it's impossible to diet because all they give us are starches. I feel fatter and fatter every single day, plus there's a cut on my head that I think might have gotten infected. All I want is to get out of here and start taking Fenisec [fenproporex] again, and to use scarves and hats again. The only thing that makes me feel better is the length of my eyelashes. Right now, though, what I most want is for Tuesday to come so that I can hear my mother—that is, if she talks on the radio at all. I don't understand why she wasn't able to talk on Thursday.

I want to run away from here, I want that so badly. Oh, how I envy those birds. I sit here watching them for hours and hours, thinking about how happy I would be if I could fly. . . . My father told me not to worry, that someday, in some other life, I will be a bird.

Tuesday, September 7, 1999

148 days. Last night I dreamt about Diego and a little dog.

The day has gone by more or less as they all do, except for the fact that today is Tuesday and I am hoping to hear messages from my mom and everyone else.

On the news all they talk about is the people in Cali, which really makes me mad—just because the church is in the middle of it, those hostages get released before we do. These people are so inconsiderate. We've been in captivity for two months more than them, and our families have really behaved with a lot more consideration: they don't draw up petitions, nor do they go around blaming the ELN for every-thing, or signing letters swearing that they'll never pay a ransom—they haven't even demanded that the government swoop in and rescue us. That really makes me furious, and it only makes me feel more impotent. The fact that we are at the mercy of these people is so hard for me to believe sometimes. Lately I feel like crying all the time. I hate this: it's such a dirty game they're playing with us. I'm furious at God, and even more furious at the church, which has always been and always will be nothing but a bunch of pharisees. It's all a big farce. And they are all a bunch of hypocrites. I hate churches and I hate the people who go to church, because most of them just go to wipe away the latest bunch of sins they've committed over the past few days, for a clean slate that will allow them to go right back out and commit the same old sins all over again.

I feel as if I am in another world. That is the best and most honest way I can describe what I feel: I am in the same world, but in another dimension. I feel like I'm in a huge labyrinth and I can't figure out how to get out. Sometimes I think I can see a light somewhere along this dark road, but then I realize it's just an optical illusion, that everything is still the same. The feeling of crisis comes over me again, as does the hellishness of this reality that torments me, day in and day out.

I didn't eat today. I wasn't hungry.

If it weren't for these pages, I would have no way of letting go of all the things I feel. I would feel so much more alone. This experience has really taught me an important life lesson about understanding and cherishing the things I once had, things that I never really thought or cared about before. But now that I have learned the lesson, why can't I just go back? It's like that story I wrote a long time ago, about how I had this revelation and floated out of myself: I began to see my house, my neighborhood, the trees, the mountains, and the rivers, and I suddenly realized how marvelous everything was. As I moved upward, going higher and higher, I kept on thinking that I would be able to go back, that the higher I went, the more I would understand about the marvelous world we live in. But by the time I finally came to appreciate the grandeur of the world and everything in it, truly seeing all the things I had never noticed before, I tried to go back down, back into myself so that I could live with all the new things I'd learned, and I realized that there was no way back down. The more I wanted to go down, the higher I floated up in the air, and I grew more and more frustrated. I couldn't understand why I had been allowed to see things and to learn how to appreciate all those wonderful things, if I wasn't going to be allowed back down to earth. It seemed so illogical. But then, all of a sudden, a great sense of peace came over me, and I slid into that all-encompassing tranquillity and I stopped caring about going back.

Now I realize that the very same thing is happening to me. And I ask myself the same question: Why have I been allowed to see all these things if I can't go back? The only difference is that before it was a dream, a figment of my imagination, and now it's real.

Dear God, I hope I will soon feel the peace I describe in that story so that I can finally stop worrying, and most of all so that I can finally stop punishing myself. Lots of times I try to make light of this situation, but there is really no humorous side to any of this, and that is one of my greatest battles. And the absence everyone feels back at home is nowhere near as overwhelming as the void I feel inside of me. I can see it already, an avalanche of anguish that is about to crush me—I know that I must find my reserves of inner strength, but . . . where? How? I analyze this situation from every angle, searching for the place where I will find this valor and strength, but it is unrealistic to think that I have either. I fall into the abyss. No, it's worse than that: I *let* myself fall.

I am crying. I can't decide whether it is from the loneliness or the impotence I feel. What a phony society I live in, what phony people I live among, what a phony world I was born into. Fine. But now my question is this: am I phony, too, for living in this phony world? I hope not. Every day I grow more and more convinced that God really screwed up, a few things at least: for one, bringing me into this earth was a mistake, because I feel like an outsider here. People kill for the sake of killing in this world, people chop down trees just for the pleasure of watching them fall, they kill little animals, there are people out there who live to wreak havoc on others, even in the most insignificant way—whether it's making someone feel bad or attacking someone where it hurts the most. I don't see love anywhere here on this planet: nobody really loves anyone—this is just a great big theater where everyone is putting on a big show, and those of us who speak the truth are pushed to the side and banned from taking part in the show. But I guess that's better than being part of the farce.

What is the point of loving someone or something with sincerity, when we live in a world where true, sincere love is too great a thing for most people? That's why people go crazy searching for things that are fake and phony, because fake and phony are all they know. In this world, people like me get left out of the mix, they never really understanding a damn thing. When that happens, I think, that's when we realize that to be "happy" we have to live a life of deceit and lies, we have to sink into this hypocritical society, because otherwise there is no way to live, or survive. It's so sad ... but that's why we are the way we are. Society makes me sick. Everyone makes me sick. Life makes me sick. My life in this horrible world makes me sick, sick!

I wish I could say everything I feel to everyone I know in the world, just to see who would support me, to see if maybe I'm not the only person in the world who feels this way, to feel a little less alone. I hope to God that there are other people who feel the way I do, just so that I can find a reason to say that not absolutely everything is bad. But why, why are we made to endure so much suffering that we cannot understand, why is the world like this? Maybe it's because we're in that antechamber, yes, that's it, the antechamber of the universe. Yes, yes. I hope so.

Wednesday, September 8, 1999

6:07 in the afternoon. Today I began reading the book *En secreto* [In Secret] by Germán Castro Caycedo. I love the way he writes— I've read almost all his books—I start reading and I can't put them down.

Today has been a little slow, a little boring. Last night I dreamt that I escaped, that I ran and ran until I reached a village. There wasn't a single car willing to drive me anywhere, though, because nobody wanted to get into trouble with the ELN. At the entrance to the village, where I walked out, a few guerrilla soldiers fired at me twice, but they didn't hit me. Then I ran and ran, until finally an army patrol car passed by and a soldier asked me who I was, and I was so happy because finally, finally, I was going to get to see my family.

On the news, all they talked about was the bishop of Tibú. I am really losing my patience. This morning, while I was still half-asleep, my father told me he had an idea about why they stopped covering my story in the news: he said that it was likely that the news shows had probably been silenced because of the negative thing my mother had said about the president.

Yesterday was an awful day for me. I had a run-in with one of the guerrillas about food. Then we felt the helicopter pass by overhead, but not so close. Right now I am sitting at the table where we eat, looking at the photos of Che Guevara, Karl Marx, and Lenin that they tacked up. Juan and Uriel are eating. Every day it gets harder and harder for me to tolerate their moronic faces.

I look up at the sky; it's raining. A gray, dark day, with a ghostly feeling about it. God, I can't stand the green anymore—everywhere I look, it's green and mud, green and mud, green and mud everywhere. I'm tired of wearing the same clothes all the time, seeing the same faces over and over again. I'm so limited in every sense here. And everything, everything is so unpleasant: the hens, the hog, the three dogs named Fokker, Lander, and Tico—that last one is the little one. I think they named him that just to annoy me. Then there's the supply lady's daughter, the one with the annoying voice who watches TV all day long, I know she hates me. Just yesterday as I was going down to the river, the supply lady, just to make my life even more difficult and exasperating, told me that there were operatives in the area and that I couldn't spend more than half an hour down there.

Right now the hens are going back into their coop, which is right next to the pigsty. Oh, those poor animals, what a sad life they lead. All they ever get to eat are leftovers, and the problem here is that nobody ever leaves anything over, so they always end up having to munch on all the little insects that cross their path. They also don't ever get any water: they have to make do with the puddles that form when it rains. People watch them grow, and they get used to being around people, and then, just when they least expect it—*bam*! They get killed. You should see the way they kill the hen: first they break her legs so she can't run, and then, in the most merciless form imaginable, without a second thought, they grab her by the neck and wring it and wring it until the poor thing is finally decapitated. These people are complete savages. And what they do to hens is nothing compared to what they do to the hogs. They have it even worse: the guerrillas give them names, teach them things, and by the time the poor little animals actually start feeling a bit of affection for them, the guerrillas tie them up and stick a knife in their hearts.

The trees around here don't fare much better, either. The guerrillas are completely addicted to the chain saw: they just love to watch the trees fall. I would say they chop down about 150 trees per campsite: to make kindling, to make planks, to let the sun come through. . . .

It's awful. It breaks my heart to watch them ravage those trees and not be able to do a thing about it. To have your hands, feet, and body tied like that—not physically but psychically—is so unbelievably frustrating, so humiliating. Those are the moments when I have to wonder if there really is a God on this earth.

And then I ask myself, if this is the way things are here, what is the state of things in the city? A thousand, or even a million times worse, I suppose. Does God exist? I don't know. All I know is that there is no justice, at least not on earth. I don't know if there is any justice in the heavens. I hope so—I hope that justice exists somewhere, because if not it would be very sad to go on living without the hope that when you "die"—and for me, "death" means rebirth, just in another place—things might be different from what they are in this crap world where all you do is learn to suffer and hate. I live with such rage in this world because everywhere I look all I see is injustice. This world is completely backwards, I have no doubt at all about that. I could care less if I died right now, now that I've lived for as long as I have—that is, if you can actually consider that what I have here is actually some kind of "life."

I can't write anymore because Francisco and one of the guerrillas are talking so loudly, I've lost my concentration.

Thursday, September 9, 1999

Today I spent all day reading and I finished *En secreto,* by Germán Castro Caycedo, which I started yesterday. I learned a lot about all the conflicts here in Colombia. If you really think about it, everyone is right in some way. Before, I never understood why the paramilitaries stage so many massacres, and now I understand a little more about the situation, though I try to stay neutral about it. The book talks a lot about the guerrillas and Don Pablo, the drug lord, and the M-19 and their struggles. . . . They all have their reasons, in some way, no doubt about it. But the main problem is the Colombian government: these groups would never have a reason to exist if there weren't so much corruption at the highest levels here. The government must be thrilled that poor people are running around killing each other, the way the guerrillas and the paramilitaries do. If only they were a little more intelligent and a little less proud, they would realize that the war shouldn't be about the poor killing the poor. The real battle should be between the rich and the poor, the rich and the not-so-rich.

For me, the kind of people who deserve respect are the ones who make their money through hard work, people who try to help their country, not people who steal from others and abuse their positions or their power to steal and undermine the interests of people who struggle and suffer. If you really think about it, neither side of the conflict has any interest in ending the war, because what would become of their lives if the war were to end? They would have nobody left to fight and their businesses and interests would be dead. It makes me so mad when I realize that this is the way things are.

Today when I went down to take a bath, I ran into the head guerrilla, and took a few minutes to express these feelings and thoughts. The guerrilla tried to explain the reasons behind many of these acts that I cannot seem to understand, no matter how many times they have tried to justify them for me. Why are there so many kidnappings? I cannot understand this. He told me that they only demand ransoms from rich people, from the oligarchs of this country. That made me completely furious, and I spat back at him:

"You know something? For you people, anyone with an apartment, a car, and a little bit of money saved up is rich. And that's just not true. There are a lot of people who earn their money through sacrifice and hard work. But you people seem to despise anyone who lives or tries to live in peace. As far as you're concerned, 'the Colombian people' are only those people without a roof over their head, and you're wrong. There are plenty of people all the way up the ladder who are corrupted as hell, and you don't ever lay a finger on them—you just screw over everyone else. Us."

"Leszli, that's not true," he said.

"Well, then, I guess I'm just an idiot," I said, "because that is how I see things. And let me tell you something else: I'm not the only idiot out there. Forty million other Colombians are idiots just like me, because that's how all of us feel about this situation."

And he said, "No, no, that's not true, you're wrong: the ones to blame in all of this are the government, and the big corporations that run this country, like the Santodomingo Group or Adila Lulle. They're the ones we are fighting."

When I heard that, I replied, "Well, gee, that's funny, because I don't see any one of those capitalists, from any of those groups, anywhere around here. All I see here are seven airline employees. But you know what? Your hatred runs so deep that you've decided that all of us deserve to be here, just because my father happens to work for that company. Is it so terrible to work for a successful company? According to you people, it is. And you know what pisses me off even more about all this? That me and my father and my entire family are stuck in this mess because of the government, just as you say. And yet, you know something? I am not a particular fan of our government, either. It makes me furious to see how much corruption there is in the government, and it breaks my heart to see how they squeeze taxes out of everyone, for everything, because in the end, that money never goes back into the country, it always just ends up in the pockets of a few people who split it up among themselves. But us? What do we do? Do we drop everything and come here toting guns? Good God, no! You people, you talk a lot, you judge everything and everyone, but in the end you don't bring any real proposals to the table. And I hope to God you don't go and get mad at me. Just try to understand what I'm telling you."

He listened, and then replied: "I know you don't understand us, and that you're angry at us because you're here. That much I do understand. . . ."

I went on: "I think a lot about things, but I never tell you what I think. And if I were out there instead of here, I'd think the same thing. This country is in terrible shape: everyone fights and fights, and everyone kills everyone else, and there is bloodshed everywhere, but the saddest thing of all is that nobody is capable of proposing a rational solution. It makes me so mad to see how this country is rotting away from all the rage people feel, and yet nobody does anything. It's easy to talk, and everyone talks about peace, but nobody practices what they preach. People can never be bothered to simply bow their heads and acknowledge that they have made mistakes, that they have done something wrong. People have let pride and hatred destroy whatever love they ever felt for the country that raised them and nurtured them. That is so sad to me. I hope and pray with all my heart that one day I will be able to do something for this country, because I love our country, it's my home. Colombians really do have a great capacity for hatred, and it makes me so sad to see that."

Just as I predicted yesterday, there were no messages for me on the radio today. I am seriously thinking about not eating as a way of pressuring these people to bring messages to my mother.

Today I wrote all over the outside of the hut, even more than I did before. I wrote things like "Let us not look back in anger, nor forward in fear, but around in awareness" and "Since April 12, we have been living in hell for 151 days. How much longer will we be here?" Then I added another mark on my walking stick, like I've done every day since the hijacking. I also drew my favorite cartoon character, the one I always draw, the one with the little moon above his head. And I drew a calendar from April 12 up until the present, and another big sign in red, saying "Hijacking of Avianca's Fokker 50, April 12, 1999."

Then I made another sign, a very big one this time: "I have been kidnapped by the ELN." I do this so that every single day I am reminded of where I am and how very desperate I feel. To remind myself every morning that I am yet another victim of this war, enduring an experience that will mark me for the rest of my life. I do this so that I never forget how much I am suffering right now. These signs are to remind me of the injustice I have been dealt . . . and yes, to fill me with even more hatred.

Oh, God, I don't know what to think anymore. I feel that you abandoned me a long, long time ago and it feels awful. I am in such agony! Do you not see me? Or is it that I don't feel your presence? Give me a sign, oh please, a sliver of hope, something that I can cling to, to keep me from falling. Just do it already! I can't be any stronger than I've been. Get me out of here, please, I beg of you, get me out of here.

You know that in this life I have never done anything evil: I love animals, I adore my family, injustice makes me furious, I love with a true, pure heart. . . . I don't mean to say that I've never made anyone feel bad, but I try not to do things like that. I forgive and I try to forget. I don't commit sins, I don't steal, and I have never killed with my intentions or feelings. I know that I have done bad things but I have atoned, and besides, they are nothing too terrible. Anyway, I think a few bad acts can be compensated by a few good ones. Now, I have kept the promise I made to you a long time ago, about remaining a virgin until I marry, and not because I want to give the man I marry some kind of gift, but because I promised it to you as an expression of respect and thanks for the trust my mother has placed in me and for so many other things that you and I know.

So, with all that in mind, I still don't understand what I did that was so bad. Please, tell me: help me to see what it was so that I can try to make up for it. You know that I am a good person, and that if I ever wished harm on anyone it was in a moment of rage, and if someday I ever have the chance I will ask that person to forgive me for having hated him or her.

Oh, Guardian Angel, Guardian Angel who looks over my father and my entire family, and all the people I love . . . please look after us night and day until we finally achieve peace and happiness. . . . And to my loved ones who are dead, if you are out there, I ask you for protection and peace.

10:20 P.M. I have turned off my flashlight now and am thinking about everything and everyone, just as I have done every night here. I definitely feel that I am able to connect with the people I love through my thoughts. The only time I can do this is at this late hour, and maybe that's why I love the night so much: at night I am free to be with whomever I please, even if they don't want to be with me. I do what I feel like, in my space and my mind. Nobody can take that away from me, ever. I love the night.

Friday, September 10, 1999

Today I got up late, at 11 A.M., and on Laureano's radio I heard that this Sunday a mass will be held in our honor. This Sunday will mark five months in captivity. Changing the subject, my father told me that last night Francisco heard on the radio that Navarro Wolf recommended the ELN release the hostages before December 31, to start the new year with the so-called National Convention, the dialogue space they keep pushing for. At night, one of the guerrillas called us in to a meeting and told us that the head commander in the region of Magdalena Medio is working hard on the negotiation process, and that he sends us his regards. He also said that if things keep on going as they've been going, our release won't be far off.

Nobody seemed very moved by the news. Personally, I think they were just giving us a cheap thrill.

Saturday, September 11, 1999

Boy, did we have a scare tonight when we were watching the 7 o'clock news on Caracol. There we were, all of us sitting around, when suddenly we heard a thunderous explosion. It terrified all of us: some people ran, I grabbed my father and hugged him tight, and then we gathered together to sit with the others while the head guerrilla called out to us to remain quiet and calm. But they got scared, too: immediately they dispatched two guerrillas to see what was happening. Then they got their rifles out and told us to turn off the TV set.

I said no, because I was afraid whoever it was might fire at us, thinking we were guerrillas. I said I thought we were better off leaving it on, so that they could see us and recognize who was who. Right away they lowered the volume on the TV set, told us to not make any noise, and insisted we stay very calm. A few minutes later we found out that a tree branch had snapped off and activated one of the land mines they use for security.

Once they confirmed this, they all calmed down, and so did the rest of us. The head guerrilla then told us that they always place land mines around the perimeter of the camp, for security reasons, and that we now had 29 instead of 30. The commander that arrived last night, who we just saw for the first time today, told me and my father that if we ever found ourselves in a situation like that again, the best thing to do was to fall to the ground and drag ourselves to safety. Even so, he said, they already had an emergency plan: one group would go down to fight, and another would be in charge of getting us, the hostages, to a safer place. No matter what, they said, we didn't have to worry because everything was under control. God, was that scary! It happened at 7:15 P.M.

On another note, I started a new book today, a novel called *How the Steel Was Tempered,* by Nikolai Ostrovski. A beautiful story.

Today my father told me stories about my grandmother Gisella. When she was a little girl, he told me, she would go out to the concentration camps and throw bread and fruit to the prisoners inside. There was one woman in particular, a very young woman, who would often talk with my grandmother and thank her for the food she brought. One day she asked my grandmother her name, and my grandmother told her. The lady then asked my grandmother if she could find anything out about her family at a certain address in a certain town; she wanted to know what had become of them. My grandmother obliged, and found out that there was nobody at all in the lady's old house; it had been abandoned. She reported back to the woman at the concentration camp, who was extremely grateful to my grandmother (still a girl at the time) for all her kindness and generosity. The people in the camps had no idea what was going on in the outside world, and the lady was completely in the dark. My grandmother just told her not to worry, that the war would be over soon, that the Russians were going to arrive soon, that they had already crossed the border. She told the lady to stay calm, that everything would be all right. Through those exchanges, a bond of friendship formed between the lady and the 14- or 15-year-old girl who later became my grandmother.

Not long after that, my grandmother had to leave the country with her two sisters; they went to France. From there, the Red Cross sent them on to different countries: my grandmother went to Toronto, her married sister went to New York, and the other one went to Caracas. Sometime after that, my grandmother reunited with her married sister in New York, but she was actually much closer to the sister who had gone to Venezuela. So she saved up her money, bought a ticket, and set sail for Caracas. In Venezuela she met my grandfather, and they were married in San Antonio. Then, practically penniless, they went to Bogotá. They had virtually nothing, but they had heard there were Hungarians in Bogotá, Hungarians who were very good about helping one another out. After they arrived, my grandmother got a job sewing in a factory, and my grandfather, who knew a thing or two about diesel engines, worked as a mechanic. In addition to her factory job, my grandmother had a Hungarian friend who helped her get work sewing made-to-order women's clothing. One day my grandmother was sent to a private home to take a lady's measurements for a suit, and the two women began talking.

"Where are you from?" my grandmother asked the woman.

"I'm from Hungary," the lady said.

"Ah . . . so am I. . . ."

The lady was very wealthy; she had married an American man, the president of an oil company.

"Really? What part?" My grandmother told the lady the name of her town, and to the lady's surprise, it was the same town that she was from.

"I can't believe it! That's where I'm from."

"Where were you in prison?"

When she told my grandmother where she had been held, my grandmother answered, in shock: "You can't be serious! I used to bring those people bread and fruit."

The lady then replied, "You are Gisella Daniel, aren't you?"

"Yes," my grandmother said. "I'm Gisella Daniel."

"I don't believe it."

With tears in their eyes the two women embraced, and that day my grandmother's life changed: my grandfather Nandor, who had been a mechanic in an auto shop, was given an extremely important job in the oil company run by the lady's husband. According to my father, he went from earning around 300,000 pesos to something like 7 million pesos. Their luck changed overnight, and the two families became very close.

What an incredible coincidence.

"Think first, then act." That's what my father always says. "Everything in life is based on logic. Everything can be resolved with logic."

Then he recounted some other memories still floating around in his head.

While my grandmother Gisella was still in Hungary, some Russian refugees came to town. One of them knocked on the door of the house where Gisella lived with her brothers. There was a piano in the house. The Russians played piano beautifully but they were really quite ignorant: they actually drank her perfume thinking it was alcohol. Very heavy drinkers.

My grandmother was orphaned at a very young age, when she was around 13. Her mother was a Russian Jew and died of cancer, and her father also died around the same time. He was Hungarian, though, not Russian.

Sunday, September 12, 1999

It's 2 in the morning and I'm listening to *Amanecer en América* as I draw on my mosquito net with my magic markers. I rarely receive messages on *Amanecer en América*, but I always listen because Lucía, Judith, and Esperanza often talk to my father through this station.

Today they are airing the program from Vélez, in Santander. Juan, Laureano, Francisco, Uriel, Diego, and Fernando have all received messages. As usual, I didn't get any, nor did my father this time around.

On the TV news, I saw that our families held a mass and released 16 doves in honor of the 16 of us who are still in captivity. I didn't see my mother or any of my relatives, though. After that I watched a karate movie on RCN.

When I went to change, I walked past the playing field and stood there for a little while looking up at the stars and felt myself being transported up, up, and away, and just as I was wondering if there is life on other planets, I saw a shooting star. It's a beautiful night out tonight, cold and lovely, and as I gazed up I thought a lot about my family and all the people I love. I want to see them so badly. . . . I hope I get back home by December, most especially so I can celebrate my birthday with them on December 11. My mind and spirit are with them.

Oh, this is all so hard!

Today I talked to the head guerrilla about books and about the ELN. He told me that he had heard my mother on the radio criticizing Pastrana and said she gave him a good laugh. The ELN's chief guy in Magdalena Medio was listening to the program along with him, and he said, "No wonder the daughter's like that—her mother's even worse." And he laughed.

Today I swept everything up and got rid of a lot of roots sticking out of the ground. There's a guerrilla here who's a painter, and I like him a lot: he seems like such a nice, wise person. Plus he's very serene; talking with him is such a pleasure. He told me that the door was open whenever I wanted to come back—as a visitor, of course, not a hostage. He also told me that the others had warned him about me, that I had a terrible temper, that I had shaved my head, that I was depressed. He knew all that before he arrived at our campsite, plus he also told me that he knew about my trip to Israel. Right now I'm listening to La Mega and thinking about my family and my friends. I wonder what it will be like to see each other again. . . .

On the news I watched a report on foreign hostages in Colombia: Daniel Hoffmann and Nicolás Pérez, of the United States and Panama, respectively, were both mentioned. To fight the loneliness, I reread the letters that were written to me on July 4. I'm still listening to La Mega, and I just heard a song that I love.

In a dictionary that the guerrillas brought, I read a page that lists the gestation periods for all kinds of animals: zebra and donkey, 375 days; sperm whale, 480 days; possum, 13 days; mouse, 21 days; marmot, mole, hare, 40 days; rabbit, 30 days; fox, 54 days; guinea pig, she-wolf, 60 days; panther, 93 days; horse, 335 days; giraffe, 440 days; rhinoceros, 560 days; lion and tiger, 106 days; pig, 115 days; beaver, 128 days; sheep, 150 days; badger, 180 days; gibbon, 210 days; deer, 235 days; fallow deer and hippopotamus, 240 days; grizzly bear, 260 days; manatee, 270 days.

There were no messages for me or my father on UIS. I'm so angry, not because of that but because of what the priest from the Cali church asked for. He said that it was time for the ELN to offer another goodwill gesture by freeing five more people from the church. Oh yeah, and what about us? We don't exist? We don't count? We don't suffer? That pharisee only cares about the release of the people in the church, and doesn't even realize that those of us from the plane have been in captivity for a lot longer. The church in this country is such a farce, and the same is true in the rest of the world. I hate churches because they prey on people's faith just to get charity money from them—and they're the richest people in the world! Isn't that something else? It also pisses me off that the ELN goes and releases the other people first instead of us, when we've been in captivity much longer.

Today they killed a little cow and brought her back in pieces.

It's late now, and they just switched on the light. Everything around me looks so pretty, just as I always imagined the setting of Snow White: the shadow of the trees, the clouds, the mist. And with the cold we've had lately, it really does feel just like a fairy tale.

My back is hurting from these planks, because they're uneven. Today I started spiraling into those feelings of despair again, but I controlled myself. I didn't take a bath, because it was just too cold. Thank goodness I have a wool blanket; when I bundle up in it I don't feel cold at all, except for my feet.

Francisco was kind of gross with me today, but I can't tell, maybe it was just me. It had to do with a soap opera. . . . I would like to think I just misinterpreted what he said, because if not this will only make me more furious with that guy. On top of the fact that I absolutely cannot tolerate him, I have to pretend that I think he's all right. Of all the things about him that make me mad, this would really top the list. But my father said something the other day about calling a meeting among the hostages and patching things up between us. That's another thing that has me really irritated—to think of my father initiating something that, really, Francisco should have initiated. I hope my father changes his mind and ditches the idea.

Wednesday, September 15, 1999

Today I talked for a while with the painter guerrilla. I showed him the drawings I'd done, and then gave him one as a gift. He told me about the ELN and said that he liked the way my mind worked. What he liked most about me, he said, was my honesty. He asked me to read "I am not a shield" to him, if I didn't mind, and I said of course I'd read it to him. That was something I wrote specifically for them, and he liked it! He also told me he liked to draw, and that he liked deciphering my drawings.

Today the health aide gave me a very pretty piece of paper that says "Happy Day of Love and Friendship," and tomorrow I'm going to give him and everyone else the same thing. Today I also made a card for the painter guerrilla that says: "Your efforts will come to full and total fruition only when you have refused to abandon the struggle. Keep the faith, and keep up the fight. Happy Day of Love and Friendship. Leszli Kálli, September 15, 1999." I think he likes me. But I just felt like doing that.

Either this morning or later tonight, after everyone else has gone to bed, I'm going to make another card that says, "For the ELN: Happy Day of Love and Friendship . . . and peace. Yours sincerely, the Kállis."

Thursday, September 16, 1999

We've been here for 158 days now. Everything has been more or less the same today, except my mother spoke on the radio at 5 A.M.— that's what Francisco told me, anyway. I didn't hear her myself. Today, in Caracas, they held a meeting with Gabino and the commission appointed by the government to deal with our situation. On another note, I didn't receive any messages on UIS, although Lucía, my stepmother, did send a message to my dad, something about two stars in the sky. . . . God, that woman can be so corny!

Four years ago today Carolina got married.

I feel like eating some chocolate and vanilla ice cream. I feel like going to the bathroom. And I want to see my mother and everyone else. I'm dying to know how Danielito is.

Friday, September 17, 1999

Today there was a meeting in the TV hut. The painter guerrilla told us that the enemy had entered the area and he wanted to give us some recommendations of what to do in case anything happened: first, he said, we should all have a change of clothes ready; those of us with suitcases were to hand them in so that they could hide them away; if we heard shots being fired near the river, we were to go straight to the TV hut and if we heard them anywhere near the TV hut our meeting place would be the kitchen or meal shack. He also told us not to spend too much time down by the river, and that if we had to evacuate the camp we would be paired up in twos with two guerrillas assigned to each pair. He also told us not to make too much noise, and that if we heard a helicopter overhead we should just look for cover under a big tree.

Saturday, September 18, 1999

I dreamt of my grandfather last night. Nothing. Same old story. I am afraid there's going to be an armed conflict.

Sunday, September 19, 1999

It's been 161 days. Last night I dreamt of a combat scene: several guerrillas were carrying a stretcher with an older man, and I watched as they carried him along in a kind of a ceremony. Then I heard shots ring out and I began to run, but I left my flashlight behind and then I started to panic because I couldn't find my father. When I turned to go back they started firing at me. Then I woke up. In another dream sequence, I saw Cristhian. Lately I've been feeling death very close by; I feel as though something could happen to me at any moment.

Last night I sat up with the guard: first with a regular guerrilla soldier, then with the health aide. She told me that the most critical hours are between 8 and 10 at night and then again between 3 and 6 in the morning. She said that if you end up in the front lines, it's almost certain death, and then she told me about her first combat experience: one of her fellow soldiers was killed and they ambushed 15 police officers.

I also talked to the painter for a little while. He told me what the ELN did yesterday in Medellín—they captured 30 people, and it wasn't a random bunch of people, either, he said. They knew exactly who they were going after, because it was a totally economic maneuver, just like the operative in Barranquilla and one of the kidnappings in Cali. They went straight after politicians who everyone says are completely corrupt, but the government refused to identify them because the story would only stir up a lot of bad press for them, since several of the hostages had financed the present administration's electoral campaigns. He also told me that they're trying to get money from some of the airplane passengers, and of course they're trying to get money from Avianca, and that in general things were going well.

My mom spoke on the radio this morning, but I missed it because I was asleep. She said that by next Saturday I should be back at home. Now, I don't mean to seem negative, but given the situation I think we're better off being realistic. I don't know why she says things like that.

Just today the guerrillas held a little cultural event, a kind of chat session where they all get together and tell jokes, read one another's fortunes, sing, perform pantomimes, read poetry, and do some other things. We were allowed to attend if we wanted. They said to us, "Today we're going to hold a cultural event. Do you want to come?" Uriel went and recited a poem.

Monday, September 20, 1999

23 weeks, 162 days. 1:20am. Today I spoke with the Nice Old Man about my thoughts on life, death, and what it means to be here, in this place.

I'm not tired at all. I am trying not to think about my mother or my brother and sister—I don't want to feel worse than I already do. It's better that way. I think it's a good idea to try to sleep during the day, because it allows me to kind of skip over the harsh reality of all this. That way, I can stay up at night, which is always so relaxing for me. At night I feel as though I am alone with time; I don't see anyone, I don't talk to anyone, and I have the entire campsite all to myself. Also, for some reason I don't feel quite so anguished and desperate at night—I don't feel pressured, I don't feel watched, and even the weather is easier to bear. There are fewer insects, and it's not so hot.

9:25 P.M. I watched two soap operas: *Me llaman Lolita* [They Call Me Lolita] and *Marido y mujer* [Husband and Wife]. Today I explained my theory about life to the painter guerrilla. I also made some corn pies and left some lentils in water so that tomorrow I could make meat pies and ground lentils. Today I wore my black pants and the shirt I painted pink. I also played Parcheesi.

Tuesday, September 21, 1999

163 days. Last night I dreamt of a broad, rushing river of the most intense shade of blue, with huge, billowing waves. I was flying in some kind of biplane and arguing with someone. To keep him from getting away, I drove the plane down into the river. Both of us fell out and then we drifted away from each other; otherwise we would have drowned. I made my way to the shore and trudged my way through the underbrush and then I went further inland. It was pitch-black because of all the trees and plants, and I saw all sorts of long snakes, and I mean a ton of them. Just as they were getting ready to attack me, when I was totally scared out of my wits, I woke up.

I didn't make any pies today because the health aide was on duty up here and she was in a really bad mood.

Before I went to bed I did something really dumb: I looked outside, saw a tree, and freaked out because I thought it was a person.

No messages today on UIS. The truth is, I don't care that much about getting messages, but I do think it would be really terrible if my family weren't able to talk to me because they got into some fight with the radio station—I mean, in this situation, me being a woman, and the youngest one here, it really would be the height of unfairness. I don't think I'm going to write any more letters, just so they realize that it stinks to feel so alone. Tomorrow will be another day, I suppose. But who knows when this problem will get resolved? The only thing I feel pretty sure of is that this was more of an economic than a political kidnapping, which means that things are going to happen even slower than we thought. What a drag! Oh, I hope I can spend my birthday, and Christmas, and the New Year with my family. All I want is my freedom, the same freedom you gave me the day I was born. Freedom—freedom—freedom.

Thursday, September 23, 1999

Today my dad and I cleaned up the hut a little. I swept, made coffee, and ate my three meals. There was a meeting in Venezuela today with the heads of the ELN and the commission. Victor G. Ricardo was there, among others. Yesterday I slept all day and didn't take a bath. I dreamt that I was dressed in a nun's habit, in a black dress with a hood. I was with Juliana Toro, I have no idea why.

Today I made a calendar for October and November, and stuck it on the dressing table that my dad made. Today a few messages came in, but as usual none of them were for me.

Today a mass was held in an Avianca hangar in support of our release. Right now I am sitting in the chair drinking some coffee. Today, the painter guerrilla told me that he drew a picture of me, but he hasn't given it to me yet. I played Parcheesi with Diego, Fer, and my father. Last night while we were watching a soap opera Uriel said that the painter is always contradicting himself. I disagree: I think he's a very smart, serious guy. Uriel also said that he heard we were going to be separated. I'm going back out to play Parcheesi. It's exactly 5 P.M.

Today I made cream of mushroom soup for Diego, Fer, Laureano, Uriel, and me. Afterward, I hung around in Diego and Fernando's hut, talking with Laureano. It's 11:25 P.M. now.

The moon is full and very, very lovely tonight. I'm not even asking God to get me home by the next full moon—all I ask of him now is to let me see the moon again from my house one day. I'm really angry at God about this—I know that's bad, and that I could be a lot worse off. I know that there are people who have been in captivity for much longer than we have, but it still makes me furious. Fernando tells me not to lose faith, to stay calm and hang on to my belief in God, but I can't: I just don't believe anymore. Right now, it feels like getting out of here would take a miracle; it feels like something that just isn't part of me, something very detached. The truth is, getting out of here is looking pretty impossible, and I think I'm only going to do more damage to myself if I listen to my mom again, because listening to her will only make me feel hopeful again, and that will make things even harder on me. If in fact I am never going to see my mother and the rest of them ever again, with all my heart I hope they stop receiving news about me. Because, I mean, what's the point? It would only give them false hope. In some way, they have to have resigned themselves to the possibility at least.

I wish God would kill me already, clean and fast, and free me from this anguish once and for all. The suffering is so intense; it is pure torture. I have lost my strength, my faith, everything has crumbled to the ground. All I ask for is mercy, not to get out of here but to die soon. And I'm not saying that to be selfish, either: I think it's more selfish to remain alive when your loved ones have no idea if you're okay or not. It's better to just amputate the suffering. It's like when a person falls into a coma and stays like that for a long time: the person in the coma suffers because he can't disconnect from the world, and the people around him suffer, too, from the desperation, the agony, the impotence. Well, that's how I feel, as if I've been in a coma for six months. My life went numb on April 12. At that moment, I was disconnected from reality and came to dwell in a hell that I sink deeper and deeper into with every passing day.

Friday, September 24, 1999

Today I heard something on the radio that I did not like one bit. They said: 99 days until the year 2000. When I heard that, I started to cry and went to talk to the painter guerrilla. I told him how I felt and he said he'd try to help me get out before 2000. We talked about a lot of things. I told him a lot about my life and I think he really listened to me. I hadn't gone to him intending to talk about that stuff, and I don't even remember when or how I ended up doing it. But anyway, he told me about his life, too. I really like him. I think he's a sincere person; he has a good heart.

Today my mind is flying high, very high, liberated from my body, feeling the blessing of freedom.

God and I are the only people who understand the true essence of my life.

I close my eyes and in the middle of all this fear, I ask God to take care of you, Mom, because that is what will bring me peace right now, because you are the person who gives me strength to go on living.

Saturday, September 25, 1999

In the morning I played Battleship with Francisco and, as usual, I won. I just took a bath and now I'm sitting around, thinking about writing a letter to my mother.

8:20 P.M. I was watching *Sábados felices* [Happy Saturdays] in the TV hut but after a while I got bored and came back here. As I walked past the playing field I looked up at the moon: it was so pretty, so full, and there was a rainbow around it. Awed by its beauty, I thought back to the last time I saw a full moon, when I asked God to release me before the next one. Today I ask God for the same thing. I hope he grants my wish this time.

Amanecer en América is on today, and I hope I don't fall asleep because I want to hear my messages, if there are any for me, that is. In the last month I haven't heard a thing from anyone back home.

Today I asked the head guerrilla about the statement one of the ELN commanders made on the news; he said that more people would be released soon. I wanted to know if the ones getting out were in the other group of Avianca passengers, but he said he didn't know. I asked him if he could ask someone via radio if they had heard anything about it, and he said sure. After a little while he came over to me and told me no, the people being released were the ones in the Cali church. That made me very sad.

It's 11:30. I just went to the kitchen, made some cream of chicken soup, and gave it to the painter guerrilla, who was on duty. We talked about my mother, and the kind of person she is, and I told him about my grandfather. He had a lot of property and rice crops, and one harvest he mortgaged his land so that he could plant on another man's land in addition to his own. That way, if things went well, he'd earn back the money he made off his own land plus half of what the other man earned. In those days, people did business with a handshake, on their honor, because back then you could still trust people. Well, the harvest was a plentiful one, but two days after they gathered everything the man died and his children came around and ruined my grandfather's business. That destroyed him, because he had put all his money into that business of his. I also told him about our life in the U.S., when we were little, and I also told him about my more recent family life.

Right now I'm listening to the radio station Amor Stereo.

Sunday, September 26, 1999

96 days to go before the year 2000. Last night I dreamt I saw my mother in a big pool filled with cloudy water. She was on the other side, and to get over to her I had to glide over the water on a kind of board, but I was very afraid of falling and had a tough time figuring out how to get to her from where I was. Finally I got up, and just as I was reaching her, I fell in the water. I was very scared, and all around the pool there were tree trunks, bushes, and everything was dark and creepy. I quickly grabbed on to a tree trunk, or maybe it was a branch, to keep from sinking and also to try and get out, but there were flies everywhere and they were stinging me. I asked my mother to give me her hand, to help me out of the water, but she refused. I felt more and more scared, and then suddenly I woke up.

Today the painter guerrilla came by to say goodbye and left me with four drawings. He told me that we'd see each other again soon enough, and that if I wanted I could write to him through the head commander.

Later on I talked to the head guerrilla and the painter in the studio hut. They told me a little about how the hijacking had been carried out. They said they imagined that the ELN had decided to hijack that particular plane because of the region it was flying in, because they had received orders from the COCE people to prepare a campsite for 16 people. It wasn't until after receiving those orders that they learned that it was for the plane hostages—meaning us—and that we would be the ones occupying the camp. We also talked about life, and about a bunch of other things.

It's been exactly two months since I shaved my head. The vine we were using to swing from and play with just broke. In the afternoon I took a nap and dreamt I saw a full moon, surrounded by lots of clouds. After a while they cleared, and I saw a ton of stars. A very beautiful dream.

I have the worst stomach cramps. I'm listening to Soda Stereo: *"Té para tres"* ["Tea for Three"] and *"Trátame suavemente"* ["Be Gentle with Me"]. "I don't want to dream the same things a thousand times" is one of the lyrics.

When I got back to the hut I spotted a huge cockroach. My father said it must have been 10 centimeters long. I asked the guard not to kill it, but still, it was pretty disgusting. My mother would have died if she'd ever seen something as revolting as that.

If I had the power to turn back the clock, I would do it. Without a doubt. First and foremost, I would tell my mother how much I love her, and I'd say the same to Danielito, such a beautiful little person, and I'd smother him in kisses to make up for all that lost time. I would tell my brother and sister how much they mean to me, and I would thank them for all the support they give me. I would treat everything I possess as magnificent; no matter how small or seemingly meaningless, I would take care of my things and learn to cherish them. I would tell all the people close to me how much I love them, and I would take care of them, too. And as for all those other people who are just random people, I'd act more or less as I've always acted: I wouldn't criticize them; I would just try to do the best I could, and maybe I would study them a little in order to learn how not to be like them. And I would do all these things without ever judging anyone.

But since time is not in my hands, all I can say is that if God gives me the chance to go back home, I will do all these things and more. Every day will be filled with great miracles. There is no question in my mind that it would be a kind of rebirth, in the very greatest sense: a rebirth in which I would be aware of the value of things, of every step, every act. I would take the time to grow as a person and give the very best of me to the world I live in and to the people I love and cherish.

Last night I heard something on the radio that I liked a lot: "Love and sadness go hand in hand: while one is sitting at your table, the other is lying in your bed, and they take turns. . . ." It's like what they say, there's no reason to worry about things, because after something bad happens, there's always something good, something better around the corner. That's life: things go up, things come down. The world never stands still: it is in a constant state of motion.

I think that every situation, no matter how awful, has a positive side. Tough times are what make us stronger, because they fine-tune the soul. Jairo Jaramillo said something that I like a lot: "Good things hurt." Life is just that, the continuous give and take, and that is what makes it interesting. . . .

Monday, September 27, 1999

Day 169. 96 days until the year 2000.

1 A.M. I am thinking of Diego. I feel like writing him a little letter. . . .

Hello, Diego,
I want to tell you that I am happy you are back at home with your parents. They must be really glad to have you with them again. I don't know how things went for you in Canada, but I guess everything went fine, that you learned a lot and that you know a lot more about so many things, like what I wrote to you in the letter I sent you. The truth is, I don't really remember what I wrote to you, but I do know that I said something about how I hoped that you learned about both the good and the bad, and that you learned to value all the things that you have. Or something like that.

Today I am writing to you to say that when I wrote that letter I probably didn't really know what I was talking about—I don't think I appreciated things the way I do now, because I have learned a lot in that sense, and so much more. How ironic, little did I know that all those things I said to you were for me as much as they were for you. But that's life, I guess, full of surprises. . . .

As for me, my life has changed a lot. And when I say *a lot* it's because I really mean it. After all I've been through, I have learned that our plans and God's plans can sometimes be very different. Nothing in life is written in stone, anything is possible. The things you least imagine can happen, and those are the moments when you realize that nothing in life can be taken for granted. For example, I always thought that nothing could ever happen to me, because I'm Leszli, I'm strong, and nobody can do anything to me. Boy, does that make me laugh now. Who is Leszli? Just another person who, like everyone else on Earth, is at the mercy of God, at the mercy of all the good and bad things that life has in store for her.

Have you ever stopped to think about how things, life, people can change? Yes, people, too. Here I have learned a lot about both the good and bad things in my life. The good: my family, my friends, my life, freedom, the wonderful moments and all the things I once had. And the bad things? There isn't much, but it's always something involving my bad temper, my moods—I used to want everything *now*; I was always so impatient. My mom always called me *la fregadita,* because I've always been so complicated, so picky about things. Well, that's one thing about me that has changed since I've been here—not completely, but now, at least, I try to change it a little. Before all this happened, I never realized I had personality flaws. I always just thought I was perfect. But that's all in the past now. The only thing that matters to me now is the present, and though for the moment my present life is far from ideal, I don't care. This is my present and I try to take the best I can from it so that I can learn about myself and the people around me.

Life has given me a tremendous test: to learn the limits of my endurance, to learn how to get through certain circumstances, and to ponder my methods for dealing with them. With this in mind, I can honestly say that I do want to keep on going; I most certainly want to keep on living to prove to myself that yes, I am able to handle these things. The situation I'm in is hard, very hard, incredibly difficult to tolerate, and there are moments when I think I can't take it anymore and then I start thinking about all the things I'm telling you now and you know what? Those things are what give me strength.

To make a long story short, I will just say that I have grown up a great deal here, and I now have a very different vision of life. Jairo once said to me, "Good things hurt, and more if they are difficult." I really learned the meaning of that here. And like they say, every cloud has a silver lining. But that's life for you, full of surprises at every turn. . . .

So I send you a big hug, for you and everyone else. I miss you all so much, and I hope to see you one of these days. . . .

I love you.

Yours,

Your little Leszli Kálli

Later on, 1 P.M.

Pablo Beltrán spoke on the radio. He said that people were going to be released. As always, we all started to guess who it would be.

Lunch today consisted of lentils, rice, *arepas,* and yucca. To drink, they gave us lemonade with fresco Royal. Pretty gross.

Last night I dreamt that I was with Juan Carlos, the Spanish man, and Julio Ochoa. Juan Carlos was interviewing me and I was washing my hands with something blue while talking to Ana María Gómez. I was very nervous because I was about to get married and the apartment was full of people. Juan Carlos was wearing an ELN

T-shirt and refused to talk to Julio because they had gotten into an argument.

Right now I'm listening to the song *"Diana y Miguel"* by Mecano. It's all about how the sea falls in love with Diana and feels very jealous of Miguel, who is a fisherman. The sea, wracked with jealousy, takes Miguel away from Diana. And she suffers, she suffers and she waits for him to return. A very sad story.

I just finished watching a movie called *Fled,* which was filmed in Atlanta and shows Stone Mountain. What a horrible memory: those streets, and everything so ugly and depressing. Without a doubt, 1996 was definitely a bad year, maybe my worst. I suffered and cried so much that year. But the experience did make me grow up a little, that's for sure. That was around the time I broke up with Diego, and my mother got married. . . . I felt that everything was crashing down around me, and so I decided to move to Atlanta and leave everything behind: my hypocritical girlfriends who, I have to admit, I did share some special moments with; my family and Diego; my school . . . I gave all that up just to run away, to escape the loneliness and the rage I felt toward everything that I had once believed to be secure.

The good thing that came out of that experience was that I realized the mistake I'd made and when I came back I confronted all my fears. Also, rather unwittingly, a very special person came into my life, someone who helped me a great deal, who helped me to feel joy again. I owe him a lot, and though I never told him so, as time went by I do believe I began to love him and I had such a wonderful time with him, even though it didn't last very long. After a while, he changed, but he never hurt me. He was honest with me and for that I will always be grateful: he treated me with total sincerity. He always respected me, even though we were very different—opposites, in fact. Once our little passion died down, we both realized that if we stayed together we would only hurt each other, so we ended it. But I still feel a great deal of affection for him, and I truly hope he finds someone to love. Whenever we see each other we always talk, and I know he has very special feelings for me, too.

The last time I saw Christian was at Mesa de los Santos, March 27.

He told me that his dad was about to leave home. I hope he's all right and that his father didn't leave them. . . .

Tomorrow is another day, but . . . how many more tomorrows will there be for me? I have no idea. All I can speak of is yesterday, the day before yesterday, and all the days before then.

God, please let me and my father out of here soon, and please send peace and calm to my mother. Enough of all this!

My father has told me that if I get the chance to get out of here, I should grab it. But I could never leave here without him. That would be a very tough decision to have to make. I want to stay with him—I would never forgive myself if something happened to him, though the alternative would allow me to tell my family in person that we're all right and that would certainly be a big relief to them. But I don't know . . . if it were up to me, I'd just stay, but my dad gets angry when I say that. He tells me it's doubly stressful for him that both of us are here, and that he would rather not have to worry about me here. But I don't buy it. Anyway, we don't even know if they're going to let me go. God willing, they won't let me go without my father. God, please hear me out on this . . . !

Today I went over to Fernando and Diego's hut. Laureano was in there, too. They told me that they'd heard Pablo Beltrán on the news, saying that he expected the National Convention would take place before the end of the year, and that one of the issues to be discussed was the release of the hostages and some kind of official commitment to put an end to the *pesca milagrosa* [miracle fishing] and kidnapping. Sounds like good news to me, but we'll have to see what the great president of Colombia, Mr. Andrés Pastrana Arango, has to say about it. I can't wait to see what brilliant idea he comes up with. God, please, illuminate him and help him, and please help all the people who are responsible for our release. . . .

Mom, I have to say that this news makes no difference to me: I just don't believe anything, because by now I have heard so many people say so many things that I don't believe any of them anymore. Maybe I feel this way to keep myself from being disappointed. Mommy, wherever you are I hope that you are calm and at peace. I miss you, Mommy. I want to see you soon. I love you so much.

I dream of the day when I will be home, in my room, walking through the apartment, sitting in the dining room, the living room, looking at the painting I made with acrylic over foam, eating with my silverware, preparing broccoli and mushrooms in the oven with lots of cheese, making pineapple juice with lots of ice, sitting on the second-floor sofa watching TV—me, the lady of the house and of the remote control, cruising the channels. And then I think about seeing Pablito and gossiping with Carol, letting my mother spoil me rotten and listening to her tell me how much she missed me. Or I picture myself with Nandor, listening to everything he has to tell me, especially about Danielito and all the little games he plays, or I see myself listening to Mauricio's jokes and enjoying those juicy stories he likes to tell; or answering the phone when Jairito calls and telling him that I want to see him and everyone else, and figuring out where to meet, who's going to come. . . . Then I imagine a stroll through the city, going out for ice cream, pizza, hamburgers, juice, snacks, and then heading out to whatever place is "in" at the moment in Bucaramanga. . . . But before that, I see myself taking a nice long bath and spending lots of time putting on my makeup so that I look really pretty, curling my eyelashes, applying a good coat of mascara and putting on a pretty scarf, a nice perfume. . . . Aside from that, what else can I ask of life? Oh and yes, after it's all over I see myself going out to the terrace and thanking God for this great joy I feel.

Tuesday, September 28, 1999

Day 170. 95 days until the year 2000.

It's 7:05 P.M. Juan Carlos García sent me a very friendly long-distance hug. He said he was convinced that I'd be coming home soon, which cheered me up a lot. Yesterday I started taking the pills Diego sent me to help my depression. No change so far.

Another day just like all the rest. We watched the movie *Mortal Combat* and then I took a bath, ate some rice and beans, or *moros y cristianos* as they are called, and slices of fried plantain. I put on my red pants and my gray shirt, white socks, and red scarf.

As I walked down to the bathroom, I had a little scare when I passed by the guard; I think I scared him, too.

"Who's there?" he called out.

"Leszli Kálli, held captive by the ELN since April twelfth of this year."

How creepy. It was very dark out, and when I focused I could make out where he was, but I hadn't been able to tell where the voice had come from.

They just laid some planks down over the swamp; now it looks like a catwalk. Two guerrillas just butchered a pair of chickens; they were very violent about it. . . .

Later on there were messages on the UIS, but since there haven't been any messages for me lately, my father told me some very good little stories. Here are the ones I liked the best:

Two men are studying the sands in the desert. One of them spots a yellow dot off in the distance, so he pulls his binoculars out of his backpack and takes a look. Then he says to his companion: "Oh, man, a huge tiger is coming our way and he just saw us." Then he pulls a pair of sneakers out from his bag and prepares to run.

The other man says, "Listen, man, you're real naïve if you think that tiger isn't going to catch up with you. Do you actually think you can beat out a tiger?"

And the man with the sneakers says, "Not the tiger, my friend: you."

Once, a little chicken was idling in a pasture full of cows when suddenly a hawk flying overhead spotted the chicken, who immediately sought shelter between the back legs of one of the cows. When the hawk veered close to one leg, the chicken moved toward the other leg, and the hawk followed suit, chasing the chicken from side to side. After a few rounds of this back-and-forth game, the cow took a dump on the chicken, who ended up smothered in shit. And the hawk, not having seen anything, went away. The little chicken was practically drowning in excrement, and as soon as he was able, he cleared his face and began to squawk. The hawk heard the chicken, turned around, and successfully trapped, cleaned, and ate the little chicken.

The moral of the story? Not everyone who buries you in shit is your enemy, nor is a man your friend just because he pulls you out of shit. The moral of the story is that when you're in shit up to your ears, the best thing to do is to keep your mouth shut.

A street urchin is out on the sidewalk, scratching on the side of the door of a car with a little coin. A policeman stops him and says, "Why are you scratching that car with a coin?"

And the kid replies, "Hey. I can do whatever I want with my money."

"Mommy, Mommy, my father is a magician!"

"What gave you that idea, honey?"

"Because he took two wires, hooked them together, and then a bunch of sparks flew and he disappeared!"

A man walks over to the three biggest liars in town and says to them, "Listen, I'll give 500 pesos to the man who tells me the best lie."

The first one says, "Once I was in the jungle and a tiger pounced on me and I whacked him so hard that I knocked him upside down."

The second man says, "Just picture it: there I was, in a room full of people and someone was laying farts but nobody knew who. And so I grabbed a can of spray paint and painted the guy who was being such a filthy pig."

Finally, the man turns to the third liar and asks, "And you? What's your story?"

And the third man says, "Listen, I'm not going to tell you a bunch of lies. I am a witness here to swear that what these other two men say is true, because these two eyes saw them do the things they say they did."

My father has a pretty decent sense of humor. I love it when he tells stories, because his faces and his gestures are so funny. He's really a very amusing guy; people love to listen to him. Here, of course, those stories are a form of escape for us.

Oh, Diary, I don't know if I've already told you but this is our fourth campsite, the one we've been at the longest. All 32 of us were at the first campsite for about a week; then there were 16 of us at the second campsite, also for about a week; and then we spent about two months at the third one.

All of this has been so hard: it's been so hard to get used to the mud, the discomfort, and so many other things. The first days were very rough: the food was shit. . . . Then, once we got used to everything, it got better—better and better, in fact, and everything started to change. Only after that, once we were finally settled, did the serious depression kick in. Desperation and depression, because there's no longer anything to do. Thinking is the only work we do, and that's the problem, our minds just wander off. . . .

That's why I think that if we keep ourselves occupied, the time will slip by without us even realizing it, and that will give us a bit of a break from reality. Any way you look at it, though, it's still boring and horrible. I have to say I think that only those of us who have been through a kidnapping can understand the meaning of the word *boredom,* and all that it truly represents; it's situations like these that really give you a full understanding of what boredom is.

In two days this month will be over. I hope we get out of here next month. I don't care what day, even if it's the thirty-first of October. Just to get out in October, any day of the month, would be fine with me. But that's the problem around here: I don't know if it's going to happen in October, November, December, or when. No idea at all.

I just can't understand why these people inflict so much pain on other people. They just don't seem to give a damn.

Wednesday, September 29, 1999

171 days. 94 until the year 2000. My father has the flu. He asked me to make some hot chocolate and keep it in the thermos. The Nice Old Man came by today and gave me a lollipop, which I gave to my dad. I told him that the Nice Old Man had brought me two, but that I already ate mine, and he was so happy. I enjoyed that more than if I had eaten it myself.

Today I cleaned up the hut and yesterday I washed my jeans and hung all the clothes to dry. My father is depressed. He hasn't taken a bath in two days. As for me, I got up at noon today. I'm back to my old schedule, just like at home, but I'm in good spirits today—I think it must be because of the antidepressants I'm taking.

Sad news: three of the seven policemen that the FARC kidnapped were found dead today. Their poor families . . . I can't even imagine the kind of pain they are in right now. How terrible.

Today I am once again thinking about the day of my release, and about how hard it will be for me to let go of my dad. Before this, we never lived together, but in captivity I've gotten used to it and now I actually like it. He truly understands me and we get along a lot better now—we have great conversations and I have a very good time with him. This situation has brought us together, helped us get to know each other. And that was something I really needed.

Right now I'm thinking about something very real for me: before, I used to say that if I could turn back the clock I would, but now I feel the opposite, because everything I have gone through has helped me grow up in some way. And this present, in turn, will become part of the past and I know that I will also grow from this present situation. You just have to let life take its course, I guess.

I had a talk with Uriel and Laureano about what's going on here in this campsite, and after Uriel went to bed, Laureano told me a bunch of things about Francisco—things that only confirmed what a hypocrite he is. I may have disliked him before but now I think even less of him—if that's even possible. My father tells me I have to pretend to tolerate him.

I told my father what Laureano told me: that Francisco goes around talking trash about us, just to get the supply lady on his side. She's such a sucker for gossip, she loves to hear stories about other people, so of course with Francisco she is an absolute darling. What idiots: he and Juan sell out the rest of the group just so they can get a couple more eggs in the morning. I find it hard to believe that someone can really do things like that. What kind of creature is that slime?

I would love to be able to tell all this to Diego González and Fernando, because I think it's always good to know who's a hypocrite and who isn't, and also because I feel they deserve to be clued in. They should know that people say nasty things about them behind their backs. Today I swallowed a mosquito and an ant: the ant found its way into my coffee and the mosquito flew into my mouth while I was eating. Very uncomfortable.

The thing that really has me angry, though, is that Francisco said my father is a jerk. Oh, I hate him so much, most of all because he is such an unbelievable hypocrite! It is so horrible to have to deal with people like that. Today Fernando said something that I totally agree with: he said that confrontational people are always better than hypocrites, because at least with someone who's confrontational you know what you're getting whereas you never know what to expect with a hypocrite.

Thursday, September 30, 1999

I'm still furious over what happened yesterday. My father and I are waiting for Francisco to go to breakfast so that my dad can confront him and see what kind of face he makes when my dad gives him a piece of his mind. Uriel, Francisco, and Juan always stick together: the fantastic three, they like to call themselves. God, please don't let this get any worse, because I could easily start getting nasty with more than one of them, and if this keeps up, then I am going to tell them what I really think of them and of what's been going on.

But most importantly, they better not mess with my dad. I'll mess with them before I let them touch him. I'm going to talk to Fer and Diego about this today.

I have literally been invaded by ants: they are a veritable river, millions of them all over the place. I had to get totally undressed because they got into my clothes and started stinging me. Diego and Fer got a good laugh out of that, watching me jump around like a madwoman without any clothes on.

It's Thursday and there are no messages for me today. But I don't care, really. It's better this way—at least I don't have to live with the stress of wondering whether or not anyone's going to send me messages. Today I had a very cool conversation with Diego and Fer. We talked about hypocrisy and I read to them what I wrote in my diary about that. They thought it was pretty funny.

I think the ants have gotten under my clothes again. Today Piedad Córdoba said she was going to quit because of the threats she's received. So now what's going to happen to us? No idea. All I know is that I don't know a thing.

On the Caracol news, they said that the ELN is not delivering the letters that family members have been sending to their relatives in captivity. That makes me furious, and we can't do a thing about it!

Oh, God, please end all of this, and soon. Every day it gets worse; every day it's harder and harder to put up with this. It's like a time bomb that could explode at any moment. Please keep sending strength, to me and my dad, and to Diego, Fer, and Lau as well. As for the others, I hope they go to hell for being such miserable people, for screwing us over for a couple of eggs. Please send a big good night kiss to my mother; please fill her with serenity and interior peace.

Tomorrow, September will be over and still nothing will have changed. We've been here now for six months, God, six months and still nothing. So please, let October be the month of our release; dear God, don't make us celebrate Halloween or our birthdays here—my father's birthday is October 21. Get us out of here soon! I want freedom for my father, for me, and for everyone else, so that we can stop living with all this pain, so that we can feel we have a reason to smile again. Please stop killing me slowly. Get me out of here already!

It's 10:10 P.M.

Friday, October 1, 1999

Day 173, 92 days left before the year 2000.

I can hardly believe that I am writing the word *October* on this page. I feel as if I am trapped in April: for me, everything stood still on the day of April 12, and I truly can't believe that it is already October, that time and life have marched on as always. These people have robbed us of all that time. It's so unfair, it hurts so much.

Oh, what I wouldn't give to close my eyes, and then open them to find myself back at home, so I could chalk this all up to a bad dream.

Sometimes I dream that I'm home with my family and I ask God not to wake up, to let me continue dreaming, because it is so clear to me that I have every right to be there. I always feel a tiny bit afraid when I dream, though, because I know that when I wake up I'm going to have to come back to this situation where fear, boredom, impotence, and frustration rule my life.

The hypocrite said hi to me with a friendly face and I answered back, "Yeah, right!"

I've had some awful menstrual cramps lately. Tonight, one of the guerrilla women had a strange fit of some sort, it was very disturbing.

I'm listening to Amor Stereo right now. Someone named Diego just called in to the show to request "Taxi" by Ricardo Arjona, and I swear he sounded exactly like my Diego.

Fer, Diego, my father, and I have really bonded. We give each other a lot of support, which we all need around here. Tonight we played Parcheesi and I won. Fer is kind of annoyed because of something Uriel said about his sister, and frankly, I don't blame him. To tell someone that their sister has a voice like a horse is very offensive. Plus it's not even true: he just said it to have something stupid to say to Francisco and Juan. These guys, the way they act, they really make me sick. And let me tell you, when I decide I can't stand someone, there is no way I will ever change my mind about them; it's terrible.

If something were to happen, though, I do want to make it very clear, first and foremost, how much Francisco and Uriel despise my father. There is something very sinister about the friendship they have struck up with the guerrillas. They pit us against them, saying nasty things about us all the time. Sometimes I actually start to get scared. I worry that maybe my life is in some kind of danger, and that maybe my dad's is, too. I pray to God that all this will come to an end soon. Oh, Mommy, why can't you be here with me? I miss you so much! How much longer do I have to endure this? How much longer do I have to put up with this suffering? It is so unjust; I feel consumed with rage and hatred when I look around and see these things happening around me.

At night I dream, but I don't remember what I dream anymore, which makes me so mad.

Today we ate rice and beans. As we finished eating, my father and I talked about the past for awhile, about his separation from my mother, about how he met her, and then about how he met Lucía. I told him, more or less, how I felt—about how hard it was to see my mother married, and then to see him with Lucía. . . . Oh, I don't want to think back to all that. It still hurts so much, even when I think back just a little bit. I would give everything I have just to not feel that pain whenever someone brings up the past. But in the end, I guess the past is the past and it ought to just stay there.

I hope to God that when I get married it will be for good, because separations almost always involve suffering, and the kids are usually the ones who bear the brunt of it. I hope to God that I marry a good person, but most of all someone who respects me and loves me, and who won't be unfaithful. For my part I hope to be a good wife, one who's not jealous, a good mother, and I hope that both I and whoever I marry can keep ourselves from getting wrapped up in things like pride. But the most important thing is that it has to be love, true love.

I think a lot about marriage. Before, it always seemed like such a lovely thing, and yet the older I get the more the word scares me, I guess because it means so much. That's why I'm always asking God to send me a good person. I think a lot about that person, and I wonder what he's doing right now—if I know him or if I've seen him before in my life, if he lives in my city or somewhere else. And I wonder what he's like, who he is, how it will be to meet him for the first time if in fact I still don't know him. Such a mystery. And does he have any idea who I am? When will he know? When? Is he awake or asleep right now? Do we look alike at all? What will his voice be like? I ask myself millions of these questions all the time. The day I finally meet him, I am going to tell him about all of this, about all the things I wondered about him, and I will definitely tell him that I asked God to take care of him and protect him, even when I had no idea if I had already met him. But one day he will be the father of my children, and I intend to love and look after that person. And though it may sound really strange, I love him already, even though I don't know him or have any idea who he is.

I also think a lot about my children and what they'll be like. Well, in reality I only want to have one child. I ask myself about that a lot: what will he or she be like? Will he or she be ugly or pretty?

Oh, God, what a bunch of junk I am writing! It must be because I am wide awake and that's usually when all this nonsense about the future comes into my head, and I start writing about it. As they say, though, when someone offers you a future, they deny you the chance to live in the present. Or, perhaps more to the point: everything in due time. Right now, I'll stick with the here and now, and that's it.

Until tomorrow, Illak, my friend. Why did I give you that name? Because nobody around here hangs on to their head for too long, everything is upside down, backward. There are no secrets here, in this diary, none: we speak the truth, and that is the most wonderful thing about having you with me. The only person I trust is you—that is, me. My best friend, my confidante, my ally, you never let me down. We always have each other, here and in any other part of the world.

Yours,
    Leszli Kálli López
    Goodbye, Illak

Saturday, October 2, 1999

Day 174. I feel paralyzed by these cramps.

I'm sad to see that this is just one more day, that it's already October and that we are still here in the middle of nowhere. I find it hard to process the idea that we are in Colombia, because this place is much farther away from home than Israel in many ways. Soon I will have been here for as much time as I was planning to spend in Israel. To think that it has been six months since I last spoke to my mother. Who knows what she thinks of me now?

Sometimes I wonder if these people have any feelings at all: I don't think so. Wherever they go they just step on the people in their way, as long as they get what they want. With so many people suffering because of what they do, I have to wonder if they can be good people, really, and if they will ever achieve their goals. Because things should not be this way. If there is one thing that's clear to me, it's that justice does not exist, and I am not talking about the kind of justice dished out by the government here in Colombia. No, I am talking about real justice, the kind that *should* exist in this world.

These people really do contradict themselves: they are always talking about how they are fighting for the Colombian people, and I have to ask: what about me and my family? Aren't we "Colombian people," too? Why are they causing us so much pain? That is what I fail to understand. Maybe I'm just really thick, or else I don't make the cut to be categorized as part of the "Colombian people." But as far as I know, I was born here and so was my family.

Francisco just walked into the hut and told us that they're releasing Daniel Hoffmann in the next few hours. Good news. Very good news.

Today is the birthday of one of the guerrillas. Those men in our group are celebrating with them; they are such hypocrites. They didn't invite my father and me. Now that Francisco has turned them against us, I'm afraid they're going to do something to us—especially now that they're drinking and the head guerrilla is nowhere to be found. They give us dirty looks a lot these days, and it really gives me the creeps. I wish that other guerrilla, the painter, would come back so that I could ask him to move us to another campsite, or put us somewhere else. What did that hypocrite Francisco say? This really has me worried.

I hate it when the head guerrilla leaves, because then the other guerrillas act completely different. Everything becomes much more chaotic; it's awful. I hope to God he comes back soon.

Sunday, October 3, 1999

Day 175. 90 days to go until the year 2000.

This morning Diego asked me if I would have it out with Francisco, to make it clear to him that we aren't idiots, that we know what is going on. He told me that this morning, when he went out to go to the bathroom, he bumped into Francisco and Juan, and Francisco said to him, 'Hey, you know it's possible that Leszli will get released before the rest of us, and then she'll tell everyone how bad they treated her—how bad we treated her."

Diego didn't say a word. He asked me if I wanted to respond to that, and I said yes, that I have no intention of keeping my mouth shut. Just now Francisco went in to talk to my dad, probably about this very topic. I'm very curious now to see what they're saying.

Every time I think about the way me and my dad are getting treated here I want to cry; they act as if we didn't exist. What really makes me furious, though, is what they're doing to my father, because he spends all his time and energy trying to do good things: he talks to everyone, he tells jokes, he gives advice. In general all he wants is for us to feel united as a group, and look at the way they pay him back for that. It's so unfair that people like that exist; people who have such little capacity for reflection and rational thought, people who are concerned only with their own well-being, even if other people have to suffer for it.

Last night my father told me that he wrote a book: he called it *Ice, Glass, Second Infinite, and Last Hope,* and the main character is called Simeón. The sheer breadth of his imagination, quite frankly, leaves me completely speechless. He is amazing!

My father finally came back and told me about his conversation with Francisco. He said that Francisco realized what he'd been doing to us, and that he was going to try and patch things up and make up for all the misunderstandings, because he had been very unfair. Personally, I don't think we should believe a word he says, because that guy is a major hypocrite. Who knows, he probably just invented it all that so we would think he changed his ways. I'll believe it when I see it.

I went out to watch TV and Daniel turned it off, like a jerk, saying that since I'm the only one who watches TV, it was time to turn it off. It was so humiliating. All I keep telling myself is that the present will soon become part of the past, and the future will be filled with present moments that are much more pleasant than these. For him, on the other hand, this present will become a part of all his future moments, and in that sense his past must be filled with moments like these, too. This is just a bad moment that will soon pass, and I am going to try and put it behind me.

Life keeps on placing obstacles before me, and this time I am going to overcome them. I got stuck with a bunch of obstacles, all at the same time, and I think it was to show me that the only way I am going to overcome them and get out of here is with my head held high. Once I get out of here, I will be confident in the knowledge that I was able to confront them, not just one by one, but all together. It's funny, the things that seem like such big problems right now will soon seem so insignificant once the worst is over. There will be calm after the storm, I know this.

The hypocrite sits down and asks me if we can have a talk. I say yes. He tries to convince me that he hasn't done a thing, and then he asks me how he has offended me; he wants to know why I am so angry with him. And so I tell him, at least in part: that he always gets everything he wants, he hoards things, and then teases me with them just to upset me. But not this time, much less now that I know what he's really like. I didn't flash him even the tiniest little smile; instead I shot him a look that let him know just how mad I was. I really do despise hypocrites. When he tells me that he senses this very poisonous attitude from me, I feel like blurting out to him just how poisoned I feel, so poisoned that I have to bite my tongue.

I cannot believe the show this guy puts on. The most incredible thing is that he has actually convinced himself that what he is saying is sincere. What a revolting person! I fell for this routine the first time around because I was naïve and stupid. Then, the second time, because I believed him; but I'm not going for it a third time. No way. And if he says sorry to me, well, you can't just boil everything down to a question of saying sorry. If he wants forgiveness, he'll have to earn it, he has to fix the mess he made for himself, and if he doesn't get the picture, I'm going to really tell him what I think. Everything.

I'm looking up at the stars now; I can see them all. They are so beautiful, and there are so many of them. I'm sitting in the chair my father built, and on the radio I can hear the song by Diego Torres *"Sé que no volverás"* ["I Know You Aren't Coming Back"].

Sé que muy lejos estás
Que buscas otro lugar
Sin mirar para atrás

[I know you are far away
That you are searching for another place
Without looking back]

Monday, October 4, 1999

25 weeks. Day 176. 89 until the year 2000.

My father got up in a pretty good mood. He said he's going to call a meeting so that all of us can make up, once and for all. I'll write more later. . . .

Happy ending! We are all friends again. Everybody was really glad, and best of all, Uriel is talking to my father again, plus he even gave me a couple of lollipops. It's incredible: after 176 days we can all live in peace, finally.

With this whole episode my father taught me a very important lesson that I will never forget: to learn how to forgive and how to ask forgiveness of others. I feel so proud of him, of the way he spoke, of everything. . . . We all came out of the meeting really pleased. We wiped the slate clean and have started anew. Thank you, God!

It's 11 P.M. The day went by quickly. Diego and I swept the entire campsite and it looks terrific. It's raining, but it's not cold. All afternoon the sky was gray, but it was sunny in the morning. My father and I bathed in the river.

Juan Carlos García sent his regards over the radio, on La Mega, and Lucía sent a message through Caracol, but she didn't send regards.

I have a feeling that this is going to end soon. I don't know why, I just have a feeling. . . .

Tuesday, October 5, 1999

Day 177. 88 days until the year 2000.

Today I played volleyball but I got sick of it after a while and went to take a bath. My father and I spent some time talking about life, about how I shouldn't worry so much about everything, and how it's not worth it to be so stressed out because you only go around once, and before you know it life is over and you're up there in the great hereafter. We talked about Carol, Mauri, and my mom. I made him see how I feel about everything, and I think he took it pretty well. We all ate together. A guerrilla just arrived and now I'm listening to La Mega. The atmosphere is really different now, much better. I like the fact that we can all live together as human beings now, and not like animals, or worse.

Eloy David, my cousin, just celebrated his birthday. I wish him a very happy birthday from far away.

My father and I talked for awhile just now. It was really great; he has such a special way of helping me see things in a better light. One of the things he told me is that the only thing that doesn't have a solution is death. I told him that I'm very worried about my mother, because I don't think she's been able to work very well on account of me. He told me not to worry, that they've all had to go on with their lives, because life goes on and you can't just sit around nursing your memories. . . . That left me thinking, and I asked him again: "What if we had died?"

"Honey, they would have buried us, they would have cried for us, and they would have grieved for us. They would always remember us, but they would have had to go on, too. They can't die with us, or let themselves get buried alive, either. It's just life. If someone dies unexpectedly, well, that's destiny, but it doesn't mean other people need to die, too. Life is a constant series of ups and downs, and we can't let ourselves get bitter because of it. Listen, Leszli: before this happened, your mother worried about money and other things. Now, do you think you can imagine what became of those 'huge problems' the day they called to tell her that you might be dead? Those problems went down the drain! Do you realize that? None of that matters at all now.

bolibol que tiene 220 cuadritos 9
de ancho por 80 de largo [image] la luna
esta por la mitad y yo
No puedo controlarme.
lalucano escucha musica a todo
volumen y metal que mamera.
Dios necesito tener la mente quieta por un
segundo no pensar me preocupa mucho el
futuro que hacer para no sentirlo. yudica me
dice que lo que me tiene asi es ver que ya
se aproxima navidad y yo esto aqui.

19 octubre 99 Marzo

...que no hablan pero en resumidas
hablan y hablan pero en resumidas
no dicen nada.

amor, disculpándote

"Me hundó en el empíreo
de mi día hoyo grande
y oscuro en el que caigo
con una rapidez, voy
en demencia al infinito

What she cares about right now is that you are alive and that you'll be coming home soon. But until that day comes, life has to go on. Don't you see?"

I'm so glad we talked about all those things today. These are lessons I have learned and will keep with me for the rest of my life. I will always remember this day: it is one of the greatest gifts life has ever given me. My father's advice is truly the best advice in the world.

Today I got some messages on La Mega, and on UIS, too. First, Nandor spoke; he told me that Carol, Danielito, and Mauri went to live in Brazil, in a city or town called Guaruya. He also said that things are pretty much the same as they were when all this began: that they don't know anything, that they hadn't sent me any messages for a while because they had thought we were walking, because we were going to get released soon. Later, when I got home, he said he would explain why they thought that. My mom said the same thing: that she hadn't spoken over the radio in such a long time not because she doesn't love me but because of what Nandor said. Then she told me she adores me and thinks of me every day, that she misses me a lot and hopes I will be home soon. She also said that she fails to understand why the people from the ELN don't do anything, since it's been six months now. She said it's time for them to regroup and do something. Poor thing. She also said that Diego Plata is very concerned about me, too, that he calls three times a day to find out if they've heard anything. And she said that everyone—cousins, friends, aunts, uncles, my grandmother—sends me lots of love.

All I want to do is cry, after hearing how much everything has changed out there in the real world. So Carol left with Dani and Mauri. Now, nothing will ever be the same again: that adorable little baby boy, and all the noise he made and games he played around the house, will be gone. It hurts; but that's life, I guess: things change from one moment to the next; everyone has to go their own way. Still, how rotten! I cried and cried and cried over that.

Carol, I miss you so much. You and your little family were part of my life, and knowing that you're not there anymore fills me with such sadness because, in a way, it makes me feel that my family is falling apart.

Our house must be such a lonely place now. I am so afraid of going back and facing all the pain that is waiting for me now that the three of you are no longer there.

Day 178. 87 days until the year 2000.

I am drowning, I have no strength left, and I don't see any way out of this even though I am trying my best to look beyond what I can see with my mind and my eyes. There is no hope left here. The day is long and my desire to die is powerful and strong. I feel that my life is like a long, long night and that I have been abandoned in the middle of the ocean with big waves all around me, beneath a gray sky and in the middle of a terrible thunderstorm, swimming without knowing which direction to go in, my arms aching from the effort I have to make not to drown. My heart is screaming at me, telling me to give up the fight, to let it rest already, but I know that if I do that I will die. My entire being is yearning for peace, peace.

Today they released a man from the group of hostages at the church in Cali. These releases have slowed down to a trickle.

A letter for Diego:

Darling, if you only knew how bored I am in this hell. I can hardly describe how difficult it is to bear this awful reality. The days are like years here; I feel as though I've lived an entire life here, but truly, this life is not a real life anymore.

I have asked God to give me the strength to withstand this, but lately I really get the feeling that he has forgotten about me. I have asked him to tell me why this is happening to me. Over and over again I've asked him what I did to deserve this, and I ask him to forgive me if I did something bad, but the more I think about the past, the more I realize that I haven't done anything wrong, I haven't hurt anyone, I haven't killed anyone, I haven't robbed anyone. On the contrary: I have always tried to make the world a better place, I love the people who are with me, I love animals, I am against all injustice . . . which makes this even more confusing to me, and so I ask for some explanation. Over and over again I ask the question, *Why this?* And then I feel consumed with rage and frustration when I think about the fact that this kidnapping has happened to good people, while the bad guys are as happy and safe as can be. That's when it hits me, that's when I realize that this world is full of perverse people who derive joy from doing terrible things to people, crushing them in the name of their so-called "ideals." They don't give a damn about anything as long as they get what they want.

Diego, the world we were born into is unjust. It is completely upside down—at least, that's the way it looks to me. The truth is, I feel completely uninspired to climb up and look out over this world or to participate in this theater that is called "humanity."

Diego, I hope you never change, because you are one of the people who help me keep moving forward in life. Take good care of yourself. Remember always that I think of you often, and that I love you for yesterday, today, tomorrow, and always.

Yours,

Leszli Kálli

Thursday, October 7, 1999

Day 179. 86 to go before 2000.

9 P.M. They found a snake in Rosalinda's tent today, a lovely 5-foot-long bushmaster. They removed her fangs and told us that she was very, very poisonous. Then my father gave me an hour-long lecture about how I had to be very careful with those snakes, and that I shouldn't be so cavalier with them because they could easily kill me. It drives him crazy that I trust these animals. I should try not to worry him so much—the poor guy lives with so much stress because of me.

Tonight the sky is completely clear: you can see all the stars, and it's so pretty. Oh, I want to be home, where I belong, enjoying the things I deserve to enjoy. God, get us out of here soon!

Day 180. 85 days until the year 2000.

It's 1:45 A.M., and I just had a talk with Laureano, who came in after watching television. Laureano is such a nice guy, I really admire how calm and collected he is. We discussed a little bit of everything, and I think the talking did both of us a lot of good. At least, I felt a sense of relief afterward, and that was nice.

I just brushed my teeth and now I'm in bed. I turned the radio and the candle off, and I'm writing with the light from my flashlight now. Right in front of me is the calendar that I drew up for the months of October and November, with a few important dates singled out: October 9, which is Diego González's birthday; October 12 and November 12, which mark our six- and seven-month anniversaries here in captivity; October 21, which is my father's birthday; and November 28, Nandor's birthday.

It's such an awful feeling to be stuck here, especially inside the hut, which makes me feel as if I'm locked away, and then when I see the hut full of faces, eyes, sayings, and calendar dates I scrawled . . . well, it's kind of weird.

The night is still as clear as ever, and it's very cold, too.

Today makes exactly three months since I let my eyelashes grow, and every time I look at them I feel so proud of myself. I never thought I would let them grow. My mom is going to be so happy when she sees them. . . .

I'm not tired at all, because I slept the entire day yesterday. I'm going to stay up for a while with the flashlight off, and dream of all sorts of things about the people I love.

Yesterday a fly flew into my left ear and it still hasn't come out. I hope it doesn't create some kind of problem for me, or start hurting.

It's 4:15 P.M. I got up at noon. Navarro Wolf said there was a meeting yesterday in Caracas and that he was very optimistic. We'll see what comes of it. . . .

My father and I just got done cleaning up the hut: we made two boxes, which I lined with notebook paper and painted, so that we wouldn't have stuff strewn all over the floor. As far as my spirits go, I feel much better, very calm, and that is a real relief. It's nice not to worry so much.

I found a snake when I went down to the river this afternoon. I picked her up, brought her back to the camp, played with her for a while, and then let her go. She was about 30 centimeters long, very thin and dark, and with black lines that ran the entire length of her body. I showed her to the Nice Old Man, who chewed me out and told me to let her go immediately because she might be poisonous. She was very smelly, I have to say that, but she was so docile and calm.

I stopped writing for a moment or two because the ants are patrolling their territory; they are like a rushing river, it's unbelievable. We had to stop everything. I had never seen anything like it, not even on one of those Discovery Channel documentaries. Only here in the jungle have I ever seen so many ants all together. The guerrillas call it the great march. It is, literally, an army of thousands—no, millions of ants, rivers of ants, like a massive moving tablecloth. They usually come out at night, and they destroy just about everything in their path: from the underbrush you can see and hear the crickets, cockroaches, frogs, and snakes running for their lives. Even the cockroaches run for cover in puddles so that they don't get eaten by the ants—I just saw at least 20 cockroaches cram themselves into one little puddle. And to think—a cockroach is much, much bigger than an ant. What happens is, the ants travel in such vast numbers that all the animals—not to mention the humans—in the vicinity run for their lives when they sense the onslaught of the great march. The ants may very well be the greatest example we have for learning how to solve the problems of Colombia: if we all joined forces, we would find peace. I am sure of it.

Later on, my father and I went to sit down outside and started to talk about what everyone must be thinking back at home. My father said something that I liked a lot: that he would have died if this had happened to me alone. And I said, "Well, listen, Dad. Here I am with you in captivity. God wanted you to be here with me," and he said, "Yeah, thank goodness."

My flashlight stopped working, so my father lent me his, so I could write.

On the news they talked about the meeting with Pablo Beltrán and the commission. They say the president of Venezuela is willing to allow the ELN to hold their National Convention in Venezuela, but only if President Andrés Pastrana gives his consent. If he says yes, they will get together once more to decide on the dates of the meeting and of our release. God, please let Pastrana say yes so that we can get out of here sometime soon.

Oh, it would be so wonderful to get back to Bucaramanga and for Diego to tell me he loves me and ask me to think about getting back together. That would really be an incredible gift. But something inside of me says no, that everything will stay the same, that he must have a girlfriend, or who knows, that he loves me but just as a friend. No, no, I'd better not think about it because it's only going to make me all bitter. Everything in due time. I have to put it in God's hands. I promise I will not force anything. I will simply let life take its course. What's mine is mine. Nobody can take that away from me.

I ask God over and over to let a good man into my life, a good man who loves me deeply, as Christina says, who would kill and kill himself for me. That line is from a song by Christina y los Subterráneos; it's a very pretty song.

A plane is flying overhead—around here we hear planes a lot, and we can see them, too, but they always fly very high. It's clear and cold out tonight. I don't know what else to write.

Right now I feel like writing a letter to my brother.

Nandor:
I am very proud and happy to have a brother like you. Here, sometimes, I feel very much alone even though my father is with me. It feels as though I'm in another world altogether. Technically, you and I may be in the same world, but honestly I feel that I am in another dimension—it's like being in a huge labyrinth where you can't find the way out. All I know is that the one thing that keeps me hanging on is that all of you are

somewhere on the other side of this enormous labyrinth. That is what drives me to get out and to try to survive all of this.

Here, I do have moments when I feel happy and at peace because I feel that very soon I am going to see the light at the end of the tunnel. But then there are times when I realize that the light is only an optical illusion and everything is still the same. Then I sit down, trying hard not to go mad from the frustration, though I can feel the strength and the enthusiasm I once had slowly fading. I realize that I have a promise to keep, to get out of here alive and well so that I can be with you, and only then do I feel my strength return, like it was in the beginning. That is how I make it through these crises, and keep on going, even better than before.

These ups and downs are a constant in my life; they are my daily bread around here. I know I'm not the only one, either: everyone goes through the same thing even though we all pretty much keep it to ourselves. For me, this has been going very, very, very slowly. It seems that the negotiations have gotten stalled, and this drives me crazy, although not as much as it did during the early days. I just hope that they reach an agreement soon and leave us all in peace.

Nandor, I love you and miss you so much. I pray to God that I will see you again soon.

Take care, and take care of Mom. And stay close: you, Carol, and Mom. I will always love you.

Yours,

Leszli Kálli, your little sister

Saturday, October 9, 1999

Day 181. 84 days until the year 2000.

Today I wrote a letter to the COCE men, telling them about how I feel and about my family, too. I even included names and ages. Then I went over to talk to the head guerrilla and cried the whole way through. He told me he liked my letter a lot, and that he'd send it on. I hope something comes of it. He told me that if it worked for me, he'd be willing to help other hostages do the same thing.

Today is Diego González's birthday. I wished him a happy birthday and made him a card, which everyone signed. I haven't eaten anything today, and I don't feel like eating at all. I'm wearing my jeans and my black shirt. My father is talking to Uriel about the 767, the next plane he's going to pilot.

I ate, and then I walked round and round the playing field, from side to side and then in a zigzag. Later on, at around 6:15, Fer called us over to a meeting at the playing field and told us all to hold hands. It was odd; he told us we're going to share a moment of silence or something. I stuck my foot in my mouth, because Uriel was talking, and then completely out of turn I said something about how I thought we'd be released in November, and then my father said, "I think the company planes are really nice. . . ."

The reason he said that—bringing up something that had absolutely nothing to do with anything—was to make me realize that the point of the little gathering was to talk spontaneously about whatever came into your head. A serious storm is about to start. It's thundering a lot and the sky is thick with clouds. We don't have any candles so I'm writing by the light of the flashlight. Today we watched *Sábados felices* [Happy Saturdays] and another show called *También caerás*. [You Too Will Fall].

My mind is off somewhere else, far away from here, in a world that isn't really a world, where the air is peaceful, where there is always a full moon to shed light on everything. It's a very flat place that looks like a desert but it's right next to a very calm sea with no waves. From there you can see all the stars, and the night air is balmy and mild. I'm relaxed, alone with my thoughts, lying naked in the sand, with my arms extended and my eyes gazing up at the sky, the stars, the sand, the full moon, and the sea, which almost seems like a lake, that's how calm it is. Nothing matters to me right now. I don't want to see anyone and nobody wants to see me. I am very happy. I don't want to close my eyes, because I am so amazed at this beautiful natural spectacle. There is no time, no pressure. I can take all the time I want here. I am neither cold nor hot. I am calm, I am happy. Nothing matters to me right at this moment.

Day 182. 83 days until the year 2000.

Today on *Despertar en América* my mother and Nandor spoke.

Good news: the president of Colombia said yes, he agrees to the meeting. So now we have to wait and see what happens. I didn't even want to watch the TV news. I don't pay attention to any of what they say anymore. All I want is freedom—for me, for my father, for the 13 others from the plane and for the 2,000 people in this country who are presently in captivity.

On TV I saw a really sad advertisement. It started off with no sound, and then a bunch of black-and-white images flashed across the screen as someone said: "More than 2,000 hostages, so many deaths . . ." and other things. And then: "Is the war worth it?"

Diego González came over to me and said, "Leszli, why do you have this feeling that it's going to be in November?"

I told him that it's because back in April when I was talking to Diego Plata I said, "All right, Diego, I'll see you in November."

And the truth is, after I said that I sat around wondering why I'd said that about November. I don't know, but something inside tells me that I'm going to get out of here in November.

I find it incredible that Ruben has not sent me regards through anyone. And I thought I was his best friend. When I get back I'm going to tell him what I think about that.

I'm listening to the song that Pacho dedicated to me, *"Nunca te olvidaré"* ["I'll Never Forget You"] by Enrique Iglesias. . . . It reminds me a lot about those long-gone days . . . really corny, right?

While I was bathing in the river today, I saw a helicopter fly overhead, very high and very fast. I haven't eaten yet. I asked the supply lady for some jam and crackers and I distributed them around. Everyone liked that. Fernando started imitating my mother, and Diego and Fer painted the green "no more violence" symbol on their shirts. Then they asked me: "Leszli, what are you going to wear when you get out of here?"

"My red pants and my black shirt." I was making a joke: red and black are the ELN colors. They laughed at that one. Of course I would never wear anything like that, not even as a joke.

My father and I just went to watch the news. As we sat down in our chairs he said, "Hey, let's go to the playing field to listen to the news on the radio." We went out, and the sky was totally clear, so clear we could see the stars. I started walking around the playing field, round and round, until I got woozy.

Today, before the news, Laureano, Diego, Fernando, my father, and I talked about drugs. Laureano asked who had tried drugs before and some of us said we had. We all took turns telling our stories. It was very funny to hear what everyone had to say.

I just drank a cup of coffee and now I'm all jittery. It's so annoying when that happens, especially here where everything is so dull and boring.

Mommy, what are you thinking right now? What are you doing? Who are you with? How are you dressed? What did you eat today? How many cigarettes have you smoked? Is Nandor with you? I have so many questions, and so few answers.

Today a new guerrilla arrived. He's very rude: he glares at all of us with pure hatred in his eyes, and he doesn't even say hello or look at you so that you can say hello. These people are really the worst!

Illak, what would become of me if I didn't have you by my side? What would these days be like if I didn't have any way to confess these things? Illak, you are so important to me.

With you, I talk about everything. This is my life. The day I die, everyone will know what I thought, what I felt. Maybe nobody will care, but for me it would be so sad to pass through this life without leaving a testimony of some kind. Good or bad, something should come out of this place.

Right now I'm in the tent with my dad. I told him to put on the radio, but he didn't want to. I don't mind, I guess. Then I told him that I was going to sing a song, and I sang something by Christina y los Subterráneos.

Then I ask him to sing me the song he dedicated to me in Bucaramanga on the night of October 10, 1996, just before I left for school in Atlanta. I left Colombia on the eleventh, and on the night of the tenth we had a going-away party at La Carreta, a restaurant, with Carol, Lucía, and my father. The song is called *"Reloj"* ["Watch"]. I love it! I remember just how my father dedicated it to me; he was very emotional that night. Then he sang the song *"Un barquito chiquitito"* ["A Little Boat"] to me. I loved that one: it's a song my father made up when I was a little girl, and I always loved it.

A little boat
Sailed on the high sea,
Sailed from wave to wave,
Sailed on and on
(repeat)
Until one day one of the waves
Almost sank the boat.
And the sea . . . was the sea,
And the waves did not
Want to let him reach the shore safely
But the little boat
Sailed on and on.
And this little boat
Managed to escape the waves.
And the furious sea
With the claws of her waves
Tried to sink the boat again
But the little boat
Sailed and sailed
Sailed on and on.
And that little boat
Arrived and weighed anchor
And the sea, with her claws
She laughed on and on.

I still think back to those times when I was a baby and how he would sing me that song, and rock me back and forth, pretending I was the little boat and he was the sea. It's incredible, how time really does fly by, how I've grown—I'm almost as big as he is now.

It's so wonderful to remember those nice things, but it's also kind of sad, because those days are over; we'll never get them back. At least not in this life. Maybe one day I'll talk about those memories with my children.

All of a sudden I feel this need to know everything about the man who is my father. The son of Hungarian immigrants, his father was called Nandor Kálli, and his mother was Gisella Daniel. She lived long enough for me to know her. Her mother was a Russian Jew and her father was Hungarian. My father was born here in Colombia, in Bogotá, and he has a sister, Judith, who lives in Seattle, in the United States.

My grandmother died on November 19, 1992, of pancreatic cancer. My grandfather died of a heart attack when my dad was 18. My father was born in 1950, on October 21; that makes him 30 years older than me.

My grandfather Nandor was born on the same day as me: December 11. I was my grandmother Gisella's favorite. She loved me very much, but there was something else, something more than that. I think there was something about my personality that she responded to in a very special way. I don't know what, or why, but I was definitely her favorite. Just like my grandfather, she was in Europe during World War II. They escaped, and through the International Red Cross, they traveled to various places before settling in Colombia: my grandmother first went to Toronto, Canada, and then she went to New York and Venezuela after that. Venezuela was where she met my grandfather, and then they went to Colombia, where my father and Judith were born.

I'll come back to all this tomorrow, or maybe I'll talk about other things. . . .

Day 183. 26 weeks. 82 days until the year 2000.

For some reason I couldn't sleep at all last night, so I got up and walked around the playing field, from side to side, back and forth, over and over again. Then I sat down, listened to some music, and I felt this void grow inside of me. After that I went back to bed and slept until about 5:30 A.M. My father brought me some chocolate at around 9 A.M., which I ate and then went right back to sleep. I dreamed about a giant plane that had been hijacked, and when I looked at the list of passengers I saw that my father and I were in the second group of hostages.

Today we played the percentage game: basically I write down my name and the name of the person I'm thinking about. Then I assign every letter a number that corresponds to its spot in the alphabet— e.g., the letter "a" is 1, "b" is 2, and so on. Then I add all the numbers and the sum at the end is the percentage of that person's thoughts that are dedicated to me. For example:

$$G \quad A \quad B \quad O \quad + \quad A \quad D \quad E \quad L \quad A$$
$$7 \quad 1 \quad 2 \quad 16 \qquad 1 \quad 4 \quad 5 \quad 12 \quad 1$$

Total: 26   Total: 23

26+23= 49%

I haven't eaten anything today, and I don't think I will, but if anyone asks me I'll just say that I did because I don't want my father to worry about me.

If this situation doesn't change, I don't think I'm going to be able to live with it anymore and I'm going to take matters into my own hands so that I can put an end to this nightmare of a life I've been forced to live. I am not going to let them kill me this way, slowly, dragging me through all this anguish and misery. I'd rather just kill myself and get it done with. God, forgive me, but I just can't take it anymore.

Enough already! I hate my life, I hate this present moment, I hate breathing, I hate looking out at the world from here, I hate all the green, I hate the earth I walk upon, I hate everything. Life, goddamnit, I want to live you! My soul is slowly being destroyed and nobody can hear me. Mom, please forgive me for this, forgive me for wanting to die, but I just can't take it anymore. I don't want God to send me strength anymore, I don't want peace: I just want to be out of here! But this is impossible, because instead of being your decision, it's in the hands of a bunch of cruel, heartless people. So I'm screwed. Forgive me for thinking this way, but this is how I feel. God has abandoned me.

Tuesday, October 12, 1999

Day 184. 81 days until the year 2000.

Today is our six-month anniversary here. Today, two of the guerrillas found a squirrel monkey they called "Chita" and brought her to the campsite. I spent all day with her, which cheered me up a lot. My father played volleyball today and yesterday. I took a bath and then bathed Fokker, the dog that's been with us since he was born. He's huge now.

I've been having stomach problems lately. I've been constipated for four days now and today, when I tried to go to the bathroom, a lot of blood came out. It doesn't hurt, though. I asked the health aide for some *chicha* [traditional Columbian drink]; maybe that will help a little since it has alcohol in it and it's pretty strong.

Today we received messages on UIS. My mom said that she loves me, that unfortunately the COCE officials are men and not women, and they can't possibly imagine what it means to have your children held hostage. She also told me that she is willing to do whatever she has to do to get me back, that she wants to come here so she can be with me, and then she said that once she has me back she'll never let me go. She also suggested that I present my case to the ELN people, and explain to them how much I am suffering. Then she said that I would fly high, very high, and one day come back to my nest.

Mommy, I am drowning here. I just want to die, and fast. This is unfair. Mommy, I already presented my case to the COCE people, I told them everything and now I'm just waiting for an answer. Mommy, this is not life. I am simply vegetating here. Mommy, I love you, I love you. Please forgive me if I end up doing something stupid, but you have to understand: this is so hard, and I just don't have the strength, I'm weak, there's no way I can win this struggle against a giant void. I am so fragile; this is all too much for me. Nothing means anything to me anymore. I feel so guilty for everything that has happened.

A Letter to the ELN

Central Command, Ejército de Liberación Nacional

I would like to take this opportunity to write to you once more to let you know, once again, how unhappy I am here. The problem is not so much physical as it is mental. It is a question of depression. In general, I feel like crying all day long, I barely sleep at night, and during the day, on the other hand, I sleep as much as I can because it makes things easier, it makes reality much hazier. I don't do any physical activity here: my one and only form of exercise are my brief walks down to the river, to bathe and to go to the bathroom. I have no interest in watching television, or eating: I only eat because if I don't my ulcer will flare up and that only makes things worse. Every five minutes I ask the time, to see if the hours have gone by, but the day drags on forever: seconds become minutes, minutes become hours, hours become days, and the days . . . one day is an eternity. At night I start to feel so desperate that I start walking, from one side of the playing field to the other, back and forth, back and forth. I smoke a lot here, too, around a pack a day. I constantly feel as though I am drowning; my soul aches and my mind begs me for a rest from thinking so much. 24 hours a day, I am always thinking: I think about all this, I think about my house, and most of all I think of my mother, my brother, my sister, my cat . . . everything. I don't know what to do to make you understand what a tragedy it is for us to be here. I feel that I am vegetating. This is not a life, and if this doesn't end soon, very soon, I will do something, anything. I have asked God to let me die soon. I don't want to go on living like this. I can't take this anymore. It is so excruciating to be stuck here, and now I ask you to take pity on me and my father, and release us already. You cannot be as bad as they say you are. If there is one thing I know, it is that you are men of flesh and blood, with feelings like everyone else, and you must have children. Think about it: how would you like to go through something like this, how would you like to be denied your freedom in the company of one of your children, held captive for no reason?

Sirs, I have written to you before with a detailed explanation of my case. Please, please have pity! I beg you to have pity on me! Put an end to all this suffering! The joy of my home, my life, and my father's life are in your hands. All it takes is a few words from you to put an end to this hell that my family and I are living in.

Help us. Today, for me, and tomorrow for yourselves. We are all brothers, children of the same God. Please put an end to this nightmare. I am down on my knees begging you for mercy. I am losing my mind here. I cannot take it anymore.

And please consider one more thing that is absolutely irrefutable: my father and I have not done anything to anyone. So please, let us go. Freedom. Put an end to this already. Enough!

Yours,

Leszli Kálli

Wednesday, October 13, 1999

Day 185. 80 days until the year 2000.

Today I decided to build a new chair, and it looks pretty good. The squirrel monkey left, which I'm glad about. I ate and then vomited. My breath stinks from the five pieces of garlic I ate.

My mother spoke today on UIS. She told me how lonely she feels, and how Pablito comes into the room thinking I'm about to come home. Carol calls three times a day from Brazil, and Diego calls every day, she says. Nandor is in the hospital; he feels very lonely, too, she said. Then she told me not to worry if I'm fat, that when I get back home I can go on a diet and she will spoil me rotten. Today, she said, they released a man in Cali and announced that they would be releasing more people soon. She thinks I might be one of them. I was with my dad and Uriel when I heard that message, and it made me cry. The tears just came out and when she said goodbye over the airwaves, I called out, "Goodbye, Mommy."

I am lost. I am so, so scared. God, get us out of here already! This is not fair!

Thursday, October 14, 1999

Day 186. 79 days until the year 2000.

On the radio they're already playing Christmas songs, which only makes me feel more frustrated and distraught. My father just came by and told me, Laureano, and Francisco that on the news they just said that Faciolince announced that everything is in place for the conversations with the ELN, and that this coming Monday in Caracas they'll set the date. Apparently, once the conversations get under way, they will free all the hostages—those from the Fokker, the church in Cali, and the church in Barranquilla. I am unmoved by this. I'll believe it when I see it. They talk so much shit but none of us believes a word they say.

Last night I dreamt about Juan Pablo. I wanted to buy a ring from him but then I ended up buying a bunch of Jet chocolate bars. Tatiana Lara was in the dream, too, and she said to me, "Leszli, tell Juan Pablo about everyone you know."

And so I said, "Well, I know the Moras, Beto and David."

Then my mother came by and said, "Leszli, don't buy that ring, it's so ugly!"

Then I woke up. What a strange dream. Yesterday my mother said that I might be home by Halloween. I hope to God she's right.

I am sinking deeper into the inferno of my days here. It is an immense, dark hole that I plummet down. I am traveling to the infinite with a demented mind. I want to leave already, I want to escape, I want to run freely through an open field where there are no trees and nothing green, and I want to rest at the end in a complicated compromise where chaos exists in every world but the one I inhabit, so that I can dig a furtive hole where happenstance may occur, and I want to be a hapless Cinderella where funny things are the norm, and find a hermetic world where we make too many decisions and sit far away from one another amid the unknown, and the slenderness of life leads us to spend our time dancing under the stars. Great challenges take the place of hardship, which becomes a great and sweet desire, and all of us are in the phase of force in which physicality no longer matters and in an efficient scene with everyone, where nobody can fulfill a reason for happiness, where nobody has real reasons for anything, where nobody has to be a creep, because only those of us who are slightly great ride on the ship of the greatest people on earth. The labyrinth becomes clear, and it is no longer dark: everything is luminous. And I am experiencing a grand illusion in the middle of hell.

I just finished writing and I have no idea what I wrote. I just let my hand, with a pencil stuck between my fingers, work its way across the page, and scribbled everything that was going through my head at that moment. Right then, I felt something that I'd never felt before: I hit bottom, and captured just what I was feeling in these pages. It lasted around 10 minutes, but they were very, very intense minutes. Then everything returned to normal. I am scared to death to look at what I wrote: it's as if someone else said those things. But no: it was me!

I'll write more later.

———————

It's nighttime now, 11:30 P.M., and I am at wit's end. I have two pimples on my head and they hurt. The squirrel monkey came back and spent all afternoon with me. She's very affectionate, and when the guerrilla tried to take her from me she didn't want to leave me. My mother didn't talk on UIS today, and I didn't get any messages on La Mega, either.

Right now I'm listening to the news on Radio Noticias Caracol. They're talking about the Millennium Plan, about the drug traffickers who have been captured. At night, after watching TV, I found my father, Francisco, Diego, Lau, Fer, and Juan sitting around talking. Juan was saying a bunch of stupid things about his dogs. I find all that stuff about pedigrees so unbelievably stupid, and it sounds even dumber when he talks about it. Instead of running around breeding show dogs and paying a fortune for supposedly fancy animals, he ought to have a child who he can spoil rotten, or else give his money to poor children. I love animals, but as far as I'm concerned, an animal with a pedigree is worth the same as any old mutt you run across in the street. When someone shows interest in an abandoned dog—now that is what I call proof of someone who truly cares about animals. I think it's sickening to only love the ones that cost a lot of money. It's completely idiotic, just like everything else that comes out of that guy's mouth. I just don't understand why that man refuses to act his age. He thinks and acts like an 18-year-old when he really should just accept his age and act it. Whenever he starts talking, though, I just keep my mouth shut, I never tell him what I really think. After all, what good would it do? It's better to avoid problems and let people do their thing.

Friday, October 15, 1999

Day 187. 78 days until the year 2000.

5 P.M. I'm sitting outside on the chairs with my father and Pacho. Today was boring. I think I feel the beginning of a flu coming on, because the roof of my mouth itches and I have a little cough. My father played Parcheesi today with Uriel, Fer, and Diego. The batteries in my flashlight are running out. We're listening to *La Luciérnaga,*

another radio station. It's such a bore. Today is Friday. If I were back at home, I'd already be figuring out a plan for the evening. I wonder what my mother and my cat are doing right now. . . .

A flock of green *guanacayas,* around fifteen of them, just paraded by. So pretty. I'm all alone now. Everyone else got up to watch the news on TV.

Oh, God, to think of all the days that I was free, all the dreams and goals I set for myself, and all of it for nothing. My hands are tied, and my soul has been crushed. I don't have the strength for this anymore, everything is dark and cloudy. I have begged you to get me out of here but you don't listen. My life right now is so ugly, I am stuck in complete nothingness and I want to die. For some people, I must already be dead: by now they must think I'm never coming back and the truth is, that's what I think, too. I think this is punishment for what I did one night in March of 1998. God brought me here to tell me what would have happened to me if I had died, but instead he brought me here alive.

I don't want to live this life anymore, in this little corner of dark feelings, in this immense labyrinth. All I want is to see light, peace, but in 187 days they have refused me these things . . . and I don't think they will ever give in. I am in the middle of two roads that lead to the same destination: one road is this one, long and difficult, and the other one is swift but cowardly. But why should I keep on putting up with this, this stupid life! I want to end you already.

It's 11 P.M. I didn't go to watch the soap opera. Anyway, they didn't turn the TV on because the electric generator isn't working right. Diego was by the chairs. When I went out and asked him what was going on, I realized that the poor guy feels more or less the way I do right now. We talked, and I told him that I felt the same way, and the truth is I think all of us are in exactly the same boat in that sense.

I used to think that the world would come to an end without me, but the simple fact is that everything goes on as usual. The world put an end to me—that's what really happened.

Today my father told me that my personality reminds him a lot of my grandmother Gisella, and physically I resemble Nandor. Carol has bits of him and my mother as well: she gets her serenity from my father, and her bravery from my mother. She's very cautious, very intelligent. My brother Nandor is exactly like my grandfather Nandor, he says. And me? I am a mixture of him, grandmother Gisella, and my mother. He says that my half sister Lauren is exactly like Lucía and that Marcelita, my other half sister, is identical to him and has my grandmother Gisella's eyes.

I feel so badly for my father because he isn't happy with anyone. The other night he told me that the happiest times in his life were during the fifteen years he was married to my mother, but then they started having so many problems, so many fights that they had to separate even though they still loved each other.

Today the wife of the governor of Caquetá was kidnapped. Poor thing: she doesn't know what she's in for. It was an ELN job.

I am marking off the days on the calendar that I put on the wood shelves that my dad and I use to store our things. And I marked another day on my walking stick.

Francisco told me that he writes on the quiet so that they don't find out and try to take his diary away.

Saturday, October 16, 1999

Day 188. 77 days until 2000.

Today I got up at 6:30 A.M. because I had to go to the bathroom. It's raining, and I went down to get two *arepas*—one for my dad and one for me. I didn't eat any chocolate: I'm full. I'm not going to eat any more. My father is fixing—or trying to fix—the radio. The supply lady is sitting in for the administrative guerrilla today. They've got the squirrel monkey with them in the kitchen.

It's 7:15 A.M. and I am very much awake. I already can feel the oppressive weight of the day bearing down on me. I feel the agony, drop by drop, and I can sense the feeling of impotence come on, the same feelings with which I begin every day here.

Yesterday afternoon I got into an argument with my father because I wanted to fix one of his shirts, and he got snippy about it. I was almost finished with it, though, and I said yes, he said no, I said yes again and we went on like that until I finally got hysterical and left the thing on the wooden plank and went to bed. After some time I got up, cried for a little while, and then went back to bed. Later on I got up again and he told me that the guerrillas had let the squirrel monkey free, and that he called out to her and she came down but then disappeared up one of the trees again. Immediately I started calling out to her and she came back. I put her down on the wooden plank but all she wanted to do was hug me and climb all over me. It was so funny. Then, in a nicer tone of voice, I told my father that I really wanted to rework that shirt of his and he finally said yes. I fixed it up and in the end he really liked it. With the leftover fabric remnants I made the squirrel monkey a shirt and I put it on her. That was my dad's idea.

I didn't take a bath but I did eat today, and my father washed the dishes. I sat down to listen to some music, and then I listened to La Mega for messages, but there weren't any, so I switched to Corazón Stereo and sat there listening to the love line. At one point I actually thought I heard Diego's voice calling in to Juan David to talk on the show, but he hung up.

Later on, the head guerrilla and one of his underlings came by, said hello, went to bathe, and then went to bed. I felt very angry for a while, and then I got to thinking and sat around wondering what my husband would be like. What a video! as Salvador would say. I dedicated the entire night to that stuff. I walked around the playing field, then gazed up at the sky for a while. It's cloudy. I'm not tired, and it's 11 P.M. I took off my watch because I kept looking at it all the time, but I couldn't stand watching how the hands just didn't budge. That stressed me out even more.

Nothing much to say except that I hope they bring more candles soon. We're running low on cigarettes. We've only got seven left and they're my dad's.

I just saw the prettiest snake under the spot where the squirrel monkey sleeps, but I'm not going to tell anyone because I know they'll just kill her. She's orange with little black dots. My father just left the tent to go to the bathroom, saw the snake, and told the guard to come in and kill her. Damn! He's mad at me because I didn't say anything about it.

Day 189. 76 days until 2000.

I couldn't sleep last night so at 3:30 in the morning, I went out to the playing field and then over to the kitchen. As the sun began to rise I went down to the river for a bath, and washed my aqua blue sweater, the pink shirt I reconstructed, my black pants, and my burgundy shorts. I came back up, put on my jeans and my Nike shirt, and went to the TV hut to cut my nails. While I was there I talked to the head guerrilla, who told me that he showed my letter to the painter guerrilla and then sent it off. He said he liked it a lot but that it would have looked even better if I'd included a drawing of some sort. I asked him how things were going, what the COCE people had said, and he told me that they would be holding a meeting soon, and that we would have to wait and see what happened. I think it's the same old story: nothing. I stayed there a little while, and then headed over to the kitchen to warm up because I was freezing—my hands and feet were all purple. Before going over, I put on my dad's jacket, and afterward I walked back up and went straight to bed. I got up around 2:30 P.M. and had rice and beans with little pieces of fried plantain for lunch. After that I went back to the hut, smoked a cigarette, and now I am sitting in the chair I made, watching a soccer game as I write this.

Here the soccer games almost always happen in the afternoon. The teams are always the same: the men from the Fokker 50 versus the guerrillas. How ironic: kidnappers versus hostages! Very funny. As they play their game, though, it does seem that the men are capable, at least for a few minutes, of forgetting that they are the victims of a kidnapping, and they really seem to enjoy themselves while they play. The same is true when they play volleyball: it's always the guerrillas against the hostages.

Tonight at around 6:30, the head guerrilla said he wanted to talk to us, and we all gathered in the dining room. He was pretty annoyed about some things that the Nice Old Man had said about us. At first he was very tough, very hard on us, but when Uriel started telling him what things are really like for us, he shut up. In the end he admitted that we were right and now it seems that the supply lady is going to be removed from the camp. He told us that the guerrillas understood perfectly that all of us are completely beside ourselves, but so are they, he said. The end result of the chat, though, was basically a lot of talk, but the same as usual. Nothing new.

As the head guerrilla talked on and on, I made a little figurine out of a candle. Francisco was sitting in front of me and just sat there staring at me, mesmerized, as I did this. When I was through I gave it to him as a little gift. I just suddenly felt like giving it to him. Then I got to thinking about why I had done that and I couldn't figure it out. I told him to hold on to it, that it was a gift, and he found this very funny.

I ate three meals today. It's 9:15 P.M. and I'm tired even though I slept all day. In the morning I played with the dead snake and told the older guerrilla that it was a *mataganado,* the "cattle killer," not a coral snake. That's what they call these snakes, and they're apparently quite dangerous: when they bite into human flesh, the skin will slowly begin to rot.

In this place, I always feel that time doesn't depend on me or what I'm doing. This is a test of my resistance, I know it. I have to endure this as long as necessary and suck up all this boredom for however long I have to. I'm going to try. My father often says, "All of us here are like chickens, waiting for someone to define our situation. We eat and we wait. At any moment they can give the order to kill us and that will be it: that will be the end for us. Or they can free us and then we'll leave, and that will be it."

Time, please pass quickly, very quickly. I beg of you. Help us not to feel you so intensely. Please pass by in a blink of the eye, so that before we realize it, all of this will be an ugly, unpleasant bit of history.

It's 12:06 P.M. and I just got up to go to the bathroom. It's raining, and I'm scared. It's this terrible omen—of what, I don't know, but it's terrible. I turn some music on. I control my mind and think about something I have no reason to think about. Shakira is playing on the radio: *"Mis días sin ti"* ["My Days Without You"].

Oh, how I would love to be at home, to turn on the light, the television. That would be so nice. Instead I'm stuck in a hut that could topple over at any moment, clutching a flashlight to stave off the fear I feel. I identify strongly with the song playing right now. That is how I feel. I go out to the bathroom and get wet. Now I'm cold. I am thinking about my mother right now, wondering what her nights are like. I wonder what she's doing these days—this is usually my favorite season of the year.

Monday, October 18, 1999

Day 190. 75 days until the year 2000. Week number 27.

Today a meeting will be held in Caracas, run by the commission headed up by the attorney general of Colombia, María Emma Mejía, Antonio Navarro Wolf, Pablo Beltrán, and some other people. I hope they reach an agreement and put an end to all this. The face I drew on the mosquito net down by my feet lights up when I shine my flashlight on it.

Last night, my father told me that he doesn't like the way I think, and that he was very worried about the idea of me going to Israel. This made me think about the kind of person I am, the way my mind works, and the truth is, I like both of those things about me. I am sincere, I say what's on my mind—what I like, what I don't like. I am a bit headstrong, and I know that's not the best quality; I also know that because I am so sincere I can be demanding sometimes: I want everything done *now*. I adore animals and I see no reason why they should ever be killed. I like simple, honest people who are loyal and who tell me what they dislike about me. I love being alone, because I consider solitude to be the most natural condition in the world. Sometimes people make me uncomfortable, and I guess that's why I like to be left alone sometimes. I love to look up at the sky, the deep blue firmament, and see how the stars and the clouds travel around, even when I can't distinguish them very well. But that doesn't matter—I imagine them in formations that suddenly occur to me as I look at them. I love to walk barefoot in grass or on the earth; that always relaxes me. There are days when I feel sad, usually just before I get my period, and other days when I feel excited about a million things and I want to do everything. I feel happy when the moon is full . . . but it's strange. I adore the sunrise and the sunset. Rain makes me sad, brings my mood down a bit. I am romantic, which means I love it when the person who loves me shows his feelings; I love all those tiny, silly but original gestures that come from the heart; classic, romantic music that touches my soul, or songs about war and peace, like the kind by Pablo Milanés or Silvio Rodríguez. I like it when the person I'm talking to looks me straight in the eye, because I'm one of those people who believes that the eyes are the mirror of the soul.

With some people I can tell I'm going to like them from the minute I meet them, and then there are others who I just can't stand, who annoy me just because. I like it when people listen to me, and I also try to be a good listener myself. I like to draw strange things that I don't quite understand. I like the colors black, white, and most especially aquamarine. I believe in God but not the church—although I do respect it—and I believe in marriage. I like to respect others and to feel that they respect me, too. I adore people who say what they feel, without thinking. My favorite animal is the cat, in part because I identify with cats: they like to be spoiled, they like to know they're appreciated, but then sometimes they recoil and refuse to let you touch them. They like nighttime better than daytime, just like me; they are careful in everything they do, every movement is beautiful, singular, well defined.

I love chocolate and chocolate ice cream. I adore adventures, and even a little bit of danger. I love the idea of breaking free from everyday life and entering strange, unreal worlds. I am a decision-maker: when I make a decision, I follow through. I am totally crazy about traveling and seeing new things, strange places. I despise monotony and can't bear to see the same old things all the time.

I daydream a lot—that's something I really like. I believe there are other forms of life in other worlds, that death is one of the many phases of the soul. I believe in true love and I hope to find it with one person. When I feel that someone has deceived me, I make sure to let the person know how badly I feel, so that he or she knows what it's like; only then can I turn around and start over. I believe in forgiving but not forgetting. Whenever I make a mistake, I become very cautious, because I'm always afraid of doing the same thing again. I believe in friendships but not cliques.

I love to spoil the people I love, and I love to be spoiled, too—I dance to the music you play for me, if you know what I mean. I can be the sweetest, most gentle woman in the world, and I am never clingy, but I can also be hateful and mean. My moods change very easily, which is something I don't particularly like about myself. I'm very unpredictable in certain aspects, but not as a general rule. I love to watch birds fly. Cockroaches send me into a panic. I adore my family—I love to feel the warmth of home, to see my house filled with life and activity, to celebrate Christmas with tons of people, with a giant, full Christmas tree. I like sunflowers a lot, that's my favorite flower. I love to walk around in sandals. I adore them, and comfortable clothes, too.

It's 6 P.M. I'm sitting in a chair with my boots on, plus the white socks I was wearing when I got here, and the pink shirt that I just sewed up. Today I shaved and washed my blue sweatshirt. My father played all day. Today's a holiday.

I just heard on the news that the government is meeting with the ELN in Cuba instead of Caracas, as they had said they would, but the results have yet to be made public. Antonio Navarro Wolf did say, however, that he thought things would move a lot faster with the ELN than the Fuerzas Armadas Revolucionarias Colombianas [Revolutionary Armed Forces of Colombia], the FARC. That's good. Today I put on some makeup and my burgundy shorts.

There is a kind of flower here that grows on the treetops, it's absolutely huge. I can see it from where I sit in my chair and it looks so pretty; I like it a lot. Francisco told me he'd never seen anything like it before, and he thinks it's pretty, too. I asked him how much he thought it measured in diameter and he said about a meter.

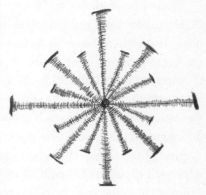

On *La Luciérnaga*, the show on Radio Caracol, they just reported that the meeting that was supposed to happen never took place because Pastrana wouldn't agree to it. Laureano got really upset and said that we'd just gotten a death sentence.

As all of us started talking—except my father, who was sleeping—the other guys started making little jokes about my mother, about witches and white candles, calling her "a witch who reads people's cards" because my mom sometimes makes predictions about when we're going to get out of here. They said a bunch of other things, silly things that made me laugh at first, but then I started to feel uncomfortable and asked them to show a little more respect and to stop making jokes about my mom, since they don't really understand why she says those things to me. Fernando didn't appreciate my comment, not one bit, and he got kind of nasty with me but I don't care. He can fuck off for all I care—let him make fun of his own mother, or brother, or other people's relatives, just not my mother. After that, nobody said anything for a little while, but then the conversation picked up again.

On TV I saw a very nice advertisement about the peace rally that's going to be held on October 24 all across Colombia. It says something like this: "India achieved this, Germany achieved that, Spain achieved this, England achieved that. What about Colombia?" I hope to God that the people of Colombia will go out and support the rally for themselves, for us, and for peace.

Tuesday, October 19, 1999

Day 191 and 74 days to go until the year 2000.

Today I cried all day and had the most awful dreams: I dreamt that both Mauricio and Diego's fathers died, that Diego was feeling horrible and there was nothing I could do to help him, which made me feel miserable. Then I also had some ugly dreams about Kika, but they were all very convoluted.

My mother sent me a message today through UIS; she said that the damage being done to us is unspeakable; that we have nothing to do with this conflict; that she works as hard as she can but still feels helpless; that Carol calls every day from Brazil and feels very depressed about my father, because now she realizes how much he means to her; that Nandor is also very depressed and dreams about us every day, just like Carol; that at night when it's cold she gets up and thinks about how I'm doing; that she has to remain strong and calm because if she doesn't everyone else will start to droop, which will only make things worse. I could hear a cat meowing in the background as she talked, and she said it was Pablito.

I could no longer hold back the tears, and once again I began sobbing, from the sheer frustration and pain of it all, but also from the joy. She said such pretty things. After the radio show ended, I went over to the head guerrilla and told him about the message and how it made me cry out of desperation. I also asked him if the people at COCE had received my letter, and then I begged him to help me, to put himself in my position. I know he can't get me out of here, because the decision is simply not up to him, but his superiors can certainly listen to him and take his opinion into account. I asked him to talk to the COCE people again, to help me, and then I reminded him that I'm only six years older than his own daughter, that I love and need my mother, and that I am going crazy here. I don't know if he paid much attention to what I said, but I hope so, because it is the truth.

I just can't believe that people can be so evil. If they knew what my life was like, what my father's life, my brothers and sister's lives were like, they would let us go in a heartbeat.

Dear Lord, I cannot abide any more suffering in my life or in the lives of the people I love. I know that I have my life ahead of me, but my father only has thirty years left at the most. Tomorrow he'll be 49 years old, and it just isn't fair of you to make him waste away here. I walk from one side of the playing field to the other: 50 paces long and 30 paces wide, and in the middle there is a volleyball net that has 7,200 little squares: 9 high and 80 across. I counted those little squares one by one. As I look out at the half-moon tonight, I feel that I am losing control of myself.

Laureano is blasting heavy metal music. So annoying.

God, I need to feel that my mind is at peace, even if it's only for a second: I just want to stop thinking. I'm so worried about the future. What can I do to make those feelings go away? The head guerrilla says that I feel this way because Christmas is coming soon.

Day 192. 73 days until the year 2000.

I haven't smoked a single cigarette today; my ulcer flared up again. Last night I dreamt that I was with Diego in some kind of country estate. We were talking about Paloma's suicide, and I got very sad and Diego told me that she was alive. But I said no, she's dead, I'd been to the funeral already and knew for sure. In the dream I also saw myself on the Pacific coast of Colombia, in Chocó, and I didn't want to be with Diego.

Today I got up at 6 A.M., went to the kitchen, and watched them kill Chispi, the hog. It was pretty revolting: they plunged a screwdriver into her heart and hacked into her face with an ax.

I just smoked a Poker cigarette that one of the guerrillas brought me and drank a cup of coffee. The supply lady just gave me a lollipop, but I gave it to my father. It's his birthday tomorrow and I feel so badly that he's going to have to celebrate it in captivity. We don't have the ingredients to make a cake, and that makes me feel sad, too.

The head guerrilla hasn't shown his face to me today and to tell the truth, I understand perfectly. It must be hard for him to look me in the face these days. But if I can't tell him the things I tell him, who else am I supposed to talk to?

I don't think I'm going to take a bath today. I don't feel like doing much of anything, in fact. I am completely miserable, and I don't know who can help me.

It's 7:10 P.M. I look at the calendar and start feeling distraught again when I see all the days crossed off and still everything is the same, nothing happens. What can I do? I don't want to see those days march on while I'm stuck here, unable to live for real. I feel more dead than alive right now. Life goes on for everyone but me, my father, and the 2,000 other hostages in this country. Oh, God, I pray that something comes out of this rally, that it can move a mountain and get us out of here.

Nobody understands the pain I'm in. The guerrillas are tough as nails; their hearts are like stone: they don't feel, they don't cry, they don't despair. They are very hard people, and I am too weak to make it through this war, which is bleeding our country dry.

Nandor spoke on UIS today. He said that an NGO held a meeting to see if they could do something for me. He told me that he had had to bring photographs, and that later on he would tell me how it all went. My mother didn't talk today.

My father has been complaining a lot lately that his body aches, especially when he walks. I don't know what to do. Tomorrow I'm going to talk to the head guerrilla to see what can be done about it.

Yesterday in the river I cut my father's hair, about a finger's length, and he liked the way it turned out. Today there's a Colombia-Mexico soccer game in California. My father and I just came back from watching the news and started talking about our situation. I told him how happy I am that we aren't alone in our suffering, that there are so many other people who are in this together with us. I also said that things are going to have to change in Colombia because people are tired of this war. I really feel that with all these kidnappings—ours, plus the churches in Cali and Barranquilla—people woke up and realized that this could happen to absolutely anyone. Tons of people in this country travel on planes, go to church, drive on highways—all the places where the guerrillas carry out their *pesca milagrosa,* the so-called miracle fishing, rounding people up and kidnapping them in big bunches.

The protest march on October 24 is going to be massive, and I think it will inspire the government and the groups responsible for these kidnappings to sit down and negotiate peace once and for all. In Colombia, we are killing one another, beating ourselves to death. And everyone, all across the country, asks the same questions: Who really wins in this war, this senseless battle in which all of us suffer, both the perpetrators and the victims? Who are we killing for? Who do we suffer for?

Good God, we are all human beings, and we are all Colombians, which makes the whole thing even sadder. Who can go to bed with a clean conscience when all this is happening? Is it worth living if you have to live like this? Why is there so much hatred among us? This country needs to change, and it needs to change now. I know it's very easy to say and very easy to demand, but in order for a change to happen all of us have to work toward making peace a reality, and I mean we really have to strive for it and not wait for other people to do something, so that we can all finally go back out onto the streets and enjoy what we have earned for ourselves. We can do it if we want it badly enough.

God, please help this country. Please change the minds of the people who steal so much from the Colombian people. That is our problem: the goddamn corruption that exists here, and the fact that in the end the righteous always end up paying for the sinners. The real problem in this country lies way up in the upper reaches of the government, and with the despicable people who are rich because they steal from hospitals for the poor, and everyone else. It is so disillusioning to pay taxes in this country because all of us know that instead of going where it should, all that money is just going to end up in the pockets of the people who are responsible for making Colombia what it is today. Those people have no interest in working toward peace, because they know that they will be the first ones to lose out when that happens.

Thursday, October 21, 1999

Day 193. 72 days until the year 2000.

Today I am going to write a letter to my father and give it to him tomorrow at dawn.

Dear Dad:

On this day I want you to know that I love you and I am so happy to have you at my side today.

I want you to know that it would make me so content to have you with me always. I just ask the "greater power" to help you so that you never let me down, because I want to learn everything I can from you, because you are the best father in the world. If there were more people in the world like you, we would all be so much better off. I only want to follow the example you have set for me, and I hope to practice that example with my own family one day. But before I do that, I want to take this present moment and hold on to it in my memory and cherish it, for it is a great treasure that I hope to open up again and again as an example of all that is good in the world. Dear Daddy, even though Nandor and Carol are far away, I want to tell you over and over again how much we all love you. On behalf of them, I send you this message.

Oh, Daddy, thank you for being who you are: the wonderful, sensible person to whom we owe half of our lives. We hope to be with you always, and we also hope you feel you can be with us as well.

Thank you, my father. I thank you once and a thousand times over, for being a truly unique man, like no other.

Happy birthday, Daddy. I love you so much.

Yours,

Leszli Kálli López

Your daughter in captivity

They dedicated the entire UIS program, from 7:30 to 8:30, to my father. Lucía, Cony, Catuto, Rodolfo Peña, Orlando Beltrán, Carlos Ortiz, and Esperanza Duque all said a little something. Marcelita sang "Happy Birthday," and they all gave him a serenade, too. Then Nandor said a few words, and my mom read something very pretty about how happiness is just around the corner, and that triumph is the reverse of failure. She ended by telling me to be strong, and that she loves me.

I feel so good with my father. At 6:30 in the evening we all gathered in the dining shack, sang "Happy Birthday," and gave him a card that we made together.

I took a late bath tonight and got quite a scare from a giant frog, which I mistakenly thought was a snake. Then I turned on La Mega, and just after I heard Juanca saying hi to me, I did see a snake, a *patojita*, as the people around here call them. The Nice Old Man tried to kill her but she slithered away somewhere. After that I sat down to listen to UIS, and at around 10 P.M. I went outside and started talking to the guerrilla that arrived here yesterday, the one they call Calvo—baldy. He's a really nice guy; he gives me cigarettes when the other guards say they've run out.

My mood is all right, I'm calm tonight. The news is promising and people are feeling positive. Today we have almost a full moon; tomorrow it will be 100% full.

Archangel Gabriel, please bring me good news. They say you are always the bearer of good news. Our release will be the best news you can send us. Help us.

Friday, October 22, 1999

Day 194. 71 days until the year 2000.

The night came and went. Now it is daytime. The sun illuminates everything and restores my faith: I have hope, and my mood is brighter. I tidied up the hut a little today and decorated it with palm fronds. I only managed to cover half the door with the palm fronds; the rest was still covered in plastic.

The day went by quickly today: my mind was busy and that felt very good. Diego González, my father, Fernando, and I sat around talking about things that have happened to us, and we laughed a lot. That was awfully nice.

Today, when I was in the river, I felt something very odd when I thought about Diego. I don't know what will happen when I see him again. Something inside of me wants to know if everything I used to feel for him will come back when I see him face-to-face. I don't know if those feelings I used to have for him are still in there, somewhere inside of me, or if they're gone.

Day 195. 70 days to go until 2000.

Today I got up and ate breakfast with Diego and Fer. My father went to take a bath, and Laureano went after him. Then I asked for a notebook and started to write.

I thought about cutting more palm fronds for the tent, but I couldn't find a machete. Then I went to the health aide and asked if she could order me some Fenisec. She said yes, but we'll see if they come through. Right now I'm listening to La Mega. Yesterday they made us papaya juice with milk. Very tasty.

It's funny, I just realized that I really tend to write a lot more when I'm feeling bad; the same thing happens to me with my drawings. Creativity always comes to me when I'm at some kind of extreme: either very sad or very happy. I'm never very creative when things are just normal.

Day 196. 69 days until the year 2000.

Today I got up at 8:40 A.M. and went to take a bath. It's a very gray day out here. Fernando made some signs that say "No more" and stuck them to all the huts. Then we went to watch TV, to see the great protest march that's taking place all across the country. Medellín was incredible, there were so many people. They didn't show the march in Bucaramanga. They also aired the signing of the agreement in La Uribe, in the region of Meta, between the government and the FARC. It was so nice to see all those people gathered together. We saw Otto Duarte in Caracas. He was one of our fellow hostages.

For lunch I ate beans, rice, and lemon wedges with salt and olive oil.

Yesterday I began reading *How the Steel Was Tempered,* and I'm going to read more today.

The moon is so beautiful, so mesmerizing—it's just divine, completely full and lovely. The sky is absolutely clear, and next to the moon I can see a star, and an elongated cloud that stretches out over the horizon. This is without a doubt the most incredible moon I've ever seen.

Today we got a new guerrilla, one who was with the painter guerrilla recently; he said he sent regards. I said hello back. In the dining hut I ran into Francisco: we talked for a few seconds about books, but he really isn't much of a reader, so I just hung around reading while I waited for the coffee to brew.

I think I'm going to play a little game: I'm going to start telling lies and make everyone around here believe a bunch of garbage until the day I get released—just for fun, to kill the boredom a little. If I get nervous about getting caught in my own lies, I'll just stop. But it will be a good way to get rid of some steam, and no one will know any better. That's what I thought about as the others watched television.

It really blows my mind to think that everyone I love in the world can see the very same moon that I can see.

A good sign: el Negro, one of the guerrillas, tells me that we'll be out of here by December. I pray to God he's telling the truth, because that is what I most want in the world: my freedom. I once heard some saying—something about how people don't know what freedom is until they lose it, and those who don't have it are, ironically, the ones who understand it the best. Incredible but true, completely true.

Here in captivity, I feel that I have significantly changed the way I act and the way I think about things: I have matured a great deal, and I'm glad about that. One day I just got to thinking and I realized that you often don't notice those changes from one day to the next, but you do grow and you do move on, maybe not much but a little bit, at least. After years and years, these changes become easier to see and are often quite surprising.

It's 11 P.M. right now, and it's freezing outside. I have the worst menstrual cramps. I just snuggled down under the blanket. I listened to my father talking to Uriel for a while about plane simulators for the 727, the jumbo jet, the MD Fokker, the 767, the 757, and some others, too, and then they talked about radials, vectors, and some other things, but I got bored so I left. I was kind of upset with them, actually. Then my father asked me to tell the story about when we got robbed in 1989, when seven armed men, their heads covered in hoods, came into the apartment at 12:30 in the afternoon. I told them everything: about how they put a bomb under the bed, in the same place where I was hiding . . . I didn't leave out a thing.

Monday, October 25, 1999

Day 197. 68 days until the year 2000. Week 28.

Today, while looking for scraps of fabric to hang things in Laureano's hut, I dismantled the hut that had previously been used by a guerrilla who left us a while ago, and Lau found some palm fronds. My dad advised him to put plastic over the roof. I also drank some *chicha* and brewed some more. Then I watched *Lolita* and *Marido y mujer* on television. I didn't take a bath but I did eat. There's another full moon, but it's not quite as pretty as it was yesterday. Right now I'm listening to the Enanitos Verdes on La Mega. Today I spent a long time pondering what I talked about yesterday, the lying thing. I thought better of it and decided not to do it.

The guerrillas are very decent with us: they don't humiliate us or try to make us feel bad, and in fact I'd say that they actually try to make things as comfortable as possible for us, but no matter how hard they try you just can't help feeling bad here.

It's hard to make any kind of general statement about the ELN guerrillas. It's kind of like the way it is at school: there are good people, there are generous, cooperative, and friendly people, but there are also spiteful, resentful people who stare at you with pure hatred in their eyes. And then you also come across people who are neither one nor the other: quiet, cautious, reserved people who seem removed from everyone else, and who are hard to identify as either "good" or "bad"—people who fall somewhere in the middle of the two extremes. Or, as my mother would say, the kind of people who "you don't notice if they leave, but you don't mind if they stay, either." Neutral people.

Diego, why am I always thinking about you? Why do I love you so much? At what moment did you enter my life and take control of my heart? Why is it that the more I try to push you out of my life, my mind, my soul, the more you get under my skin? Why does it hurt so much to know this is true? How long will I have to live with these feelings that are so strong, so persistent, so overwhelming? Oh, how I wish we could just end it, for the good of us both!

I will leave it in God's hands.

Tuesday, October 26, 1999

Day 198. 67 days until the year 2000.

Yesterday I dreamt that I was pregnant, and that I was looking out over the Sierra Nevada de Santa María, watching Nandor paragliding. I was filming something and I felt very sad that I was pregnant.

Three months ago today I shaved my head. Now I have about three centimeters of hair, more or less. When I went down to the river to take a bath, I saw that a new head commander arrived. He's very fat. He greeted me by name and told me that he had seen me in the newspaper.

My mother spoke on the radio today and sounded very happy: she said that I was my father's best girl and that if I heard any messages that bothered me, I should just turn off the radio, that there was no need to go listen gratuitously to unpleasant things the way I had to when I was a little girl. Then she told me that she knows I am the strongest of her three children and that in her dreams she sees me with my father, and she can tell I'm very happy with him here. Nothing is all bad, she said: there are things to be gained and learned from all experiences, even terrible ones. On the news Pablo Beltrán said that more hostages would be released, and my mom said that she has faith I will be among them.

Today I finished reading *How the Steel Was Tempered*. What an incredible book: very beautiful, very powerful. One sentence in particular stuck in my mind: "You must also learn to live when life becomes unbearable. Make it useful."

Wednesday, October 27, 1999

Day 199. 66 days until the year 2000.

Today when I got up I remembered dreaming they were going to move us to another campsite. Today I watched el Negro as he cleaned his rifle and a Smith & Wesson 9 millimeter pistol. I helped him a little, wiping the gun with ACPM and oil, and told him that my mom had a Smith & Wesson .38. When I finished he thanked me and I walked back to my hut and drank some *chicha* with my father. I think about my mother so much—I miss her so much, and I want to see her so badly. My father just told me that the government delegates and the ELN representatives are planning to meet in Havana.

I just came back from watching *Padres e hijos* [Fathers and Sons], and I have now sat down to read my diary. I was in the middle of reading when the squirrel monkey suddenly appeared and settled down for a rest on my legs. Right now, at this very moment, she is looking at me as I write and I am resting my notebook on her body. Diego and Fernando are all annoyed with me and my father, but frankly, I couldn't care less. Today the fat guerrilla left us.

I didn't feel like taking a bath today—I'm too depressed, because this situation isn't moving forward in any way, and it's just so unfair. I mean, it's getting boring for me to write the same thing over and over again: it's not fair, I feel frustrated, et cetera, et cetera.

Today on UIS, Nandor told us that we should try and keep our moods up, just like the dollar, to improve little by little every day. He also said he hoped that our names would get picked in the ELN lottery—mine, my dad's, or both, or everyone's. Because that's what this is, he said: a lottery.

My dad and I talked about the past today, and I told him what I thought about his life.

Thursday, October 28, 1999

Today marks 200 days in captivity. I find this is truly unbelievable.

Last night I dreamt that Bucaramanga got bombed and we were forced to climb into trucks that took us to a kind of parking lot. Without getting out, we all started playing with a computer.

Today a plane passed by overhead, flying quite low. My father said that it belonged to Aires, an airline. Then he said to me, "You know what's happened to me? The same thing that used to happen to you when you were little: in the morning you would get up before anyone else, and since everyone else was still asleep you would wake everyone up. It was so funny, you looked like you were counting us. Once the rest of us—me, your mother, Nandor, and Carol—were finally awake you would go back to sleep. I guess you just didn't like the feeling that you were alone."

Today, the others were playing soccer and at some point the ball ended up in the toilet. One of the guerrillas retrieved it and washed it off. I played Parcheesi with Diego, Fer, and my father today. On the radio they talked about the big party they're having for October 31. How incredible: it feels like yesterday that I was dressed up like a witch at the Café Bonaparte with my friends, and that on November first, Diego, Salvador, Pedro, Luis, and I went to Mesa de los Santos. Time passes by so fast! And then my life got stuck in April. I really am cursed.

For a while now my father has been complaining of a very acute pain in his kidneys. The head guerrilla came by and told him that tomorrow, first thing in the morning, he would radio the command center to let them know.

Two black dogs have been wandering around the campsite; the guerrillas are very worried. They sent out a group to catch them, to see if they were wild, or if they belonged to a hunter or the army.

At night I went to the latrine. As I was climbing up the hill, one of the guerrillas gave me a cigarette, to be nice. I mentioned that Christmas was right around the corner, and how awful it would be to have to celebrate here. He said, "Oh, no, don't worry about that. You'll be out of here before then."

I told him he was naïve if he thought we were going to be released before December. Sometimes I feel I'm never going to get back to the real world, because bad things always seem to happen to me.

Some people say that life is preordained, and that everything happens for a reason, that nothing happens in a vacuum. Today I started thinking about that and I had to ask myself: what could be the reason for all this? I didn't ask it from a place of anger but curiosity, I really pondered this, and I searched my soul but I just can't answer that question. Why did this have to happen to me so young—I'm only 18 years old—and last so long?

I do feel that a great change has taken place inside of me, that I have grown up intellectually, which makes me happy but also a bit sad, because I feel I am leaving behind the little girl I lived with for so long—that little girl who didn't care about anything, who was so impulsive, so hyperactive, so irreverent. And that hurts a bit. Now, before I do anything, I will always think twice about the harm my actions may cause me or the people around me. Before, I was never very responsible, and while I wouldn't go so far as to say I am completely responsible now, I have definitely grown in that sense, too.

I think I am afraid of finding happiness and then having that happiness taken away from me by someone or something. I would like to think that from now on, happiness will be something that exists inside of me, that I am the only person who can make it appear or disappear. I will not give anyone the power to take it away from me. My happiness cannot be removed by someone other than me. My happiness is part of me.

Who would have ever thought that one day we would be thrown into a situation as difficult as this? Mommy, I can't imagine how lonely you must be without me, your little girl. Do you remember when I used to say, "Mommy, will you spoil me a little?" and you would say, "No, honey, you're too old for that now." That always made me so sad because even though I had grown up physically, I still felt like your little girl. I want you to know that even when I am older I will keep on saying to you, "Mommy, will you spoil me a little?" because for me, it brings back such sweet memories, because it reminds me, now more than ever, that I was, am, and always will be your little girl. Mommy, I love you so much. If I had known that you and I were to be separated that April 12, I would have expressed this and so many more of the things I have always felt for you.

Mommy, why do these things happen? Why are these people keeping us apart for no apparent reason? Why are they putting us through this? It is so unfair—what did we ever do to anyone to deserve this? Why is life denying us the joy and thrill it once gave us?

Just as you do, I am sure, I have wondered over and over again if God really exists. To keep myself from sinking into despair I think yes, he exists, but he must be very preoccupied with other problems that are much more important than ours. Pope John Paul II called for our release and even prayed for us but it didn't do a bit of good. I mean, look at us, here we are: 200 days and nothing. You have no way of knowing what is going on with me, and I have no way of seeing you or telling you that I am alive and well, and I'm still so sad that you are so far away. When will our luck improve?

Good night, Mommy.

I love you, and hope that all is well with you.

Friday, October 29, 1999

Day 201. 64 days until the year 2000.

Today, a baby girl was born to Manuel Fernando Torres, one of the Avianca hostages being held with the other group, which includes Ana María Gómez, Juan Manuel Corzo, Gloria Amaya de Alonso, Yezid Gómez, Abner Duarte, and Nicolás Pérez. Originally there were eight of them but this past October 2 they released Daniel Hoffmann, the American. Over the radio, Isabel, the baby's mother, asked them to release Manuel so that they could share this joyful moment in their lives.

I have an upset stomach today. Today for breakfast and lunch I ate *cancharinas* [cakes made of wheat flour and sugar], lemonade, lentils, two *arepas,* and rice.

Today they released another hostage from the church in Cali, and the gasoline generator broke down. Right now I'm listening to UIS: classical music.

My father and I had a talk about my future today; we decided that the best thing for me is to study English and computer programming, and then look into the possibility of studying abroad. I ought to figure out what field is in the greatest demand outside of Colombia, and then study that, either here or abroad. I think it's a good plan, but it makes me sad about Israel. The truth is, though, I do have to get serious because I'm really wasting time not doing anything!

Juan González jokingly says to me: "Leszli, what do you say you marry me and we'll go to Canada together. That way we'll make my mother and your father happy and we'll solve both our problems!"

I had to laugh at that one. Juan is always telling jokes. Although, to tell the truth, I hadn't quite expected that one.

I am so filled with rage; I feel as though I have been split in two. If I hadn't been kidnapped, by now I would already be back from Israel speaking fluent English, and as things stand now I still don't speak English and all I have to show for the past months is a lot of lost time. I suppose I have no choice but to grin and bear it. Or, as that favorite saying of mine goes, let us not look back in anger, nor forward in fear, but around in awareness.

Saturday, October 30, 1999

The night was a long one. No television yesterday or today. My father performed the cupping glass technique on my back and in one fell swoop all the gas I had came right out of my body. Today I got up at around 6:20 A.M. because I had to go to the bathroom, and then I went down to the kitchen shack and ate an *arepa*. Then I brushed my teeth, went back to bed, and stayed there until 11 A.M. When I got up, I washed the rice for the *guarapo* I wanted to make with the *panela*, and then I went over to the dining shack and took a seat. The daughter of the supply lady gave me a banana as a gift. Why? I have no idea, she's the strangest little girl—some days she's off, some days she's on. Just like me.

Yesterday Fernando and Diego received new boots. They are so thrilled. Just as a joke, I said to them: "That's the ELN's Christmas gift to you."

"Why do you have to be so negative, Leszli? Maybe they gave us the boots because we're going to start walking."

"Or maybe because you're going to need something to put on your feet for another six months. . . ."

On the news today they said that the ELN is going to meet with a governmental delegate in Cuba next week, that things are on the right track, and that hopefully there will be good news for the country after the meeting. That's what Víctor G. Ricardo, the high commissioner for peace, said.

Today I dreamt that I was at the top of a crystal-clear river. Looking down, I could see everyone: the health aide, my father, Juan, Diego, Francisco, Lau, Fer, Uriel, and some of the guerrillas were all playing with a scarf. I was taking a bath, and when they stopped playing they came up, and I had to go down, because they were going to get the water all dirty and I was already clean. Then I had another dream: I was in a bar with a bunch of people in costumes when suddenly I fell. Beatriz threw water over my face, and then lots of people started pouring into the place, all of them pushing and throwing things on me. I was on the floor, and the music that was playing transported me to another dimension. I was completely enthralled with the music and nothing mattered to me at all. It was as if I was drugged or something!

After lunch I got to talking with the Nice Old Man. I saw he had some colored pencils so I asked to borrow them and made a picture for the supply lady's daughter. She liked it. That made me happy.

The other day, the Denorex shampoo I ordered finally arrived. I have a lot of dandruff. Today is Saturday, message day, but I don't know if I'll get up to listen to them. Today the Nice Old Man started talking to me about the hijacking, about the moment when the men pulled out their weapons on the plane. He asked me what went through my mind at that moment, but frankly, I wasn't too keen on talking about that—I really didn't have much interest in reliving such an awful day in my life. The Old Man then told me that from what they were saying on the news, it sounded like we were going to be released soon. I told him not to be so naïve, that for 202 days they have been talking and talking and talking, and I will only believe it when they tell us, "All right, get ready, because we're leaving. We're handing you over now." Only when they actually put us in a helicopter, and the helicopter takes off, will I really believe it. Until then, forget it.

The fat guerrilla who knew my name came back today. He doesn't know anything; he tells me they sent him here because they needed him to look into a few things that have nothing to do with us.

Today I ate a piece of *panela* and now I'm waiting for the supply lady to give me two big hunks of it because I want to ferment some.

I feel so, so fat! It's awful!

When I start to think about it, I can hardly believe that I have been able to survive for over six months with six shirts: two green, one of which they gave me the first week and another one that was given to me by Carlos González, the man who died here in captivity, and which fades a little bit more every time I wash it. Then there is the red shirt that I altered, and then there is another shirt that used to be my father's and a white one they gave me here, both of which I altered and ended up rather skeletal looking. Then I have another one that originally belonged to my father but I remodeled that one, too, and now it's very tight. And the last one is a Nike T-shirt that they gave me along with a flowered scarf. My flowered Gap shirt got lost sometime during the first week. As for pants, I have one pair of black pants and one pair of blue pants that I altered: now they hang low on the hips because I cut the waistband and the ankle bands. I also have the jeans I was wearing when we got here. Before, we never had towels and whenever we took baths we had to wait around half an hour, like a bunch of idiots, as we dried off in the sun. Now I have three towels. Hard to believe it's me talking—me, the girl for whom a 50-kilo suit-case seemed like precious little to take to Israel. How about that. I have to laugh when I think of that.

It was almost dark by the time I took my bath tonight, and right afterward I had rice and beans. My father, Uriel, and Laureano were already in the dining room, and as I sat down to eat with them they launched into a conversation about airplanes, as usual. Uriel told me that when he was a kid he liked to study in cemeteries because that's what they do in the little towns in Colombia—it's kind of a tradition. They say that if you study in a cemetery you'll retain what you read, and everything will turn out okay. They also talked about the *enano* [midget] Solano and his nights out on the town in Madrid with my dad. Then they said that this isn't the first plane ever hijacked in Colombia, that there have been seven before ours. Unbelievable.

Today I made a bracelet out of a bit of white rope and decided that I will not take it off until I have been reunited with all the people I love in the world.

Exactly a year ago today, if you count by the day, and tomorrow, if you count by the date on the calendar, I was getting ready for a Hal-loween party where everyone had to come in costume. I dressed up as a witch, and I looked really nice—I did my face up with frosty face paint, and then I went to Bonaparte with Diego, Silvio, Rata, and the *gordo* Manuel. We had such a fun time, although Diego did some-thing kind of nasty—it's something I remember to this day, and it still makes me mad whenever I think about it. One day I'll make him pay for that! That day he took a photo of me; I think he still has it. I know that tomorrow, all the people who were with me that day will think of me.

I'm in bed now with my super blanket, listening to Amor Stereo. I want to go home so badly! I hope this ends soon. . . .

Today, as he was sweeping up, Uriel said a bunch of things that really got me thinking. For one thing, he said that these people could kill us at any moment; if the army comes after them, he said, the guerrillas would rather kill us than hand us over alive, just to make the army look bad. But the guerrillas say the opposite: according to them, the army is actually more likely to kill us to make the guerrillas look bad. One of the two versions must be true, clearly, but what does it matter, since we get killed either way? It's so sad. Uriel also said something about how we're like slaves, that the guerrillas do whatever they please with us: they take us here, there, everywhere, they give, they take away, et cetera. . . . I don't know whether to believe him or not. Everything he says sounds pretty grim. If he's right, then the reality of things around here is very sinister indeed. I just keep hoping this will all end soon.

It's 9:30 P.M.

Triumph is failure but in reverse. Happiness is sadness in reverse. The good and the bad go hand in hand: when one sits down at your table, the other one lies in your bed; they take turns. I only hope that all these bad times bring good times. In that sense, I wouldn't mind being here five years, if I knew that at the end of those five years I would have five years of good things in store for me. That would be so nice, but of course, who knows?

I feel that I am beginning to see things more clearly now. I have no anchor because I don't want to weigh anchor anywhere. I want to be out traveling—always knowing where I'm going, but traveling just the same, forever and ever. Dear Life, I may only be 18 years old but I can safely say that I have already known you at your darkest moments. I try to understand you but you are strange and unpredictable—though maybe that is precisely what I like about you: you change so fast, you never stay the same. For better or for worse, you are always in motion.

Sunday, October 31, 1999

Day 203 in captivity. 62 days to go until the year 2000.

Nandor and my mother spoke on the radio today: first they said hello and then they said that they hoped this would be their last time talking to me on *Amanecer en América.*

My father and I had a long talk today about how everyone seems to be feeling quite optimistic except us—we feel less hopeful than ever now, what with all the food and clothes they just brought in for us.

When I went to eat breakfast I found out that the health aide, that obnoxious, arrogant wench, is filling in for the supply lady. Since she hates me and my dad, she started saying things like, "I don't give a damn about you and your problems," but before that, she said, "You know what? I feel like the other guerrilla: I wish the plague would get here already and give us some action." The plague is her code word for the army. She is really such a miserable human being: she is the vomit of human existence reduced to its basest expression.

It's 8 A.M. and Diego and Fer are listening to Sunday mass over the radio. I dreamt that Nandor bought a pretty green car, a bicycle, and a paraglider all on the same day.

My father tried to fix the electrical generator today, but it didn't work. Now, who knows how long we'll have to go without television. He knows a lot about planes and engines but I don't really know what happened with the generator.

Right now I'm making *chicha*; I made two jars of the stuff but it won't be ready for three days.

I just decided I'm not going to take a bath today, it's too much of a drag. Plus, I cut one of the fingers on my left hand when I was peeling a stick with a knife, which the boyfriend of the guerrilla who's my age lent me.

Now that December is right around the corner, I am happy to say that I have once more kept the promise I make every December: not to lose my virginity until the day of my marriage. I've made lots of other promises that I haven't kept, not intentionally but because I've been here. Very few girls my age are still virgins—I may be the only one I know, in fact. I like that, though; it makes me feel unique—I'm glad not to be like other girls. They might think it's completely stupid but it's important to me. I just feel that my virginity is to be reserved for a special person and not for any old guy I go out with!

Another important thing I have done while in captivity is let my eyelashes grow, after ten years. In December I want to quit smoking, find the right career, and start studying. I also want to take a look at my list of resolutions from last year, to see which ones I kept and which ones I didn't.

In addition to my resolutions I prayed for my family's health, and I think my prayer was answered. I prayed for the health of my parents and my brother and sister, and I think it was answered.

I hung around until about 9:40 P.M. talking with Laureano about the way I look at the world, about the things I want out of life. . . . I told him all about Diego, and Cristhian, and about the time I spent living in Atlanta, and about my dream of one day living in a tiny town in Europe, in Italy, maybe. . . . He told me lots of things about himself, too. Then Uriel came around and I decided to go to sleep because he's such a bore to talk to. With Laureano it's different because he and I are almost the same age—well, I'm 18 and he's 24.

Laureano lost his dad in a plane accident, an Avianca 727 that was headed for New York. His father had the same name as him, Laureano Caviedes, and he was the captain of the plane.

Uriel and Laureano say that they think my mother has spoiled me a lot. They say they can tell from the way I act. I reply that yeah, maybe they're right, but after being here for so long, that part of me has changed. When I get home, I will still be the same person I am here. Lau tells me that I will have to be very tough, and I agree.

Page 448 of *How the Steel Was Tempered* really stuck in my mind. Reading it, I felt as though the author was right here with me, going through all of this at my side: "What should be done? This question without an answer opened up before him, like an ominous, black precipice.

"Why go on living when he had already lost the most precious thing he had, his will to fight? How would he justify his life now, or on the sad days to come? How would he fill his days? Just by eating, drinking, and breathing? End up impotent in the presence of all his comrades who would go on fighting? Become a burden for the detachment? What if he just sent the body that had betrayed him to the great hereafter? A bullet to the heart and . . . all his pains would be over. He was a man who knew how to live and who knew when to put an end to things. Who on earth would condemn the soldier who only wanted to end his agony?

"His hand explored the inside of his pocket, patting around in search of the flat surface of the pistol, and his fingers, with movements that were already highly familiar to him, grasped the handle. Slowly he removed the weapon.

"'Who would have thought I would ever make it to this day?'

"The handle of the pistol looked him in the eye with scorn. Pavel left the pistol sitting on his knees and cried out a litany of curses.

"'All of this heroism is a great fiction, my brother, it is a fiction fit for a novel! Any idiot can pull a trigger and kill himself if he wants to. It is the easiest, most cowardly way out of any situation. All right, if life is so hard for you, then shoot yourself! But have you ever tried to achieve triumph in this life? Have you done everything to break the iron gates? Or have you forgotten how you attacked Novograd-Vlonski seventeen times in a single day, and despite everything, you conquered it? Put the pistol away and don't ever tell anyone about it. You must also learn to live when life becomes unbearable. Make it useful.'"

This is another passage from the book that I hope to never forget:

"Friendship may exist without love, but love without friendship, companionship, common interests, is mediocre. . . . That is not love, it is simply egotistical pleasure. A toy."

Of all the people on the Avianca plane that was hijacked en route to Bogotá from Bucaramanga, those of us who remain in captivity are: Manuel Fernando Torres, Juan González, Fernando Buitrago, Diego González, Uriel Velasco, Juan Manuel Corzo, Francisco López,

Ana María Gómez, Gloria Amaya de Alonso, Leszli Kálli López, Laszlo Kálli Daniel, Yezid Gómez, Abner Duarte, Nicolás Pérez, Laureano Caviedes.

After flipping through the maps in *Larousse Dictionary* here, these are the places I would like to visit one day: the thirteenth-century church of St. John of Kaneo in Ohrid, Macedonia; Cape Town, capital of the province of Western Cape, the city at the foot of Table Mountain; and the Fiji islands.

Monday holiday, November 1, 1999

Day 204, 61 days until the year 2000. Week 29.

Yesterday Juan Pablo Montoya won the Formula Cart in California. Today my father is fixing the outdoor chairs while I sit around listening to La Mega. They say that it's a beautiful, sunny day in Bucaramanga today.

Last night I dreamt about my mother, that she was so happy to see

me. I'm so afraid that we're still going to be here when December rolls around. That will make for a very difficult Christmas.

I feel like peeing but I can't— for some reason that happens to me a lot around here.

One year ago today, at dawn, I was kissing Diego at Mesa de los Santos, almost two and a half years after we broke up.

My father got rid of the planks that led to the playing field and then we went to take a dip in the river. Today I was about ready to go crazy, but Uriel calmed me down: he said he understood, and that he knew what I was going through because he was going through the exact same thing. And he said I just had to try to calm down, because there was nothing to be gained by getting worked up. The tears slid down my face anyway. There is no way to describe the impotence you feel when you've been kidnapped! On November 12 we will have been here for seven months. That is a hell of a lot of time, and yet neither the ELN nor the government has lifted a finger for us. Boy, do I wish they could experience what it feels like and what it means to be trapped here, even if only for a minute.

We just found out that they released several more people from the church in Cali. There are twenty of them left inside now.

Tonight I saw two shooting stars, one of them when I was alone in the playing field. Suddenly, for some reason, I felt like linking my arms together from behind and then bringing them forward without letting go. Afterward I showed my dad and everyone else this little feat. Then I spent some time talking to my father, who was feeling pretty low. I told him to stay calm, to remember that they are releasing people, and then he said, "Sure, right, all of us are sitting around watching them release everyone else, but they don't do anything for us."

I told him to think about the soldiers, about the people who've been in captivity for more than a year, about the foreigners. . . . That made him feel a little better, I think. Then we talked a little about me and all my drawings. He told me he thought I ought to study art, because it seems to be my calling. This caught me completely by surprise, and I thanked him for that gesture of support. I told him that secretly I have always wanted to study art but never said a word about it because I was afraid he wouldn't approve of the idea, that he would say it was for pot smokers and drug addicts. But no, he said, he totally supported it.

So there we have it: I am going to study Fine Arts. I am overjoyed, because that is truly what I want to do. What bliss!

Tuesday, November 2, 1999

Day 205. 60 days until the year 2000.

Today I woke up at 5 A.M., to the squeals of a hog being killed. Thank God I don't eat meat anymore. All of that makes me so sad.

Yesterday the FARC released two Spanish citizens. I took a bath at 6:30 and washed the woolen blanket, the top sheet, and the pillowcase, and then came back up with my dad. Together we made the desk upon which I am presently writing. I also grabbed a pole and made a little hole in one of the tree trunks we use for things around here. Then we put the chairs in place and swept the hut a little. That was when I heard about the hostages who were released from the church in Cali. Good for them! The hut looked really nice once we were all through, but now I'm feeling low again. I took a Robaxifen, a muscle relaxer, and then I took another bath. When I was done I put on my jeans and my pink shirt. I feel more optimistic now, and I hope that we will be the next group to be released. Oh, God, I wish this more than anything in the world!

Today I drank *chicha* all day, and my father and I swiped some more *panela* to make more. We heard that Víctor G. Ricardo and Pablo Beltrán had their meeting in Cuba. Apparently they hope to move ahead with the negotiations so that the ELN can finally hold that National Convention they're calling for before the end of the year. Once the government and the ELN sign the agreement to start the Convention, we will get released. What still doesn't remain clear to me, however, is whether this kidnapping was intended for political or financial gain. I have asked these people over and over again but they've never given me a straight answer. On the news they said that the ELN was demanding a ransom somewhere between four and five million dollars, but it wasn't clear whether they were demanding it of Avianca or the hostages' families. I don't know, I don't know . . . God, this is the most frustrating thing in the world—we never have any idea of what's going on here! One of the men released from the Cali church yesterday said something that I totally agree with: that this entire episode was a round-trip ticket to hell—but with an open return, and that open return is the reason why this experience is such agony, the kind that kills you little by little.

Suddenly I remember that right around this time last year, Nandor was showing me how to spot the constellation Scorpio in the night sky. Such a sweetheart, my brother. I miss him and everyone else so much.

Daniel Hoffmann said something about a helicopter, about how he thought it would never come, but it finally did. And he said the same thing would happen for us.

Wednesday, November 3, 1999

Day 206. 59 days until the year 2000.

Today was a little different from all the rest. It started pouring rain at 2 P.M.: as soon as the rain started coming down I raced out of the hut with soap and shampoo and took a shower in the downpour. It was fantastic. My father asked me if I would lend him $40 because he wanted to buy a very good 12-band radio off the Nice Old Man. When I went over to the kitchen shack, I spotted a humongous sloth, about six palms long, with gray-and-brown stripes, kind of like the stripes of a tiger. I called everyone over to see her, because she was climbing up a tree.

Over the radio today, my mother said that she is keeping the house neat and clean so that it will be picture-perfect when I get home. She also said that she is going crazy because of all this, but that I should try to keep my cool—she said I should read, draw, things like that. Apparently one of the hostages in Cali learned to sculpt while she was in captivity, and my mom said that I should try to take all of this as a kind of lesson about learning how to love and appreciate life, especially since I was not so high on life before the kidnapping. My father just asked me to listen to the song that my mother always loved, "You Light Up My Life."

Thursday, November 4, 1999

Day 207. 58 days until the year 2000.

Yesterday I dreamt that I was flying on a 767 plane, and that I was happy. My mother, my father, Nandor, Carol, Dani, and Diego came to see me off. I couldn't stop thinking about how incredible it was that after so much time I was finally able to do what I wanted.

Today, Fernando made little cakes for everyone, and lunch was basically a huge plate of rice pudding. Afterward, I sat down to read and noted down all the passages that struck a chord with me. There isn't much else to do around here. It's a cold, gray day today.

Darling, I think of you every minute, every day here. I can feel every one of your movements inside of me, whenever I feel sad and lonely. I know your thoughts are with me, and they help me so much. And in that sense, as I see how my love grows stronger and stronger, I am able to feel that my time here has not been wasted, not entirely at least.

Friday, November 5, 1999

Day 208. 57 days until the year 2000.

Today, as I walked through the campsite, my breath felt unusually heavy, labored. My heart beat fast; I could feel it pounding in my head. For a little while, all I could hear were the sounds of my body, and it felt as though my thoughts were taking place somewhere outside of me, somewhere outside of here. I sat down on a tree trunk that fell to the ground, possibly from old age, and I just stared up at the blue, blue sky. My body felt amazingly light, almost as if I could fly away if I wanted to. . . . I rocked forward and backward, and wrapped my arms around my legs, tucked under the trunk, and I felt myself transported to a place where I could see myself stretched out on the sand, looking up at the stars. As I lingered there, immersed in thought, I traveled to the stars, to new universes and imaginary worlds filled with fantastic dreams. I felt complete and total tranquillity here because, in some way, these places were like home to me; in some way I belong here.

One day I will return to the world of dreams, where every wish is fulfilled, where pain is fleeting, and the imagination lives in black, white, blues, violets, yellows, and every other color, because they are all tiny little worlds inside of this one. There are no beliefs there, except for the ones that each individual ascribes or aspires to. Everything is pure harmony, nobody depends on anyone else, and the desire to love is transformed into a desire to simply love ourselves, nothing more. And that feeling, in the end, is far nobler than that of loving others. Solitude is the most exalted state of happiness, and the company of others is simply a phase in which we listen, nothing more. Nobody feels a great need for company because the presence of other people leaves precious little time for the imagination to blossom, and imagination is what gives life to these beings. Oh, magical world, you live on inside of me even though you may not exist out there....

Last night I dreamt that they were going to kick me out of school because I was behaving badly. Then I dreamt that I asked a lady selling fruit from a fruit stand on the street to give me something for free because I didn't have any money, and she gave me an orange. Then I saw another woman selling even more fruit, and I went over to her and asked her to give me something, and she gave me an apple that looked like a peach, and then my father turned up and said: "Take all the fruit you want. Don't worry: it's all yours."

It was a very indulgent little dream, because all my senses were heightened: I could actually taste the fruit and I could see their vivid, brilliant colors.... The only problem, of course, was that I had to wake up and realize that none of this was real.

Today is Christian Gómez's birthday, his twentieth, I think. From far away and with my thoughts, I wish him a very happy birthday.

In Francisco's hut they just found a red-white-and-black coral snake, some 30 inches long, slithering around his boots—not inside the boots, just moving around them. They chopped the thing in half, and the snake's tail end kept on moving. They also killed a 6^1/$_2$-foot-long lancehead snake that's reddish and black with a bright orange underbelly. That one, they said, had come down from a big tree that's next to the dining shack. They say the lancehead is a highly venomous snake.

Saturday, November 6, 1999

Day 209. 56 days to go before the year 2000.

Last night I cried for a long, long time thinking about my mother. It's been about three days since I took a bath. The last time was when I took a shower in the rain.

I dreamt that my mother went to Atlanta, and that she had a photo album with her, and then I looked in the newspaper and saw the same photos as the ones in the album, of the Avianca plane, the Fokker 50, and an article about us. Then I saw myself combing my hair. I asked my mother if she would do my hair in a big bun and tie it up in a light blue ribbon, but she said no. I pleaded with her, and cried out loud, and then I woke up.

The rooster here crows at the craziest times of day. Today he got going at 3 in the morning.

Last night, on one of the radio shows, we heard that they freed three more people from the Cali church.

It's so nice to see people, even if they are guerrillas. They're all very good friends, I have to say—they seem to really care about each other, and I never detect the slightest bit of jealousy between them: they're like little kids, making jokes, singing. Plus, they do treat us quite well, considering, and they are equally fair with one another. And as for the commander, or head guerrilla, nobody treats him with any kind of special deference or courtesy. He is just another guerrilla, another *compa*, as they call each other. And I like that—they really seem to treat one another with respect, like brothers in the truest sense of the term.

Yesterday and today there were moments when I swear I could feel the scent of Diego Plata. I know it sounds unbelievable, but it's true, I can smell him. This, of course, gets me thinking about him, and I start to remember the days when we were together. It makes me sad to think back on all that, and then to realize that I have no way of telling him what I'm thinking about, and how much I wish I could talk to him, see him, hug him. I wish I could tell him how much I love him and miss him. . . .

Sunday, November 7, 1999

Day 210. 55 days until the year 2000.

Last night I got some messages on the radio but I didn't hear them. They told me that my mom talked about how she was the kind of person who was used to solving problems, but that this one was totally out of her hands. Judith also sent a message, saying that she had talked to her half sister, who told her mother in Hungary about us, but that she already knew the story of the plane hijacking because they had actually covered our story on the news in Hungary, on account of the fact that my dad and I are of Hungarian descent. Then the half sister spoke for a bit from Great Britain, although she spoke in English because she doesn't speak any Spanish. She said that she was very concerned about us, that she hoped the situation would be resolved soon, for the good of everyone involved, and that she loves us and hopes we all remain calm.

What do you do when life no longer has any meaning at all? How much can you do to kill time? I feel frightened. I get up, I take a walk, I sit down, I lie down, I smoke a cigarette, I take another walk. . . . There is nothing to do. It's always the same.

Monday, November 8, 1999

Day 211. 54 days until the year 2000. Week 30.

There was a tremor today that registered 6.5 on the Richter scale. The epicenter was in Piedecuesta, Santander, but nothing happened because it occurred at a depth of 150 kilometers. Two tenths more, though, and it would have done as much damage as the earthquake in Armenia. The earth trembled and shook. I was scared about what might have happened to my family, but my father calmed me down. He also lent me his watch today; mine just ran out of batteries. Today I am celebrating four months with eyelashes.

Tuesday, November 9, 1999

Today I started reading the book *16 cuentos latinoamericanos* [16 Latin American Short Stories]. I've made it to page 101, but I don't think I can take much more of it, that's how boring it is. It's 221 pages in all. I don't know what to do. I looked at el Negro and said, "Negro, I'm so bored."

He started to laugh and said, "Come on, Leszli, what can I do about it?"

And I said, "I don't know. All I can say is that I get more and more bored every day, looking at your faces all the time." This only made him laugh harder.

My waist measures 72 centimeters [28 inches]. I've gone up 10 centimeters since I've been here. I find this mortifying, and now I feel more depressed than ever.

The day is gray, and everyone's playing. Fernando is sewing flags for the ELN, and I am helping them make some patches. . . . Something is definitely not right around here. Right now my despair is at about 100 percent, as they say around here. I don't want to take a bath today. Yesterday I took a shower in the rain, like the time before.

It is 5:29 and 34 seconds in this horrid afternoon. I feel awful, and on top of it all the fingers of my right hand are all yellow. I feel horrible, sad, ugly, impotent, bitter, and I'm fat again! I am dying to take some Fenisec, but no matter how much I beg them for it they won't bring me any.

Juan Carlos sent me regards on La Mega. My mom spoke today on UIS saying that she saw an interview on TV last night with Pablo Beltrán, who told his son to stay in school and not go off into the mountains. Well, my mom said, she also wants her 18-year-old daughter out of the jungle and back in school.

Then my cousin David spoke. Among other things he had this to say to my father: "Uncle Laszlo, I hope you've taught the entire guerrillas how to make wine. I love you very much."

At about 10 P.M. I went to eat dinner. My father got there first and brought me rice. So sweet of him. We sat around talking for a while.

Wednesday, November 10, 1999

213 days. 52 days to go until the year 2000.

There's a problem in the kitchen these days with the supply lady's daughter, who's about 12. The minute I looked at her she told me to shut up. That's the way she is—to tell the truth I had to laugh at that, she is so incredibly rude. She just wanted to humiliate me a little, but I ignored her and issued my complaint to her mother.

On the news they're talking a lot about the ELN and the government; they say that things are progressing nicely.

Today I found out that Uriel lives in the same building as Gladys Guerra. He was hanging out in the Kálli tent until around nine, talking with my father and Miss Leszli. Lucía spoke on UIS today, to tell us that the pre-convention will be held in early December. I'll believe it when I see it!

The stars are all out tonight, lovely as can be. I can see Altair.

Thursday, November 11, 1999

Day 214. 51 days until the year 2000.

On the news today they reported on a car bomb that was planted in Bogotá, with some 70 or 80 kilos of explosives. They also reported that yesterday in Bogotá, Víctor G. Ricardo met with the families of the hostages from the Avianca flight and the churches in Cali and Barranquilla, but nobody knows what is happening. They said that the families seemed very optimistic as they left the meeting, but that Víctor G. did not offer any statements to the press because he had to be taken to the clinic. Apparently he wasn't feeling well.

I could just explode right now. How revolting! On the news just now I saw something that made me feel so terrible: they killed a little boy who was a year and eight months old. In the photograph he looked just like Danielito. Some despicable creature did it, apparently because he wanted to kill the little boy's puppy, and by mistake he shot the kid. He's 19 years old, and it all happened in a very poor neighborhood in Cali. I wanted to cry right then and there when I heard it, and now I feel so sad, so overcome with rage and pain. Oh, all I want right now is to see little Danielito and hug him, to squeeze that darling little baby. He's such an adorable little doll!

Today my mother spoke on UIS, and said she hopes to see me looking as pretty as I was when I left, that she feels calm and happy because she is sure that everyone is being especially nice to me since I'm the only woman in the group, not to mention the youngest. Oh, how wrong you are, dear Mother. . . . If my father weren't around, these lowlifes would have ripped me to shreds by now. They've really ganged up on me; they always do whatever they can to push me out of the way. Like, if I come by when they're in the middle of a conversation they all shut up immediately, and sometimes they even make fun of me. And since I don't let them get away with it, they say I'm rude and disgusting, and then they tell my dad I'm a spoiled brat. My father, though, always sees through it, and he always sticks up for me. What a bunch of miserable losers I got stuck with here in the jungle. And of course, they spend all their time giggling to themselves and sticking up for each other. . . . In other words, they treat each other like kings. Whenever I start to feel really bad—which happens often—I leave the hut to go for a walk, and sometimes they see me crying but they just walk right on by. I actually think I've seen them laugh when I get like that—and I'm talking about 30-, 35-year-old adults. Oh, Mommy, I don't even want to think of how many times you've been on the radio when I wasn't around, and they just kept their mouths shut and didn't bother telling me. Whenever I find out that you were on the radio and I missed you, I ask them what you said and they always say the same thing: "Nah, nothing. The same as usual."

Of course, whenever someone else sends messages over the radio for one of the other hostages, they turn up the volume, or Fernando copies the messages and sends them on to whoever the messages were for. Can you believe people like that actually exist?

Friday, November 12, 1999

Day 215. 50 days to go until the year 2000. I have now been a hostage of the ELN in the mountains of Colombia for seven months.

Last night I dreamt that these people were planting minefields. At some point they began to sing the Colombian national anthem and suddenly they realized that more and more people were singing along with them. They started firing their guns and they hit me and another girl. I told her to play dead, and we threw ourselves onto the ground as the mines began to explode and shots came at us from every direction. Somehow, in the middle of all this, I managed to keep my cool and told the girl to stay calm. Then a guerrilla brought us to the top of a house that was either being torn down or in the first phases of construction, and after that the battle died down a bit, and so I said to her, "Okay, let's go now," and we began to jump from rooftop to rooftop, over these houses that were kind of like the Quintas del Cacique houses in Bucaramanga. As we were jumping from one house to the other, from far away I saw a ton of rats crawling all over another house. It was very early in the morning.

Today my father and I went down to take our baths, and without meaning to I caught a glimpse of Francisco without his clothes on.

How revolting! He is white as a sheet, and his butt is really something else—I mean really, really white. Everyone realized that I'd seen him, and Juan asked me what I thought of Francisco's white butt. I just told him that I hadn't meant to see it, that I'd gone down to the river without realizing. And that's the truth.

After that we sat down to eat. I agreed to eat meat today, but then I vomited it all up. Then we watched the movie *In the Name of the Father*, a very lovely movie. It takes place in London and Ireland, and it's a true story.

When I was watching television, I had to go to the bathroom, and when I went out I practically stepped on a coral snake that was slithering around underfoot. What a scare! The others saw what was happening, and they killed it right away. It was red, white, and black.

Today at noon, I saw my mother on the RCN news. She looked so pretty—she was wearing a white sleeveless shirt, and her hair has gotten pretty long by now. Everyone told me how pretty she looked, and that made me feel happy, proud.

They told us that they're breaking through the security rings, that we're going to move to a new campsite, but I don't believe them. They said that the release order is coming through, that there's a 90% chance I'll be home by December 11. I have a hunch, but I don't know....

Yesterday I finished the book *16 cuentos latinoamericanos*. The Cortázar story called *"La señorita Cora"* was pretty good, but the best of the bunch was *"Un día de estos"* ["One of These Days"] by Gabriel García Márquez, though I think I read that one before, maybe it was in the book *Los funerales de la Mamá Grande* [Big Mama's Funeral]. *"Un regalo para Julia"* by Masiani was pretty good, too.... They're all pretty good, really, except for one that was called *"El Centerfiel."*

Sunday, November 14, 1999

Day 217. 48 days to go until the year 2000.

Today I woke up happy, in a good mood, but then when the head guerrilla came by, I asked him how things were going, and he said, "Oh, you know, so-so."

Hearing him say that was like having a bucket of cold water

thrown at me. He didn't say anything else after that. Every time he leaves, I always start to feel better, because I start counting the days until he returns, thinking that he'll come back with the news all of us want to hear: that we're going to be released. But with an answer like that, all my hopes go down the drain. It's like being dragged in and out of hell—the only difference being that when he returns, that hell feels realer than ever.

Oh, if only he knew that every time he leaves, I recite the Our Father . . . I feel so sad for myself. I can see how he avoids us whenever he comes back: he can barely look us in the eye, and all of us just stand there, waiting for him to say something—anything at all. Good or bad, we don't care—we just want to hear something that will break this monotony, this uncertainty of being in the middle of nowhere and knowing nothing at all about our situation.

Finally I asked him if I could talk to him tomorrow, or whenever he has some free time. Of course, it seems rather ridiculous that he wouldn't have time to see me here, since all we've got around here is time—that's why we're so bored. He said that we could talk tomorrow in the morning but still, I felt sad. And now I have to mentally prepare myself to hear the same old story all over again: that he doesn't know, that I should just sit tight, that he went away to take care of other business that doesn't have anything to do with us, et cetera.

I was just watching the beauty pageant in Cartagena, but the gasoline in the generator ran out so it got cut off.

Monday holiday, November 15, 1999

Day 218, 47 days until the year 2000. 31 weeks.

Last night I dreamt that I'd been at home for a long time, and that I'd seen everyone except Diego. I wanted to see him but he didn't call me. One night, in the middle of the same dream, I suddenly found myself in Altos de Cañaveral, a residential complex back home between the gymnasium and the kiddie carousel, and he turned up. We looked at each other for a little while, and then he came over to me and we hugged. He was wearing a black leather jacket and he looked really good. Then we jumped into a pool, with our clothing on and everything, and we moved around in slow motion. We kissed. Then I got out of the pool, and while I was washing off in the pool shower— I was now wearing a red bikini—I noticed a black line, or stain, running down the length of the pool, right down from the spot where Diego was, from his leather jacket.

Today I spoke with the head guerrilla and then with Laureano. Good news for me: it sounds like they're going to release more people, and rumor has it that I'm one of them. Nobody knows who else will get out, and I hope my father's on the list.

Tuesday, November 16, 1999

Day 219. 46 days until the year 2000.

We've run out of cigarettes, and my father is beside himself. It rained all day yesterday, and all night, too. Diego gave me a cigarette and I gave it to my father.

My mother spoke on the radio today and said that she's very happy because she heard news about me. She also said she hopes that everyone has told me all the things she said about me, and that she never stops thinking about me, and that back at home, she looks back on everything as if it were a kind of movie: she sees me, as a child, playing all my little games, and then she remembers how amazing and intelligent I was and still am; and then she remembers the song that my father always sang for me, the one about the little boat. Now, she said, that song sounds like a strange omen, a premonition of what would happen to us, but on a plane instead of a little boat in the ocean. She said that we're not going to have to wait much longer, because I'll be home in no time. She also said that Carol is ready to travel to Bucaramanga as soon as she hears that I'm coming, and that Nandor is working hard at the hospital.

I ran out, thrilled, to tell all of this to the head guerrilla. He congratulated me and shook my hand. This has to be confirmation that everything is moving ahead and that my freedom isn't so far off now. I feel that I can finally take it in, breathe it in . . . freedom. But then the feeling sort of clouds over and I start to feel sad when I think about my father, and that they may not let him go. But I beg God, my grandmother, my grandfathers, Carlos G., and Gonzalo Rodríguez to help realize the full promise and dream of going home not alone but with my father.

I am happy, so happy. God, thank you, thank you so much, thank you so very much for this. The ELN robbed me of my freedom, and the ELN taught me the real meaning of that word. This experience has taught me to embrace life, and it has made me grow up. It has filled me with sadness at times, but it will also bring me the greatest happiness I have ever known—a happiness that I could never have understood had I not gone through this pain and sorrow. Only now am I truly able to revel in this kind of joy.

Wednesday, November 17, 1999

Day 220. 45 days until the year 2000.

Last night I talked to Laureano until 11 P.M. about the news and my mother's message. He is very excited by the signs that the head guerrilla seems to be giving us.

Today two air force planes just sped by overhead, very fast and very low in the sky. I haven't seen anything like that ever in real life, just in the movies.

Then, out of nowhere, my father turned to me and said: "Hey, what if the person who called your mother was just some joker?" Then he said I ought to have a chat with the head guerrilla, and ask him to check in with the COCE people to see if it's true or not— because if it isn't, we're going to have to warn my mother.

Today, el Negro said to me: "How are you?"

"Bored. Free me already, will you?" As always, joking around.

Then he said: "Just wait and see, Leszli. There's going to be news on Friday."

"Negro, don't talk trash with me. What are you going to tell me now? Last week it was the same, and it turned out that the big news was the movie *In the Name of the Father*. Let's see, I bet now you'll just put on some other movie we've all already seen: *Antz,* or else *La estrategia del caracol* [The Snail's Strategy]. The truth is, man, you guys don't know how to keep your word, not one rotten letter of one single word you say."

He laughed at that one, and then said, "Just wait and you'll see. On Friday there'll be news." With that, he walked off, laughing to himself. "The things you come up with, Leszli ...!"

Thursday, November 18, 1999

Day 221. 44 days until the year 2000.

Today in Congress they debated over whether or not to swap soldiers for guerrillas.

Earlier today I sat with the head guerrilla and we talked about several things: we started off discussing the typical dishes of the various different regions of Colombia, then we went on to more sober subjects like my life, my state of mind, my family. I told her that my father is still not doing very well—the poor guy can barely get himself out of bed in the morning, his whole body aches. Apparently it has something to do with his kidneys, and he keeps telling me not to worry, that it will pass, but I can't help worrying, and I told all this to the head guerrilla. We'll see if anything comes of it. I also asked her when we would get news from the head in Magdalena Medio. She said that according to her calculations, we would hear sometime around the twenty-fifth or twenty-sixth of this month.

On La Mega I heard a song that goes like this:

Tal vez mañana brille el sol
Y su calor permita
Que a mi existir vuelva la illusion.

[Perhaps tomorrow the sun will shine
and its warmth will allow
illusion to grace my existence again.]

I broke down in tears again today. I am so, so scared. What will happen if my father isn't released with me? I am really stuck between a rock and a hard place now. Something tells me that if they decide to release me alone, I'll stay with him, because I belong with him. But something else inside of me, a much weaker part of me, tells me that I can do more for him from the outside.

I am also petrified that all of this is going to go wrong. If things keep going well, I do believe that sometime in the beginning of December we'll be home. And if God is with me, that means both me and my father.

Oh, Mommy, I love you so much. I want to be with you now, now.

Friday, November 19, 1999

Day 222. 43 days to go before the year 2000.

Today is the six-year anniversary of my grandfather Alfonso's death. It is also the birthday of Mauricio, my brother-in-law. Today my father and I went down to bathe. No news on the TV or radio. The head guerrilla left today, though I have no idea where to or what for.

Just as I was sewing up my black pants, el Negro came over to me and said, "Well, well, get a load of Wonder Woman." Very funny. I did laugh, though.

Lately, the guerrillas have been singing their anthem every morning.

Saturday, November 20, 1999

Day 223. 42 days to go before the year 2000.

Right now I am listening to an advertisement that says, "Come home this Christmas, come home this Christmas." God, what torture! If it were up to me, I'd already be at home! Then I start thinking about the holidays, but I just can't imagine my mother decorating the Christmas tree without me. What kind of Christmas is she going to have this year without me? God, please help me get home before then.

Today, lunch consisted of yucca soup and rice, and oats and *panela*. I spent all afternoon drawing layouts for apartments, and of this campsite. I asked el Negro for some black ink for my pen. In the morning, Juan Carlos G. said goodbye to me because he was signing off for good; he's leaving his job at La Mega. So now I'll never hear him again. How sad!

Sunday, November 21, 1999

Day 224. 41 days until 2000.

I went to bed early last night. Juan told me that my mother said pretty much the same things she always does over the radio. I don't understand why these people can't just tell me what she really said.

Today the authorities captured three people they plan to prosecute for presumably having helped hijack our plane.

Things are going well. My father tells me he's feeling low because we never do any kind of exercise or anything, and it makes him feel that we are wasting away. He also told me a lot about the 747 plane— flying a 747, he said, was quite an event, and the 767, which is the 747's successor, is also an incredible aircraft, with an amazing cockpit. These are the things that make him very happy.

After that I started staring at the ants, and my father told me that when he was a boy, he had a terrarium he filled with a bunch of dirt and made caves for the ants, because he found them so intelligent, so hardworking. I sat there looking at those ants for a long time with him, because both of us find them terribly beautiful, and both of us definitely feel that ants have a lot to teach us humans—they are truly an example for all humanity. One little ant on its own can't do a thing, but as soon as they band together, they are pure power.

Last night I heard the singsong of the rufous mourner bird, also called the *pájaro arriero*. It only comes out at night, and no matter how hard I try, I have never been able to catch a glimpse of it. Its song is exactly like the voice of a human being crying out the words "*mula, mula!*" It is very hard to listen to for long. The first time I heard it I thought that someone had brought mules to the campsite, and I ran outside to see who had come, but the guard told me that it was only that rufous mourner, not a person but a bird. At first, I didn't believe him, and so I waited around to see if it was true, and it was.

I didn't bother taking a bath yesterday, and I don't think I'll take one today, either. I'm afraid that Abel, one of the head guerrillas who was with us the first few weeks, will send news but that it won't be anything important. What a letdown that would be.

This afternoon, at around 5 P.M., I played chess with el Calvo, the bald guerrilla, and I won. The moon is full tonight. My father explained to me how every 27 days and 7 hours there is a new full moon, which means that on December 19, we'll have another full moon. I think the moon has made me very hyper; that always happens.

Today, my father, Uriel, and I sat around talking about my grandmother Gisella, about how she came to Colombia, and about her Tartar roots. I love talking with my father; I always have, in fact. I love talking with my mother, too—I know they have a lot to teach me, and both of them have always struck me as very intelligent. They are truly unique people, and I love them.

Today we ate rice and beans. I am happy, content: I feel I've got good energy today. It's 9 P.M. and everyone is in bed already except for me. I am wide awake.

I've got these strange cysts on my armpits. Right now I am listening to Amor Stereo and chewing on a pen cap. I'm taking some medicine for my staph infection. A couple of days ago I made some little protectors out of toilet paper and tape, to cover my fingers because they are turning completely yellow from all the cigarettes I smoke. A pretty handy little invention, I have to say. Just as I was coming back from my bath I saw a tiny little dandelion, which did not please me at all—they give me a bad vibe, dandelions. Every time I spot a dandelion I find out that someone I know has died, so seeing one did not make me too happy. I prayed that nothing would happen to any of my family or friends. I am going to turn off the flashlight now because the batteries are starting to wear out and the light is getting yellower and yellower by the minute, it's fading fast.

Day 225. 40 days until the year 2000. Week 32 in captivity.

Today the guerrillas swept up the entire campsite. I got my period. Lunch was rice and peas. Afterward, I washed my father's plate plus my own. My stomach started to get tied up in knots but the Nice Old Man made me an herbal infusion and I felt better. Then I played chess with my father. It's Juan González's birthday.

Last night I dreamt that my father died. Today I went to see the head guerrilla.

"I'm scared. Very scared that I am going to have to celebrate my birthday here. Do you think I'll still be here then?"

"No, I'm sure of it," he replied.

That made me happy.

Tuesday, November 23, 1999

Day 226. 39 days left until 2000.

Today when I woke up everything was beautiful, but my father was in a rotten mood, and I don't know why. I went over to the playing field to lie in the sun for a little while, because I am so, so white, and then I took a bath. They gave us each a banana. My mom and Nandor spoke over the radio. Good news: it seems that we will be leaving this place. Then I watched the movie *La estrategia del caracol.* Very good.

Wednesday, November 24, 1999

Day 227. 38 days to go until the year 2000.

I spent practically the entire day today getting my things together for when I have to start walking. Then I played two games of chess with Laureano.

My mom and Nandor spoke over the radio. My mother said that she won't put up a Christmas tree until I come home, and that my birthday will be totally amazing. I know she's right. Then she told me that my cousin David went to live in the United States—I was kind of shocked by that but still, I'm happy for him and I just know that everything will go really well for him because he's such a smart, sharp kid. I just hope to God that he doesn't get depressed the way I did when I left.

Day 229. 37 days until 2000.

My father just went down to wash what little he needed to clean, and I have taken a look around to see what I should hang on to and what I should toss. Today or tomorrow, we should hear from the head guerrilla. The guerrillas are really mobilizing—washing things, and I mean everything, getting everything together. I mean, we would have to be complete idiots not to realize that they're packing up the camp.

There's one guerrilla who I think is especially nice, and I gave him a Star of David as a little gift. It was something my mom gave me right before I left, and I hung it on a red chain.

All of us are holding our breath, waiting for the news, because the head guerrilla came back and said he wanted to talk to us. I already knew, more or less, but that didn't stop my heart from racing so fast that I thought it might explode from all the emotions running through my body. Everyone else feels the same way, I know it. It's 4:33 P.M. right now and we're supposed to meet at 6:00. I just took a long walk around the campsite, to make sure I don't ever forget it. I already feel a little bit nostalgic, actually, because after five months here, looking at the same trees, the same paths . . . you get used to things. And the people, the guerrillas—in an odd way they are like our family. Once we leave here, we'll probably never see them again. A strange feeling has come over me; all of a sudden my heart is beating faster than ever before. Fer and Diego are sitting in front of me right now, in the chairs my father built. They're sewing ELN bracelets to kill time. They seem calm and collected but I know they must be feeling what I'm feeling, or worse. Uriel is listening to music and the rest of the group is in Francisco and Laureano's tent, either playing chess or sitting around watching people play.

I turn to Juan and say, "Juan, how about a few words for my diary?"

"Oh, Leszli, come on!" is all he says. Then my father yells out, "Knock it off already!"

The afternoon is gray and cold. I am dressed in boots, burgundy shorts, and the pink shirt that I fixed up. Diego is burning some leaves; in his pocket my father has a little parakeet that, frankly, he treats a lot better than he treats me. My father says to Laureano, "All right, Laureano, go take a bath and get dressed up, you want to look nice tonight."

The guerrillas just left their meeting and are walking around, in a kind of business-as-usual attitude.

I'll be back. I'm off to the meeting now.

Yes, it is a confirmed fact. We're leaving. The head guerrilla said so: we're all leaving. On the twenty-eighth, they'll be leaving us with another group and from there we'll keep on walking. We leave tomorrow. I am so, so happy!

In her messages over the radio, my mom tells me how overjoyed she is, and that she couldn't stand it anymore and put up a little Christmas tree today. She couldn't wait—that's my mom, very impulsive.

Friday, November 26, 1999

Day 229. 36 days until the year 2000.

Today we traveled for four hours, me on the back of the best mule in the bunch. We walked along a huge river, and now we're in a little log cabin where my dad and I are setting up our beds. I'm going to eat tuna and rice tonight. Today I took a dip in a big rushing river, holding onto a tree trunk because I was petrified of falling in and getting carried off in the rapids. I am so happy. Saying goodbye to the guerrillas was really sad.

It's so incredible, after so much time living under these dense treetops, to see the sky above me so completely clear. Just now I left the little cabin and when I looked up I could see the entire sky. Then I stretched my arms and walked barefoot on the grass. The stars at night are so pretty here—there is no comparison between this and the tiny little sliver of sky we had before, back at the campsite. Here you can see everything, absolutely everything. It's breathtaking. My father just showed me the Northern Cross, a tiny glow on the side of the sky where the sun rises.

El Negro showed us how to boil water in a bag today. It sounds totally impossible but I tried it and it actually works.

Everyone is asleep now, or at least they look like they're asleep. Tomorrow, we were told, we will be transferred to the other front. Things are moving along, it seems. That is a very good thing. I am very, very happy.

Saturday, November 27, 1999

Day 230. 35 days until the year 2000.

As soon as we woke up we got back on the road: first we crossed the river by canoe and then we walked, as always, through the mountain. We walked from 8:20 A.M. until 3:30 P.M. My mule fell, and I almost got completely lost, because I started to lag far behind everyone else who was walking, and very far ahead of all the other people traveling by mule. The mule just stopped and broke into a run all of a sudden, and I had to run after her, which took about an hour. A major drag. After that, back on the path, they made us oatmeal and distributed crackers all around, and we sat by the prettiest river; it was straight out of a movie.

At 3:30 we reached a little house next to two immense and very lovely rivers that joined together at a certain point. There, we took our baths and then my dad and I grabbed the best bed and the best mattress of the lot. There was a little kitten, white with black spots, that I called "Misiá Mirringa," after the comic strip about the cat, since she didn't appear to have any other name.

Finally we connected with the guerrillas from the front that is planning to release us. There are only five of them.

Sunday, November 28, 1999

Day 231, and 34 days to go before the year 2000.

I got up today at 4:45 A.M. I am so happy but so, so tired. My legs and back are completely sore, I have a huge black-and-blue mark on my left knee, and my body is literally covered with bug bites, so many that I look like I have the measles. Today two more guerrillas turned up; we met them before, on our third day in captivity. They're pretty nice, but one of them is really quiet. Then we said goodbye to the guerrillas from the other front. My father sent the supply lady 30,000 pesos to buy her daughter a little Christmas gift, and then the group gave 10,000 pesos to the *guerrilleros* El Negro and Danielito. They were really happy about that.

Last night I dreamt that I was talking on the phone with my mother and I told her to relax, that I was coming home soon. Then she asked me, "Well, how do I know you're really Leszli?" and I told her the date, day, and hour of my birthday. It's Nandor's birthday today. My father and I spent all day today lounging around in the river, and it was delicious! I'm getting completely burnt by the sun, but who cares?

Monday, November 29, 1999

33 weeks. 232 days.

We are still here. Last night the owner of this place came by and mistook us for the urban guerrilla. Then I ate a very tasty kind of nut that grows on the trees here; it's called *arbopán*. The leaves on these trees are like giant fans. I am getting redder and redder from being in the sun so much.

The new mules still haven't arrived— that's the one thing we're still waiting for.

There are only seven guerrillas looking after us here, and we've got no radio or TV right now. All the local farmers can see us and watch what we're doing, which worries us a little. Strangely enough, we kind of feel that the ELN has abandoned us, because before we each had something like thirty guerrillas standing guard over us. One guerrilla told me that he heard about my little head-shaving episode. According to him, I have changed for the better: he said that I seem like a better person, plus I'm a lot thinner.

The guerrillas here treat us very well; they're really friendly and nice. Yesterday they went to a little store to buy food and cigarettes, and they bought me sanitary napkins. I hadn't even asked them for any and I actually don't need them right now, but still it was awfully thoughtful of them.

Today I took a bath with the soap that smells like Diego, and I thought of him—although he is always lurking in my memory somewhere.

Tuesday, November 30, 1999

Day 233. 32 days until the year 2000.

We're still in the little hut by the river. It's really nice here. Yesterday a couple of guerrillas came by, ones we hadn't seen since the first few days of the kidnapping. The mules still have yet to materialize.

My relationship with Laureano has improved tremendously: we're much closer now, we tell each other everything, and we even take dips in the river together. It's so nice to have him here with us. He's the only person outside of my father who is worth spending time with around here.

Today we had only three guerrillas looking after us, and we feel completely helpless. I am redder than ever and covered in bug bites. The guerrillas are really something else. Yesterday I cleaned the kitchen and threw out the trash for them, which totally won them over. One of them has a 9 millimeter R-15 rifle, very impressive. He showed it to me, and I totally swooned over it. Another guerrilla showed me his Galil while he cleaned it. He even gave it a name—he calls it "the barber."

Wednesday, December 1, 1999

Day 234, 31 days until the year 2000.

My mother didn't talk on UIS yesterday. Today we all woke up at 4:30 in the morning, began walking, and didn't stop for about four hours. At some point we took a little break, near a little store, where we sat down and ate some crackers, and then after a little while, I wandered around to the back of the store, just to take a little look around, and I found a poor little duck with a rope around his foot, tied to a tree. I untied it and tried to get the duck to run away without anyone seeing what I was doing, but the stupid duck didn't get it, and just stayed where he was, and after a while someone saw him and grabbed him and tied him up again.

After that they ordered us to start walking again. Eventually we stopped to take another short break, and as I sat down, completely wiped out, I looked down on the jungle floor and spotted a very narrow little path that was literally choked with ants that seemed to be working very hard on something. For a little while I just sat there observing them: innocent, lovely, calm, and beautiful, trudging along with piles of leaves upon their backs, in very well organized lines, and I marveled at how tireless they seemed. Every so often they would stop but only for a few seconds, little lapses that they took advantage of perhaps to say hello, greet one another, offer a bit of advice, or maybe flirt a little, make plans, or figure out how to keep us from invading their territory. Who knows? Maybe they thought we were gods, because of our size, so colossal in comparison to them. Then, all of a sudden and without any warning, Uriel went over to where they were and began stomping on them, killing or wounding as many as he could get his feet on. The terrified ants scurried off in every direction, hiding, disappearing as fast as they could, leaving behind their miniscule piles of leaves on the slender path they had been walking on. Poor ants, I thought. What must they think of us? That we are gods? Yes . . . the evil kind, I suppose. How innocent of them, if that is what they thought of us.

I really hope that Uriel did that just to piss me off, because it would be so sad if he did it just because he felt like it. I'm not even going to bother asking him, though, because if I do, he'll only take it out even worse on those poor ants. Anyway, the look on my face said it all. My father was pretty disgusted by what he was doing, too; I could see it on his face. But we just kept our mouths shut. Instead of reproaching him for what he did, I just stared at him like I would stare at a piece of shit.

Today we finally arrived at a new campsite, but this one is really creepy—it's the pits, in fact, with a brown, rushing river filled with giant rocks on either side.

Thursday, December 2, 1999

Day 235. 30 days to go until the year 2000.

Today I didn't bother taking a bath and I only ate two meals: breakfast and dinner. Then I made a list of the things we need the most, and after that I listened to the messages on the radio. My mom spoke for a little bit: she said that Carol is coming home on the ninth, and that all my family and friends are concerned about me and hoping for news. I have to say, though, it does make me kind of sad to think that in the almost eight months I've been in captivity, I've only received two messages from friends: Jaime Jaramillo and María Helena, Diego's mother. I guess the rest of them could care less about me. It's sad to think that nobody outside of our family seems to care much about what's happening to us. I really believed that I mattered to Diego, but now I realize how wrong I was. If he hasn't contacted me during the hardest experience of my entire life, when I feel more alone than ever before, when I feel that the world has vanished and I have been left to fend for myself in a giant void, then he clearly doesn't give a damn about me. One message from him would make me so, so happy. . . .

It hurts, but I know the pain will eventually subside. I know that someone else will come into my life. Like the song that says, "Someone to take care of me, someone who will kill me and kill for me." Oh, I feel so lonely! And what hurts the most is that I don't have anyone, outside of my family.

So many lost hours, and so many days that I believed were so full of everything good . . . and then, when the moment of truth arrived, all of those people failed me. I sat around for a little while, thinking about all that I've been through and all I wanted to do was cry my eyes out, but I held back, because crying isn't much of a release for me anymore. I accept everything—I accept it with pain, but I accept it. I move forward through this reality and I feel a profound sadness when I look at myself like this, so filled with nothingness. Just as I have said to myself so many times before, I now tell myself that it's over, that it's over and done with, that this too shall pass. I am not even a shadow of what I used to be. But I am too tired to keep fighting against this emptiness. My life got left behind and so did I, in a way, little by little, until I reemerged as the person I am today.

Nothing is enough for me, and I feel that I am not enough, either . . . I just turned off my light. But nobody can see it.

Friday, December 3, 1999

Day 236. 29 days until the year 2000.

My head really hurts today and I feel as if my strength has been drained right out of me. When I stand up I suddenly can't distinguish any colors and I feel as if I might fall, and I have to sit down immediately. Plus, I have a terrible pain in my back, very little appetite, and a slight ache in my bones. I only barely managed to take a bath today—when I got into the river I just sat down on a rock and fell asleep. Then my nose started bleeding, so I decided to come back up and go to bed, but it took me about half an hour to get back up to the campsite, and my nose started bleeding again even harder. One of the guerrillas saw what was happening and gave me some toilet paper to stanch the blood, and another guerrilla, one of the women, said that my symptoms may be signs of malaria. My father gave me an Aralén pill, which is an antimalarial drug, and then I fell asleep. I woke up again at about 3:00, but I didn't feel any better. I left the hut and went over to one of the guerrillas, who said I looked pretty pale. I started to burn newspapers to warm my hands a little, but my father got mad at me for doing that, he said I was stupid to do that and that I should just listen to him. That made me furious, but I didn't bother saying anything. He said it in front of everyone, too, to make me feel worse, but everyone knows I never do what he tells me.

After that, I went back to the hut and started to cry, about everything: the nostalgia, the despair, the boredom, everything. Then, later on, I was sitting around reading and one of the guerrillas found a gray hair in my head. I asked him to yank it out for me, which he did, and now I've saved it.

While I was playing dominoes with some of the guerrillas earlier today, one of the land mines exploded but nobody seemed too bothered by it. After that we started playing chess and I lost both rounds.

Today the ants invaded my hut and I had to leave. The head guerrilla of this group tells me that I distance myself too much from the others; according to him, that's the reason all of this is so much harder on me. Right now I am listening to Amor Stereo and writing under the light of a candle. I got out of bed because I just couldn't stand being there any longer. Outside it's rainy and cold.

Saturday, December 4, 1999

Day 237. 28 days to go until the year 2000.

Right now I am listening to UIS, to a program called *Valores humanos* [Human Treasures], about contemporary ballet.

When I got up, I started crying. I couldn't help it. It's such a pretty time of year, and to think I'm still stuck here....

Then I went to take a bath; I've got the river pretty much figured out by now. One of the women guerrillas told me that one of the men liked me, but I told her that I didn't want any problems here, that I already have a boyfriend. So on top of being bored out of my skull, depressed, and desperate to get out of here, now I get to feel uncomfortable with some guerrilla who has the hots for me. I really am so screwed. And this guy isn't even good-looking. He's ugly, as a matter of fact.

While I was writing all this, another guerrilla came by and I told him how I was feeling. Then another one came by and we got to talking, but after a while I asked them to leave because I wanted to sleep, since I have to stay up so late to hear the radio messages from my family.

I just came down with diarrhea, and now am taking a Metronidazol. Today I woke up feeling a little better than yesterday, a little more hopeful, but I'm still pretty down in the dumps. I want to talk to my mother, tell her how I feel, how much I'm suffering, and how mad I am that I haven't been able to see her in all this time. Before, she was the person who could solve anything, but now? Now, when I am really suffering, she is totally powerless to get me out of here.

The last guerrilla I saw told me he believes in God. I like that. Maybe my flagging faith in Him is what's keeping me stuck here.

Today while my dad and I were eating I suddenly felt so sad, seeing us like this. I felt like the most miserable woman in the world. To eat like this, in this hut, in this weather, at this time of year . . . this must be what poverty is like, I thought. And that was when I finally understood why these guerrilla groups do what they do: to create the conditions so that people don't have to live with hunger, to eradicate the overwhelming poverty that exists in this country, such a wealthy country at that, and to get people to stop stealing from the people who this wealth truly belongs to. All of those things make me so angry, but at the same time I fail to understand why we're the ones here instead of that other class of people, the ones who do so much damage to the country. It's always the innocent who end up paying for the sinners. How infuriating.

It's 9:20 P.M. A little fatigue and a lot of thinking. Something weird came over me when I went over and sat down on the edge of the bed. Out loud I started to say, "Mommy, I miss you so much!" and I realized I was practically shouting. I don't know what to do anymore. I want to be with her already, this is so frustrating!

Sunday, December 5, 1999

Day 238. 27 days left before the year 2000.

Another boring day just like all the rest. The more days that go by, the more unbearable they become. Ten months ago yesterday, Diego left. That makes ten months without seeing him, almost a year! I feel so sad. . . .

On the news they say that the talks between the government and the ELN are going pretty well. Yesterday, or rather very early this morning, I heard my mother and Nandor on *Amanecer en América*. I still have diarrhea and there are no drugs in sight around here.

I cannot understand what is going on in this place: these people are convinced that they are never going to have to go through something like this, and that's why they don't move a finger. The day their luck runs out I am sure they will feel exactly the same rage that I feel right now, watching on as the government does nothing, and nobody else does, either. Indifference is like a cancer in Colombia.

Day 239. 26 days to go before the year 2000.

Yesterday I decided to bring my things into the hut where my father, Uriel, Laureano, Fer, and Diego sleep, because I felt really lonely where I was, and on top of it I just felt like there wasn't any space for me there, since they kept coming in and turning on the radio at 7 or 8 in the morning. Plus, I didn't like what this one guerrilla was doing, hunting through my things thinking they were his.

Yesterday my father flipped out on me and I have no idea why. He came running down to the river, totally hysterical, and started yelling at me, just like that. I told him to stop screaming at me, and then I went to bed early, without even taking a bath. Then I got very dizzy and my father was annoyed that I went off by myself, especially after I told him that one of the guerrillas had a crush on me.

It rained all night.

As I slept I dreamt that a woman was showing me all the stars. She would say, "See, this is Sagittarius," and I would see a little arrow. Then she would say, "See, this is the Minotaur, and this is Servus," and on and on. It was a collection of stars but they didn't have any real shape, just a very bright glow.

Yesterday breakfast consisted of watered-down hot chocolate and fried fish. I didn't eat or drink anything. The food is really tough stuff here. Today breakfast was *arepas* and *agua de panela,* a sweet drink made with sugar. My father says that he thinks I must have lost at least 4 kilos over the last few days. I mean, my cat eats better than we do around here. How ironic.

This place looks like a Red Cross tent in the middle of a war zone. Every bed has a mosquito net around it. Right now I am listening to *Lunes Latino* [Latin Mondays] on La Mega.

Fernando and Diego look more or less the way I feel: sad and dejected. Everyone else is pretty optimistic—they figure this campsite is just a temporary thing and that we'll be moving on soon enough.

That may be true, but I have my doubts about us getting released anytime soon. I think they're just going to take us to a better-equipped campsite than this, or one that's deeper in the jungle. The truth is, I just don't want to build up any false hopes that I'm going to spend Christmas at home with my family. If I remain negative, then the bad news won't hit me so hard, because I had a hard enough time getting over the disappointment the last time the head guerrilla said we were going to be released.

Around here there are newspapers everywhere: *El Universal*, *El Tiempo*, *Voz*, and *Vanguardia*, but they're all very old. One article in *El Tiempo* said, "The talks between the ELN and the government are at a standstill." That was back in August. I almost had a heart attack when I saw the date.

Today Laureano got up and told us that at 6 A.M. he heard on the news that the Convention would not take place until all the hostages—the ones in Cali, the ones from Bucaramanga, and the ones in Barranquilla—were freed. Here, even the slightest mention of any of this strikes fear in our hearts, because we're the ones—the only ones—who are most affected by these decisions.

Today I put on the jeans I've been keeping in my suitcase, just to see if I lost any weight. I just put them back. . . .

Diego says they told him we would be out of this campsite by December 10. I just saw a television ad that said, "Today everything has a special glow because Christmas is right around the corner." I just lit a candle.

Gladys has returned but hasn't said hello to me. I don't care if everyone else thinks I am a vulgar, rude jerk, but I refuse to say hello to her if she doesn't say hello first. I don't give out that stuff for free. No way.

Tonight I washed the dinner plates with toilet paper and rubbing alcohol. Then I took a bath in the little gorge going down to the river, and it was so, so nice—I was all alone, without any clothes on . . . it was just the best, plus, it isn't so far down.

It's raining very hard right now. My father is drinking the rainwater and passing it around to the rest of us.

240 days. 25 days until the year 2000.

Last night I dreamt about Diego: first we were in the doorway to his building and then we were getting into the car that we crashed about a year ago this December. I said to him, "Isn't it unbelievable? It's been a year now and the car is completely fine." That made him laugh and we got in. Then I had another dream about an old key that freed a bunch of toys that went up to the sky because they no longer believed in toys.

I still have diarrhea.

Uriel is always disagreeing with everyone. Francisco woke up with diarrhea and a fever, and Uriel insists it's an infection but all of us have had it by now, and now he wants us to give him Cipro. My father asked him to please hold out until we exhausted all our other resources, because around here those pills are like solid gold. We're going to wait and see if a saline solution makes him feel a little better.

Today I cried and cried until I swear I didn't have any tears left and my eyes were all red. Diego, Fernando, and Lau told me that I have been too brave and too strong for too much time to fall to pieces now, right as we reach our last few days in captivity. Then they told me to remember what my mom had said to me: "Leszli, don't cry, because crying will only bring you negative energy." When I heard that, I dried my tears, stood up, and took an acetaminophen tablet for my headache.

My father touched my head and told me that I have a fever. He gave me a Cipro at 1:45, because the truth is, ever since December 2 I have been really sick, with a lot of diarrhea. My father is really worried about me because I've lost between 4 and 5 kilos in the last seven days.

Francisco just got here and is now resting in Diego's bed. We talked for a little while, but then Uriel came around and I shut up. The food arrived, too, and I ate, but only a little. My father got into a argument with one of the guerrillas: he said that he was looking strange, and the guerrilla told him to not be so disrespectful. My father has been telling these people for the past four days that I am really sick, but when he asked for a pot to make me some tea or something, these guys only reluctantly gave it to him. When Francisco gets sick they bring him tea with coca leaves and guayaba juice, but for me, since I'm the only woman, they just ignore me, which makes my father really angry. I lit two candles tonight to celebrate Candle Day.

Wednesday, December 8, 1999

Day 241. 24 days until 2000.

I am waiting on pins and needles because the ELN told us we're leaving—they're not releasing us but sending us to another campsite further into the jungle. And if they are going to the trouble to prepare a decent campsite, it must mean that we're going to be stuck there for as much time or maybe even longer than we were in the first campsite, from June 20 to November 25. The mere thought of this sends a shiver down my spine.

Why does Pablo Beltrán bother claiming that the people with nothing have already been released, and those who have money are still being held, when I'm still here? I don't have any money, so why haven't they released me yet? To keep the others company, because they all love me so much? Because I can give my father moral support? I have no idea. All I know is that they are being very unfair with me. Why are they so thick? I already sent them a letter explaining the situation that my family and I are in. I don't know, I guess the only thing I can do now is just wait for the head guerrilla to come back so that I can talk to him—he's an educated, intelligent man and I know he will understand my situation and explain things to the COCE. Apparently, in my own words I wasn't convincing—either I didn't say it clearly enough, or else the ideas weren't very well defined.

Now I'm stuck hanging around in my underwear, because all my clothing is wet. Actually, to be exact, it's my dad's underwear. Short white briefs that look like little shorts, and a white undershirt.

Fer gave me a few etiquette lessons today. Then I went to take a bath and they gave me three tomatoes and some potatoes. The guerrilla, a little later on, apologized to my father, and my father apologized, too.

There is one hope I still cling to: why be negative? What do I get out of not believing? Archangel St. Michael, please bring me home already.

At 9 P.M. they're going to light a red candle for our release.

Thursday, December 9, 1999

Day 242. 23 days until the year 2000.

A small plane just flew overhead, very close to the ground.

Today they released one of the 8 people left in Barranquilla, a woman.

I'm still in my underwear, but I'm not going to bother taking a bath. Today I asked Diego to lend me the manual for Avianca flight attendants, and I read it from cover to cover. I have a headache now, and when I get up, I don't know where I am, I feel all woozy. I got back into bed but time still has a way of playing games with me, because it passes by as slowly as ever.

My father insulted me and yelled at me in front of everyone, calling me an idiot. He's the idiot, as far as I'm concerned. I can tell he feels very pleased with himself every time he lets off steam with me, but then I end up with no one to unload on. I always feel like everyone is making fun of me, that nobody gives a damn about what happens to me. God, they are all such a bunch of sexist jerks. I was really cursed the day I ended up here with them. I feel like killing myself, it's so humiliating! Mommy, I miss you so, so much!

Friday, December 10, 1999

Day 243. 22 days to go until the year 2000.

They finally freed the last three hostages in Cali. So now everyone's happy except for me. I vented with one of the guerrillas, telling him about all my woes. At least he seems to take an interest.

"So then, what are you doing here?" he asked, since I had had the chance to get out at the beginning.

Day 244. 21 days to go until 2000.

I hope that today is the worst birthday I will ever celebrate. I was born at a quarter to eleven, on a Thursday in 1980.

For a gift they gave me apple juice, but then one of the guerrillas apparently didn't feel like giving me the cake that my father had asked them to buy for me. I know it must be because they hate us, me especially. I don't care, though: one day I will get out of here and will eat all the cakes I please.

There's a pack of monkeys around here, and that sicko el Negro made like he was going to shoot one of them, specifically the one I was gazing at. I didn't say anything, though, and he started to laugh like a maniac. Oh, he is so satanic—that's exactly how I picture him, just like the devil himself. He's about 6 and a half feet tall, and he is completely revolting.

Today more guerrillas and a new health aide came, but without drugs. The new guy just brought in another cake and told me that some commanders I don't even know sent it to me. I asked him how

on earth they knew it was my birthday and he said he didn't know. I was really amazed—how sweet that the top brass of the ELN thought to send me a cake, and it wasn't the same as the one my father ordered, it was totally different.

Well, I guess things improved a little today. My father wrote me a very sweet birthday card and everyone signed it. They sliced the cake and I blew out the candle. And then we got a fantastic bit of news, front-page stuff: the ELN said that they will agree to the immediate release of hostages as soon as the government names a date, location, and time for the National Convention. That announcement is supposed to happen next week. That was the best birthday gift I could have asked for.

Today I found out that the head commander of the ELN in Magdalena Medio is the direct successor to Manuel Pérez Martínez, the Spanish priest who founded the ELN, and the man who sent me the cake is his second-in-command.

This is the letter my father wrote to me:

Leszli,

A person's true valor can only be known in moments of extreme adversity and danger, and in the most demanding of tests—like that day when other people, including myself, were unwilling to look death in the eye. But you did, you faced death head-on, and you refused to let Yezid die. That is one of so many examples of the valor you possess.

Here and now in the mountainous jungle of the Serranía de San Lucas, after spending so many long, long months in captivity, in different guerrilla fronts, where everyone loved you and admired you for your character, I can honestly say that as your father, I feel very proud of you, and I feel grateful to have been able to be with you during this time. You are and always will be my strength and my support. I have always felt the deepest love for you, and it has only grown during this time as I have seen firsthand that your bravery and valor are incalculable.

On this day, I wish you a happy birthday, now and forever.
Your father
December 11, 1999

Sunday, December 12, 1999

Day 245. 20 days to go until the year 2000.

On *Amanecer en América* or in *Voces del Secuestro* (I can't remember which), Carol, Elga, and André took turns talking. Carol sent regards from my mother, and I don't know where Nandor was. Then, Gloria de Gómez, Ana María's mother, read me a message from Judith, very sweet. And María Clara Londoño, Juan González's girlfriend, wished me a happy birthday.

Today I took a dip in the river with my father. He spent the whole time singing, and it was so funny to see him like that: he jumped from rock to rock diving into the water, and I did the same, minus the singing. Then I went back up and now I'm listening to music and daydreaming about seeing everyone again.

Today is the eight-month anniversary of our hijacking.

Today I painted my nails.

On December 10 I saw a huge weasel in the river, with a coat that looked like a yellow vest. Very, very pretty.

Monday, December 13, 1999

Week number 35. 19 days to go until the year 2000, and 246 days in captivity.

Today I went to take a bath in the river and helped to make a salad—that was my idea, and it tasted really good! Everyone liked it. Afterward I spent almost all afternoon there, and I gave the hen some food and water, and stretched her little foot out so that she could move it around a little more, and I sat there playing with her for a while. Then I grabbed a cricket, gave her a few drops of coffee, and watched her as she cleaned herself. She was so pretty, and actually touched me with her antennae, and I played with her for a while. Then I climbed up and played chess with one of the guerrillas. I won, but he's playing a lot better lately.

Another guerrilla left us today. Now the supply lady is filling in as the health aide. Uriel told us some neat stories about San Mateo, the town he's from. It's 10:15 P.M., and a wasp just stung me on my right foot. I was putting on my boot to go out and drink some *agua de panela* with Uriel and Laureano, and the wasp was hiding inside the boot. I screamed when I got bitten and jumped around and around because it hurt like hell.

Good news on *Cuarto de hora,* the 9:00 show on Caracol. We

heard applause and then celebrated: the Congress announced its unequivocal support of the president. By invoking the law of public order, the Congress extended the validity of Law 418 for three more years, which will allow the government to continue working on the peace process with the insurgents, and to create a safe, neutral space for the talks. That was what we were hoping for so that the ELN can meet with the government to set a date, hour, and location for the Convention. With that in place, they can finally release us. Thank you, God.

Tuesday, December 14, 1999

Day 247. 18 days to go until the year 2000.

While I was bathing in the river, as I stared down at the water from a rock, I felt my spirit rise and I spoke to God. A great conversation, if I may say so myself. I put all my cards on the table, and finally things became clear to me. I asked him to help me, to show me the right path to take once I get home. I told him that I was afraid of failing, of facing all the unknowns that feel so overwhelming to me. And it worked. It was a singular moment for me, a very special experience.

Before that I washed my clothes, and while they dried I had a chat with my father, who said a bunch of things that made me laugh. As we were talking, one of his boots drifted off down the river and he went running after it. He managed to grab it, but just barely. It was pretty funny, though.

I have to bathe with laundry detergent because we don't have any more regular soap. Before, this would have seemed awful to me, but I don't even think twice about things like that anymore. Lunch today was rice and beans. Dinner was more of the same, plus some beets. I only ate the beets, though. The food here is completely unbearable, and on top of it we don't even have any oil, nor do we have any cigarettes. It's been raining hard since 5:30. It's 6:01 right now.

No messages today from my mother, Carol, or Nandor. I'm a bit worried about it—I don't understand why we haven't heard them on the radio. Now I can't sleep and I know I'll spend the whole night worrying about them. I have a bad feeling, something strange, and on top of it they don't send me any messages. I hope to God nothing's happened to them. It's just really odd: neither my mother nor Nandor spoke over the radio this Saturday, and I don't know anything. I don't know what's going on, and I can't understand why they've left me hanging like this. This is just the kind of thing that fills me with anxiety, which then makes my ulcer flare up, and of course when that happens I can't fall asleep. We're all out of Mylanta and cigarettes, plus I'm hungry and there's no food to be found. How can they do this to me? Really!

Wednesday, December 15, 1999

Day 248. 17 days to go until the year 2000.

Today a new guerrilla turned up with his wife and two underlings. They gave us crackers and finally, we now have some oil. I spoke to him for a little while, but he doesn't know anything. He thinks we're going to spend Christmas and New Year's here, so once again, my illusions and hopes have been dashed.

I went down to the river and cried there for a while. Then I climbed back up and washed the little monkey the guerrillas brought with them. The pack of white-faced monkeys paraded through here again. The little monkey they brought is one of them.

My soul is falling to pieces as I write this, and there is nothing I can do to stop it from happening. It's so unfair, what they are doing to us.

At 5:55 P.M., it started raining buckets. It only just began to die down a little now, at 7:30.

Víctor G. Ricardo spoke on the news tonight. He said that the only thing they were waiting for was the extension of Law 418, and now that it has passed, the ELN will meet over the next few days to establish a date, time, and location for our release, which will then take place a few days after that.

Thursday, December 16, 1999

Day 249. 16 to go before the year 2000.

At 9:30 A.M., one of the guerrillas said to us: "Get ready. We're leaving here at one P.M."

We got our things together and took off. Three hours of walking, uphill the entire way. After picking a papaya off a tree, we reached a little store where there were flashlights, batteries, knives, lighters, toothpaste, and toothbrushes. The guerrillas bought some supplies and then we continued walking. After a while we reached a little house where there was a very cute little girl. They gave us California-brand apple juice, two potatoes per person, and a can of hot dogs. I slept with my father on a mat because there was only one other mat and we gave that one to Uriel, Lau, and Fer. The three of them slept on the mat sideways, so that half their bodies were dangling off. It was a rough night.

Friday, December 17, 1999

Day 250. 15 days to go until the year 2000.

Today we got up very early and began walking right away. We had to climb up the steepest hill; it was so grueling that I almost passed out. Then we walked on for an hour and a half more until finally we reached a little hut where we ate breakfast and lunch, all together. Everyone got chicken except me and my father—they gave us four eggs for the two of us. I prepared them with scallions, and they actually tasted pretty good. I served them with rice and water. There were two cats, too—one was Siamese and the other one was a mixed-breed that looked like a Siamese but he wasn't. Very pretty. We also ate papaya and guavas and they gave each of us some biscuits.

Two new mules finally arrived today. One went to me and the other one went to the girlfriend of one of the guerrillas, because she was sick. Once we gathered our things we started walking again, although at one point my mule almost fell into the river and almost brought me down, too. We continued on for about an hour and a half, maybe more, until we reached a very pretty campground, but before that we passed by an abandoned campsite with a breathtaking natural pool and a sign that said, "Welcome to this campsite." This one was a very compact little place, flat and without any mud at all. They gave my dad the best hut—huge, really huge, though we had to make do with one mattress for the two of us because we had to give the other one to Fer and Diego. Dinner was rice, beans, and *coscojas*, banana chips. Very tasty, but now I am too tired to write any more. More tomorrow ...

Saturday, December 18, 1999

Day 251. 14 to go until the year 2000.

Last night I dreamt about my cousin Tony: we were in the city together and had to be rescued. We were surrounded by dead people, and at one point I dreamt that a snake bit me.

Today I put the little table in between the two beds. Everything looks so pretty. We gathered together some fabric scraps and used them to hang the wet wash, and then some of the men found a huge coral snake and killed her. My father went down to the river for a wash, but I stayed behind because all my clothes were wet. It started to rain today. It's 12:30pm. Last night, before going to bed, I had a little cup of milk. Then, today, I made breakfast: *arepas* and hot chocolate without milk.

One of the guerrillas made me a plank to rest my feet on, very nice looking. My father put the bed together so now, finally, we're settled. I finally took a bath and put my black shirt on.

We received some messages today, plus one of the guerrillas gave me a gift: a black felt hat.

Sunday, December 19, 1999

Day 252. 13 days until the year 2000.

Just one message today for me and my father, from Judith. She spoke live! Today I feel very happy, maybe because I really like this campsite—the river is lovely, everything is nice. I am trying hard not to think too much about my family because it only makes me feel worse. Instead, I try to keep my mind busy with other things—anything, really. Today in the morning I went to take a bath and I skipped over a bunch of rocks to a place where I could lie out in the sun. In the afternoon, I read a book about dreams. Diego just shaved his head; at night, my dad went to talk to Uriel about him because he feels Diego is straying from the group a little. I took off my black hat and put on the green one.

The moon is in the first quarter, and it looks so pretty. . . . I am horrified by the idea of having to spend Christmas Eve here, but what can I do? Nothing. I have two choices: I can either get grumpy and bitter about it, or else I can try to make the most of this experience and bear up to it as best I can. I can't do anything about the fact that I'm going to be here, but I do have the power to decide how I will deal with the situation. So I choose the second option.

Monday, December 20, 1999

Day 253. 12 days to go before the year 2000. Week number 36.

I know, I know, it's Christmas. It's inevitable. How can I help but think about it? Still, I try to occupy my mind with other things, stupid things. All I can do is kill time. The minute I get up, I am going to sweep. Yes, that's exactly what I'm going to do: sweep. I know I should get up, to get rid of this lethargy, this monotony that is eating away at me on the inside. . . .

Anyway, to pick up where I left off: I got up. Yes, I got up and I did a good job of killing some time. I got to work and with my bare hands I cleaned up our little territory. First I got rid of the branches lying around everywhere, then all the weedy underbrush. The entire thing took about three hours, all told, and my father watched me out of the corner of his eye as he worked away on a chair he was building. He's going to set it up overlooking the river. After a little while, he came over to me and gave me a homemade broom, made of dried palm leaves wrapped up around a long branch, and I got to work sweeping the entire area up. Under my bed I found the oddest thing: a perfectly formed, tiny little hill of dirt with a dead tarantula next to it: the tarantula was light brownish in color, and was missing four legs. The metamorphosis of these animals is so strange—in fact, it gets stranger by the day if you ask me. In the last campsite, there was one dead tarantula that had actually turned into a kind of plant after it died. That one also turned a strange, brownish color. God, what I wouldn't give to have a camera to photograph these things. The next thing I did was gather a big pile of white stones from the river, which I lined up all around the area, as a little border. Everything turned out so pretty, and what a difference it makes! Right now, I am sitting in the chair my father made, the one with the very best view of the water below.

Today I ate breakfast, but skipped out on lunch. Later on I ate rice with two pieces of fried plantains and *agua de panela*. My father wants to put a kind of canopy onto the top of the chair, but he's done enough work today—he only just finished nailing the sticks he's using as pillars to the chair frame. Tomorrow, when he has more light, he can attach the black plastic cloth to complete the canopy effect. We are both dead tired, plus the daylight is petering out and I don't want to use the flashlight. The head guerrilla left today.

Tuesday, December 21, 1999

Day 254. 11 days to go before the year 2000.

Last night I dreamt I was at Christian's house, a very old house with shutters that made the place look very creepy and gloomy. In the dream I was talking with Stellita about spending the night there when Christian, who was getting ready to go out for the evening, said hello to me and then told me he would take me wherever I wanted to go but I said no, I didn't want to go anywhere. I was sad because I felt so bored, and then suddenly I saw myself all alone in that big house and I got scared, so I went out for a walk. It was nighttime, and it was another year—1984 or 1985, I think. When I got out onto the street, there was no one there, and I got scared. Then I saw a house and said to myself, "That was where they kidnapped us," and I kept on walking. A black car passed by right after that and then I thought about how stupid it was to go out walking at night like that. I sat down to smoke a cigarette but then I asked myself, "Won't this hurt the baby?" because I was pregnant and I knew I had to take care of myself. Still, I just sat there smoking the cigarette. I was angry and sad that I was there. Then I saw three people walking down the street and suddenly Carolina was standing next to me, but I wasn't able to see her very clearly and I thought to myself, "Should I say hello, or not?" And then when we walked past the same house where they had kidnapped us, Carolina shouted out, "There they go, scaring us again!" At that point, I broke into a run, and everyone else started running as well. I looked over toward the house and saw a bunch of shadows that looked as though they were dancing, and then I saw more people so I turned to Carolina to ask her if I could go with her. She said yes, and I followed her until we reached another old house. Carolina opened the door, went inside, and then went up the stairs. I told her to wait for me and she said, "Close the door and come up." I tried to close the door and then I started walking up the stairs but when I got halfway up I had to go back down and close the door, because it was still halfway open. Then I woke up.

The whole thing was awful. It was around 5:30 in the morning when I woke up and I was completely disoriented—I had no idea where I was. I got up, smoked a cigarette, and told my father about the dream. Then we sat around listening to Caracol, and I went back to sleep.

Today my dad made me a little Christmas tree. Fer and Diego helped us decorate it with the edges of some sheets and with some scraps from sacks and some blue and white material from the edges of the blankets. Then we got some moss from the trees and the tops of some branches. Fer hung a few stones on the branches of the tree. Then my father made a little manger out of some rocks, and when he was done, it looked really nice. My father put the black plastic cover on top of the chair, to finish off the canopy, and the whole thing looks really pretty now, the little chair with its canopy looking out over the river right in front of our hut. Yesterday I swept up the entire tent with the broom my father made, but today the little pile of dirt I found next to the tarantula was still there, even though I thought I had swept it away . . . but who knows. Yesterday I had thought that the dead spider had piled all that dirt up before dying, but now I can't figure it out. Now I think that maybe there is another spider down there somewhere, and that maybe he killed the other spider, the brown one—who knows? Maybe he did it to protect his territory or to get rid of the other spider. . . . But if it isn't a spider, then maybe it's something else—a field mouse, probably. Because why would a spider want to dig a little hole like that? It's a big hole, around 15 centimeters in diameter, though I can't quite see the far end of it. This makes me think that we must have some other little insect or animal living with us. What could it be? What could it be . . . ?

Yesterday we got some very good news: in the next few hours a statement will be issued announcing the date, hour, and location of the Convention. Yesterday the COCE held their meeting with Víctor G. Ricardo, and today the president said that in the next few days he will be meeting with ELN delegates to discuss the details of the Convention. Hooray!

I just heard a shot go off, but by now the sound of shots being fired is pretty normal for us. Nobody even thinks twice about it. Today I feel good, very calm spiritually.

On the radio my mother said she once read that truly intelligent people are the ones who know how to take the very best advantage of things. She also said that she was counting the minutes until she sees me again, and that if we can't celebrate Christmas together, it's okay, because she is with all of us in spirit. Then she told me to just let go of whatever is too much for me to handle, and she also said that she won't celebrate Christmas again until I come home, and that Nandor and Carol are doing well.

Wednesday, December 22, 1999

Day 255. 10 days until 2000.

Today I stuck to the task at hand (that of keeping my mind as occupied as possible) and I have been pretty successful, busying myself with the little neighbor we have living in the tiny hole underneath my bed. Turns out it's a beautiful tarantula. At 6:00, just as they played the national anthem on the radio, she emerged from her lair. Dark, bluish-black in color, and very hairy, her body is the size of my fist, and each of her legs measures more or less the same as the palm of my hand, 13 1/2 centimeters. I am convinced that she's the one who killed the other spider, the brown one. . . . I wonder what she eats. Why doesn't she move? Maybe because she senses my presence, or else maybe because she's annoyed that I swept up her little habitat. I wonder how long she's been here. How old is she? How long do spiders live? My God, if my dad ever found out that I am harboring this tarantula he would go into shock. And then, of course, he would kill her. Poor thing . . . I am going to call you Tatica . . . my little tarantula. Today Adolfo the guerrilla left us. I think he might be sick; he's been looking very wilted lately. He came around to say goodbye, and we all felt bad. My father and I like him a lot.

Breakfast today was rice and vegetables, bread, and coffee with milk. What a feast! On top of it they gave me a few bottles of brandy.

Thursday, December 23, 1999

Day 256. 9 days left until the year 2000.

Today I swept up the other side of the courtyard, so that it would look nice for Christmas. I made a little fence out of some very pretty sticks, and then I went to take a bath.

We've now run out of cigarettes and are sitting around watching a sun shower.

On the news they said that Víctor G. Ricardo is meeting with the ELN people somewhere near Barranca. Today Carol spoke on UIS, with a message for me and my father. She said she hoped we were okay, and that my friends, especially Johanna Mantilla, had made a sign that said some really nice things about how friends are friends in good times and bad, and about how she was thinking a lot about the old days when it was just the four of us: Tita, Mafer, Johanna, and me. She said she felt so wistful and sad whenever she thought back to those old days, and before signing off she said that she prays every night for me and my father. I couldn't help but cry when I heard her say that. And I realized that she is such a good friend, and that I do love her a great deal. And right then I gave thanks for having such wonderful friends.

My mother also spoke on the radio today, plus she sent a message for Juan and Diego. To me she said that tomorrow will be a day like any other, and that it will only be Christmas when I come home. Then she asked me to promise her that I would stay positive and not let myself get depressed. Mentally, I made the promise to her: I vow to keep my spirits high. Tonight Lau, Diego, my father, and I drank some brandy in the hut, and Tatica came out at around the same time, though I don't know when she went back inside. Then I got sleepy.

Day 257. 8 days to go until the year 2000.

Today I woke up in a pretty good mood, and I cleared off the area in front of the chair as well as the path down to the river's edge. The men made some more chairs, and the whole place looks really nice. Fer dug out a stairway leading down to the river, which is very convenient because now we can climb up and down without the least effort, much easier than before. That, he said, is his Christmas gift to us, and he even made a little sign that said, "For my companions of the Child Jesus, from here down to the river, Merry Christmas." Then my father helped them out as they made their own chair so that they could also sit out overlooking the river in the afternoons. When he finished, he said to them: "This is your Christmas gift from the Kálli family." As for me, well, I don't have anything to give my father outside of my companionship and my good spirits, to keep us strong and positive. I did give Tatica a little present, though: two little beans that I tossed her way.

Given the circumstances, our Christmas celebration wasn't half bad. We all gathered in the middle of the campsite and drank a total of eight bottles of brandy under the electric light. It had been a long time since we'd been able to use electricity, and just having light at nighttime was a tremendous gift for me. We turned on the radio but of course hearing all the Christmas songs was kind of a drag, because they only reminded us of other Christmases, and then we all started thinking about the music that our families were probably listening to. The guerrillas seemed even more depressed than we were, because in a way, they're captives, too. I am sure that if they could, they would be back home with their families, but as they say, orders are orders.

At around 10 P.M. I decided to go to bed because I was feeling pretty tipsy, if not completely dead drunk. Before I fell asleep, though, I got up to puke, and I tossed and turned all night. It was as if I was floating, rocking back and forth, and all I wanted in the world was to feel that the bed was anchored firmly to the ground. I hate feeling drunk, I really hate it, but after a while I did manage to fall asleep. Everyone else stayed up drinking. Iván, the head guerrilla, sent each of us a Christmas card with the ELN emblem and the message "Merry Christmas" printed on the front. Inside, there was a handwritten note, but it was basically the same thing for all of us—how uninspired of him. Mine said, "To Leszli: Patience . . . to keep your spirits up." The thing was signed collectively by this ELN front. Oddly enough, everyone signed my dad's card personally, guerrillas and captives alike, and yet I got nothing. Do I care? No! Oh, yes, I do care, I admit it—if I didn't care I wouldn't mention it at all. Oh, Leszli, let go of the anger; if people don't like you, what can you do about it? Nothing. They gave us crackers, vanilla pudding, and candy, and I did not cry. Nobody else cried, either: everyone remained in pretty decent spirits. In the middle of my very nauseous sleep that night, I dreamt that we lost our apartment because of the ransom we had to pay, and had to move to an ugly, depressing house. I felt completely consumed with anguish during that dream. On top of everything, last night and very early this morning, it got really cold, and later on everyone said the same thing, meaning it wasn't just the fact that I was completely drunk. I swear I never felt as cold as I did that night, even though my blanket is half an inch thick and is made of some kind of synthetic material. I shivered all night long, especially in the early hours of the morning, and I almost got up and asked my father if I could sleep with him, since our two blankets together probably would have been enough to keep me warm, but I didn't want to bother him. Later on I mentioned it to him and he said, "Silly, you should have told me. Next time, don't worry about bothering me, just wake me up."

Saturday, December 25, 1999

Day 258. 7 days to go before the year 2000.

Today I woke up early, around 6 A.M., in a pretty good mood but I was practically dying of thirst. It seems that Tatica didn't think much of my Christmas gift because this morning before I went down to the river I saw the two little beans outside her lair. I walked down to the river with my father and the river worked wonders on our mood.

Before I went into the water I sliced some plantains for the two of us, which we gobbled down.

After the bath, we ate breakfast: sausages, two *arepas,* and hot chocolate with milk. Delicious! Plus, yesterday they brought us chocolate bars, one for my father and the other one for me. After breakfast I sat down in the chair with the panoramic view, and as I was examining my boots before putting them on, to make sure that no flies or any other insects were hiding inside, I spotted an eagle perched on a tree branch, staring at Piqui, the little monkey. Quickly sensing that the eagle was up to no good, Piqui scurried into our tent and refused to come out for the rest of the day. The guerrillas tried to get the eagle to come down, but thank God he flew off. Uriel, my father, and I sat there for a long while, just gazing at the eagle in awe. What a beautiful, beautiful creature.

Our group seems to be getting along again, which makes me happy, and I'm also feeling pretty good because I have somehow been able to keep the promise I made to my mother.

This afternoon I went fishing with Carolina, Iván's wife. She's around my age, and it's funny, she doesn't really fit the stereotype of the female guerrilla: she is pale and thin, with delicate features, pretty hair and face, and her hands are actually smoother than mine, without the tiniest little scratch. To hear her speak, she sounds like any other woman my age from the city—she doesn't roll her "s" over her tongue the way the people do around here, and she doesn't make grammatical mistakes, either. Also, she writes just like my friends do—she has that stylish sort of handwriting that I have never been able to master. When I write, I write in script, or with the letters all separated, or however it comes out, really—I never bothered to learn proper penmanship and in fact I have always kind of liked the fact that my writing comes out differently every time I put pen to paper. People are always criticizing me and laughing at me for that, but I don't care.

It's interesting, too, that Iván's wife is named Carolina, not like the other guerrilla women who have names like Leidy, Yesenia, or Patrisia spelled with an "s." I bet she just fell head over heels for Iván, and that's why she's here—out of love, not because she has some kind of real commitment to "the cause," like the rest of them are always saying. She has a very strong personality and goes around acting like she knows everything, like she's some kind of all-purpose superwoman. When I agreed to go fishing with her, of course I gave her the perfect opportunity to show off her jungle expertise, but unfortunately it didn't really work out for her because after all her blustering she only ended up with a couple of wimpy fish that were about as big as my pinky finger. She realized this, of course, and I couldn't help laughing at her big song and dance, but I did my best to hide it, because I didn't want to be rude. She tried to cover it up, saying that it had just rained, and that all the good fish were downriver, an area that was too dicey for me to handle, since you needed a lot more experience crossing the river and jumping over all the boulders down there. Yeah right, I said to myself, but still I kept my mouth shut, because when it comes to experience . . . come on. I've got plenty under my belt at this point—after all, haven't I been stuck here for 258 days? She should have just admitted that she didn't know the first thing about fishing because she only made a fool of herself in front of me, but whatever. It was pretty funny.

The important thing for me, though, was that thanks to Carolina I was able to leave the campsite. It was just for the day, but I did get to see some beautiful scenery. Down where we went, the river is much wider, the current is much stronger, and there are massive boulders lining the shore on either side.

When we came back we took a dip in the river and I took advantage of the darkness to take off all my clothes—what an exquisite feeling to slip into the water, totally naked, under the night sky. I placed my flashlight on a rock and pointed it away from me so that when I went into the water I could see the beam of light undulating and expanding in the water. Definitely relaxing.

Sunday, December 26, 1999

Day 259. 6 days to go until the year 2000.

Today at around 11:10 A.M. we heard two helicopters flying overhead, very low in the sky. My father called me over and hung on to me so that I wouldn't leave his side. The guerrillas all started running around from one side of the camp to the other, looking for their rifles, and then they summoned us for a quick meeting. First they told us to get a mosquito net and a blanket ready just in case we had to make an emergency evacuation, and then they said that as soon as they yelled out the word "apples," we were to all gather in Juan and Francisco's tent. We did what they said, but nothing happened—in the end the fat guy who started the whole fuss only yelled out the word "pears" every now and then. Still, it was pretty frightening—they turned off all the burners on the stove because they didn't want any smoke to rise up and give us away, and they suspended all cooking until the sun went down. I could tell Uriel was starving, but as for the rest of us, the fear pretty much did away with our appetites.

Monday, December 27, 1999

Day 260. 5 days to go before the year 2000. Week 37.

Today we woke up as if nothing at all had happened yesterday. Last night I dreamt that Silvia Veronica was getting married and was in a wedding gown. I also dreamt that I saw Carol in a pink dress with little white checks. Very pretty. I told her to bring Daniel with her because I hadn't seen him in such a long time. I also saw Nandor and then I saw myself on Thirty-fifth Street.

Iván spoke to me and Lau today about the possibility of us getting released. He didn't give us much hope, though.

I woke up sad today, because last night I sat up late thinking about my mom. Then my father woke me up at 4 A.M., looking for a lighter. Today is the five-year anniversary of the day I first met Diego Plata at Natalia Guerrero's fifteenth birthday. He showed up with Lucas.

Tuesday, December 28, 1999

Day 261. 4 days to go before the year 2000.

Big surprise today—the painter guerrilla turned up. I was so excited to see him that I ran up to him and gave him a big hug, but he didn't stay for long. He told me that things were going pretty well. He also said that I should stay calm, that he was on top of things and would revisit my case with the ELN authorities.

I have been feeling really lethargic for the past few days. It's been especially rough, because I've had to watch my father go to sleep without eating, hungry as hell. The portions are tiny here, and the menu is always the same: rice and pasta, rice and pasta all the time. When you ask the guerrillas what there is to drink they just shrug and say, "Nothing . . . water. The river's right over there."

I asked them to give us three spoonfuls of powdered milk so that my father and I could share a glass of milk, but they said no— not because they didn't have any but because it was for the others. It wasn't our turn, they claimed. Here, everything is a luxury. I also asked them for a can of tuna because I've been feeling very weak and know I need protein, but they said they gave all their tuna to the guerrillas.

Aside from all that, there's no sugar, no *panela,* or anything else sweet for that matter. We just eat plain pasta and rice—no salt, no nothing. They just boil the water, throw the pasta in, and when it's ready they drain the excess water and plop it down in front of us, without salt or oil or anything. Same with the rice. I don't know why the hell they bring in tomato sauce and mayonnaise and milk if they never give us any. They do throw a little milk into the hot chocolate mix, but it's greasy and gross. Who can we complain to? Nobody. If someone gets sick here, they'll just die, because we don't have any medicine, either. The river is beautiful, but we can't stay in the water for more than three minutes: we'll freeze to death if we do, because we aren't getting enough calories. We are constantly shivering from the cold, and when it isn't the cold that gets us, it's the hunger, and I have to say that life stinks when you don't have enough food to eat.

I am starving right now, and know I am going to I have to wait till morning to eat breakfast. A nice long wait for what? A plate of rice. Sometimes I think they ought to just kill us already—that way at least we wouldn't have to suffer anymore, and this whole nightmare would finally come to an end.

Wednesday, December 29, 1999

Day 262. 3 days to go before the year 2000.

Yesterday my mom and Carol spoke on the radio. Carol read something very pretty about God.

Food today was sardines and *arepas,* but I only ate the *arepas.* Then I went to sleep for about two hours while Uriel lectured my father about politics.

Thursday, December 30, 1999

Day 263. 2 days to go before 2000.

There was no breakfast for any of us today, and we're all starving. Last night I had a dream: It was nighttime, and I was with a few other people in a minivan that was going really fast. Suddenly, we veered off the road and plunged into a gorge. Somehow I managed to wiggle my way out through a window, but I still got really scraped up. Then an immense room appeared before me, and I saw this big cord, filled with blood, that was connected to my belly button. Someone pulled me and the cord broke. Then I had this other dream that I was in China, and I took lots of photos and bought lots of clothes. After that, someone started telling me how to hang a hammock that I had bought. Then I saw myself paragliding.

Lunch was pretty grim: three spoonfuls of beans and a quarter of a fried plantain. I have a headache. They also gave us coffee, but without sugar. As a kind of joke, they said to us that by tomorrow we probably won't even have a supply person because there's no more food for anyone. At 3 P.M. they gave us bread and the most delicious cheese I have ever tasted.

Two more guerrillas arrived today, with a gift for me from the mule driver: eleven bom-bom-bum lollipops. I gave one to Lau, Diego, and Francisco. Patty, one of the guerrillas, told me that a humongous shipment was on its way with tons of stuff, including a sack of tomatoes. How delicious. Uriel's medicine arrived, and he actually broke down in tears, he was so relieved. All of us felt the same. On the radio my mom, Carol, Nandor, and Mauri sent messages. It was so nice to hear from them.

Friday, December 31, 1999

Day 264. One day to go until the year 2000.

We all went down to the river and listened to the Billboard Top 40 on La Mega. Breakfast today consisted of boiled eggs, bread, and hot chocolate with milk. It was delicious. Afterward they brought me a little present from the painter guerrilla, a cake with custard, to share with everyone else. Diego gave each of us a bit of brandy and then at 3 in the afternoon we all headed down to the river for a dip, and we stayed there for an hour. We held a contest to see who could stay underwater the longest.

It's 8:30 P.M. now, and I'm lying in bed thinking about my mother, wondering how she is. I still miss her more than ever. I would do anything to be with her right now, to be able to tell her how much I love her. Today there is one question running through my head: what are they all doing? It's so hard just getting through the days here; all we do is listen to the radio—even the guerrillas look bored out of their minds. Today Diego and I talked about Christmas, about what we were doing last year at this time. Here, of course, instead of fireworks we've got gunfire and shots ringing out in the air. Oh, I wish I could just let it all out and cry. I hope that the coming year will bring freedom for me and my father. We deserve it after all we've been through.

At midnight we celebrated with hugs all around. The first person I hugged was my father, and then we all toasted to the new year. But that was pretty much it.

Saturday, January 1, 2000

Day 265.

We spent all day today in the river. The men cut down a couple of trees, and for breakfast we ate the cake from last night. Afterward I ate fried plantains with rice, and then I cut my nails. Dinner last night was chicken soup. Today I washed the wooden planks I use as ottomans, and I took down the Christmas tree. I don't have any underwear on today. Mauricio gave me some *chicha* to drink while I was in the river.

Sunday, January 2, 2000

Day 266.

Today I played chess all day with Laureano. Four games: he won two, and I won two. Last night I went out for water at about 3 in the morning. Last night and tonight it was especially dark and we were able to see all the stars in the sky: we spotted the Northern Cross, and lots of other constellations that are generally blocked by the trees. Today I started reading a book by Luis Fernando Hoyos: *Vive tu vida y déjasela vivir a los demás* [Live Your Life and Let Others Live Theirs]. Very nice. I have a serious infection in my vagina. Today I went swimming in the river.

Monday, January 3, 2000

Today, I played chess for a while with Laureano. At one point, just as I was about to make a move, my father, who has a very annoying habit of butting in to the game when he's not playing, said to me, "Oh, that's stupid!"

Now, this happens all the time, but for some reason I blew up at him when he did that and told him to butt out of the game and leave me alone, that I was old enough to figure out which chess pieces to move and where. He got really pissed off, though, and barked at me, "Leszli, who do you think you're talking to?"

"You, who else!" I snorted back.

"Well, I demand a little more respect—your attitude is obnoxious and rude. I am your father, and if you keep talking to me like that I'm going to smack you."

If he hit me, that would be the last straw. I kept my mouth shut because I knew he was right, at least in part. I shouldn't have acted like that with him, but I have told him a hundred times to let me play in peace. Anyway, to top it off, I lost my concentration and blew the game. When it was over I went back to the hut and went to bed. My father didn't sign off like he usually does by saying *viszont látasra*— which means "good night" in Hungarian.

Tuesday, January 4, 2000

Day 268.

On the news they're talking about the relatives that are going to the south of Bolívar this Saturday. Today I played six games of chess with Lau, and we tied, three games apiece. After that I went for a dip in the river. My father told the guerrillas that if our families come down to visit us, I will have to sleep with Francisco's wife. Totally unintentionally, I made a face when he said that, and I know Francisco caught that.

Wednesday, January 5, 2000

Last night I asked my father what kind of food spiders eat and he told me that basically they live on insects. If that's true, then you're screwed, Tatica, because I am definitely not going to collect insects on your behalf. I do have to say that it's nice to know you're around. I mean, if some cockroach finds its way into the tent, I know you'll be there for me. And as long as you don't sting me, my father, or the monkey, I'm happy for you to stay here. You in your little home, and us in ours. Of course, my father has no idea you're living with us.

Thursday, January 6, 2000

Tonight I stayed up talking to Lau until 1 in the morning. They brought me underwear, shorts, shirts, and toiletries today. I played chess with Uriel, too, and he won.

Friday, January 7, 2000

Day 271.

Today I went down to the river twice, and then I played Chinese checkers and chess with Francisco. Afterward, in the evening, I stayed up late talking to Lau and Francisco. Lau told me how he feels about me, and I just told him that we should wait and see what happens when we're free. Like I said before, I don't want to get involved with anyone while I'm here.

Saturday, January 8, 2000

My dad made a chess set with little rocks he collected down by the river—he spends all day there. I went in and swam for about an hour.

Another guerrilla turned up today and called us in to a meeting. My father asked him how it was possible that our families were risking their lives by coming all the way down to Bolívar just to get proof that we're alive, and then he asked why the ELN didn't just send them the letters we've written. He also pointed out that the ELN handbook is very clear about the importance of observing the rules in the International Bill of Human Rights, which says that all hostages have the right to send proof of survival to their loved ones. The guerrilla just said, "Oh, yeah, that's what it says, but nobody follows that stuff." To which my father responded: "Really? Then why did they put it in the book if it's just a bunch of garbage?"

"Hey, a little more respect—that's the ELN book you're talking about," the guerrilla replied.

"Well, what do you have a book like that for, if what it says isn't true?"

The meeting came to an end after that.

Sunday, January 9, 2000

273 days in captivity.

At 3:30 A.M., Jaime Jaramillo spoke on Caracol with the message that everyone misses me, that my friends send their regards, that I should stay strong and remember to be good to my companions in captivity. He spoke well, and it was nice to hear him talk; it made me feel really good to hear his voice. It's so meaningful to know that other people are thinking of you, it's like a little pat on the back that helps you to keep going.

I dreamt about being released last night.

Monday, January 10, 2000

274 days in captivity. Week 39.

I took an hour-long bath today. Then we had a meeting and after that Uriel, Laureano, Francisco, and I played Battleship, but the game kept getting held up while everyone took turns taking their baths. While all this was going on, Francisco and I hatched a little plan: the idea was that I would go into Uriel and Lau's hut to look at their strategy and cheat a little, but Lau caught me and the game ended on a pretty bad note.

Last night I stayed up until 1 in the morning talking to Francisco. At one point he asked me how I felt about him, and I said I didn't feel anything, really. When I asked him why he had asked me that, he said, "Leszli, I know you hate me because I was pretty rotten to you those first few days. And I just wanted to say that I hope you can forgive me for everything. I know I wasn't very nice to you, and I just want to say that none of it was your fault. I know it was my fault that we all turned against each other like we did. I just want to know one thing: do you think you can forgive me?"

I told him that I'd forgotten about all that stuff a long time ago, and that it didn't matter to me anymore if he spoke to me or not. Then he said that for a long time he'd been wanting to talk to me, to have the kind of conversations we had before he confessed his feelings for me. With all his heart, he said, he hoped I could forgive him.

I told him not to worry, that everything was all right by me, but I also asked him not to start in with all that business because it made me uncomfortable. I am sure he thinks I believed everything he said to me, and I just let him think that. I am going to have to be a pretty big hypocrite with him.

Tuesday, January 11, 2000

275 days.

Today I took a bath. Then I started reading *The Man Who Counted,* and after that I played chess with Francisco. Then the guerrillas showed us some wild mushrooms that actually glow in the dark. I talked to Lau very late into the night, and at some point a black dog came around and scared the hell out of us. I screamed and grabbed Lau, though I actually think he was more scared than I was. Then we played a little joke on Fer and Diego, making a glow-in-the-dark cross with a bunch of those glow-in-the-dark mushrooms.

Wednesday, January 12, 2000

Day 276.

Today we had a general meeting to talk about the group letter we are planning to send to the COCE. I disagreed on two points. Firstly, I made it very clear that I would not sign the letter unless my case in particular was properly explained. The way they had written it, the letter talked a lot about the "company," because all of them are Avianca employees, but that made me feel like I didn't have any say in the matter. I think they were kind of surprised by my reaction, I guess because they hadn't thought that I might disagree with them, but in the end they listened to me and gave in.

Today on the Luis Carlos Galán station my mother, Nandor, and Carol sent some very long messages. They seem further and further away all the time. Now they're going to send messages every single day. Lina spoke, too. What a hypocritical jerk! Then Diego Plata said a few words. He kept talking about how much he loves me and misses me, but everything he said felt so removed. . . . I can hardly believe it, but it seems that here, in captivity, I have finally found release from all my feelings for Diego.

Day 277.

Right now I am sitting on a tree trunk by the playing field. I woke up depressed today, so as soon as I got up I came down to the river.

Last night I dreamt about Diego Plata twice. In the first dream, he told me that he loved me, but everything he said made me feel very uneasy. Then, in the second dream, I was in an elevator and when the door opened, Diego was standing in front of me, telling me I had to stand up. I said I felt too weak to get up on my own, and held out my hand for him to help me up, which he did. Then he gave me a very lovely, very gentle kiss, and I got up.

Today on Luis Carlos Galán, Lina talked a little bit. She said that she cries at night whenever she thinks of me, and then she told me to be strong, and that she misses me a lot. Then, after her, Diego Plata spoke: "Leszli, sweetheart, it's me, Diego. I'm calling you tonight to tell you that I love you very much, and that I'm waiting for you here, and that I'm happy because I'm going to start college soon. I'm taking music theory classes with Jairo. We miss you so much, sweet Leszli. When you come back we're going to go to La Mesa, even though I bet you won't want to go! I don't care, though, I'm going to take you there with me. Leszli, I'm going to keep trying to talk to you over the radio, even if it's just to say the same things over and over again."

That was the best, the most wonderful thing to hear!

Day 278.

Today I finished reading *The Man Who Counted*. What a mystery, that book.

Francisco came by and asked me why I had been so difficult with him, why I hadn't let him heat the beans in the pot. I told him why, but in reality I know that he didn't come by because of that—he came around because he wanted to talk to me.

I stayed up late tonight talking to Uriel and Francisco. Uriel started talking about my mom again. Francisco started telling me about his life and times, and about his wife's family. I know how to listen to the tiger roar....

Saturday, January 15, 2000

Day 279.

I tried putting up the antenna today but I couldn't get a signal, and then I went to take a bath in the river but didn't bother with soap. Francisco told me that last night he was afraid that my father would catch him talking to me. I asked him why. After all, what does he have to be afraid of?

Sunday, January 16, 2000

Day 280. Today my father and I made another chair. All I ate the entire day was peas. Francisco talked to me for a long time about snakes. Juan, Francisco, Diego, and Fernando seem to have shut out Uriel. Laureano is slowly recovering from his malaria.

Monday, January 17, 2000

Day 281. 40 weeks in captivity.

Last night I dreamt that Margarita was riding a motorcycle and fell. Her right leg got mangled and she started pulling her veins out until you could actually see the bone. It was Christmas. I saw Florentina, who was very sad, and Xiomara, too.

My father told me that four congressmen are meeting today, and that the paramilitaries have agreed to clear out of the southern part of Bolivar province as long as it's in the interest of peace, so the convention can take place. Juan told us that on the twenty-eighth of this month, Pablo Beltrán and Víctor G. Ricardo will meet in Cuba.

Yesterday I put a cloth on my back to help with my posture. The morning guy is back on La Mega. The days are still unbearable, but I feel that they are starting to go by a little faster.

My relationship with my dad is perfect: we are totally united, and we talk about everything. I'm so proud of him. Everyone in the group likes him—he's such an uncomplicated man, a 100% creative thinker, as logical and as intelligent as they come.

Today the mules arrived at the campsite loaded down with

clothes, confetti, alcohol, and a can of black paint, all of which has made me very happy. Right away I started repainting the marks on my walking stick, because the ones from my first few days have already started to fade. It looks really nice now. My God, in a million years I never would have imagined that a silly walking stick would mean so much to me, but I am so attached to it! Three days after the hijacking, I kept falling down as we walked, so one of the guerrillas chopped a piece off a tree, handed it to me, and said, "Here, hold on to this, you can lean on it, and it will make it easier to walk."

Wouldn't you know it, she was absolutely right: I don't fall nearly as much when I use it. And I still have it with me. Every day I make a little mark on this stick, for each day in captivity. I plan to take it with me the day they release us, to keep it as a memento of this experience.

Tuesday, January 18, 2000

Day 282.

They distributed confetti today. I saw my mother in the June sixteenth edition of the newspaper. I played volleyball today for an hour and a half with Juan and Francisco, the fat one. Boy, did I sweat!

Uriel gave me a gift today: a pair of Puma shorts. I gave mine, the ones with the red checks, to Fer. Lau continues to get better. I played 21 with Francisco. The guerrillas brought us Listerine, notebooks, pencil cases, Jet chocolates, *supercoco* candy, biscuits, and hot dogs today.

Wednesday, January 19, 2000

Day 283.

My mom spoke on the radio today, along with Carol and Nandor. My mom says that she can't bear the thought of me crying. Carol tells me that Danielito is terrible with little animals, and that Nandor finished his rural internship, and is now getting ready to take his medical exams. One of the women guerrillas said something very insulting to Uriel, which made all of us feel bad. Francisco, Uriel, and I played Connect Four until 12:30 P.M.

Day 284.

For three days now we've been getting bread, eggs, and hot chocolate for breakfast. Uriel has rejoined the group—I'm so glad about that.

It seems that Lina, Jito, and Diego have been trying to communicate with me over the radio: Amanda bumped into Diego and mentioned it over the radio. She also remarked about how funny he is and then she said that all of them are going to make a big party for me when I get back. Tonight, while it rained, I sat up talking to Francisco until 1 in the morning. He asked me to forgive him again. I think he can tell how much I dislike him from the look on my face.

Day 285 in captivity.

Today I made a list of all the little chocolate wrappers I've collected. Lately, I've been waking up in a really unpleasant state of mind. Then, when I think about my mom, I have this feeling that she is thinking about me at the exact same time. Oh, Mommy, I miss you so much! I want to be home already. I wonder if we'll ever see each other again. It all seems so distant, so far away, so impossible.

My father isn't talking to me again. My mother spoke on UIS. Apparently the ELN is demanding money from Avianca.

Tatica, the tiny tarantula, hasn't moved much from her little lair. Early this morning when my father went out for his coffee, I tossed her a bit of rolled-up paper, and before the paper even touched the ground, Tatica scurried back into her little hole. Then she started to come back out, but stopped midway—to check out the area, I suppose, for any potential danger. Once she was satisfied that the coast was clear, she took the little piece of paper and raced back into her lair. That was the first time Tatica has ever accepted anything from me, so I ran out to ask the supply man for a bit of bread. He told me that the only bread he could give me was my portion of the bread he'd reserved for breakfast and that I couldn't come back asking him for any more. I told him not to worry, took the bread, came back, and tossed a tiny crumb into the hole.

Sunday, January 23, 2000

287 days.

Today I peered into Tatica's lair again, and found the rolled-up paper and the bread crumb outside her hole. I can only surmise that Tatica is trying to tell me, Leszli, enough with this garbage! Well, forget it, then. She can starve to death for all I care—I mean really! There I am, giving her a piece of the only bread I've got, the only bread I'll eat for who knows how long, and now it's just going to end up getting munched on by ants. Today we hung around playing Continental but had to stop at around 11 P.M., because it started raining.

It seems I have leishmaniasis, they confirmed this for me today. A snake got past the mosquito net in Francisco's hut, and then another one got into Diego and Fernando's hut.

Monday, January 24, 2000

Day 288. Week 41.

Last night I dreamt about Meg Ryan, that we were friends and that we were playing cards. Then Christian Gómez appeared all of a sudden, said hi to me, but was pretty obnoxious. Diana Sánchez and Tita also passed through the dream.

Yesterday they killed a big monkey for food. A major mistake, as far as I'm concerned. I picked her up off the ground when she fell down from the treetop, but she was already dead. Three bullets to the head. They're already cooking her up, but my father, Francisco, Uriel, and I refuse to eat it. Laureano, of course, eats everything. How disgusting. Actually, I was wrong: Uriel did eat the monkey.

It's been raining buckets lately. Francisco started demanding that someone administer the Domeboro he needs to help cure his scabies. I told him I'd do it for him, but honestly—it's so ridiculous that he can't just do it himself. He made all these faces, and of course when I asked him if it hurt he said no. He can really be funny, that guy, and very nice when he's in the right mood. He gave me a piece of chocolate because yesterday and today I spread ointment on his rash.

Tuesday, January 25, 2000

Day 289.

My mom spoke today on UIS and also on Luis Carlos Galán. I could hear the desperation and pain in her voice, and in fact she asked me to forgive her for sounding so distraught, and then she said she hoped I felt better than she did. She told me that I had to fight for my freedom, because she'd done all she could but every door had been closed in her face. She talked about how frustrated and anguished she felt, and told me to ask the ELN to release me already, because they have stolen so much precious time from me, time that I will never get back. Then she said that the silence is one of the most unbearable aspects of this situation, it only makes her fear the worst. Then she said that I am everything to her, but that she is at the end of her rope; she said that yesterday they sent letters and photos through the International Red Cross, but they have no way of knowing if they'll ever get it to me. Carol spoke, too, she called us "her darlings," and said that she loves us more than ever. She said she sent news and gossip and some other things through the Red Cross. The messages made me so sad. I can't do anything from here.

Day 290.

I'm still feeling sad about my mother's last message. Last night I dreamt that Clarita and her mother were here with us, along with a bunch of other people, including an orchestra—a whole band of men dressed up like mariachis, singing *"La Cucaracha,"* staring at me, and making fun of me.

I miss everything so much, so much. I don't know what is going on, and sometimes it still astounds me that we are still being held hostage by these people. They finally confirmed that the kidnapping was carried out for financial purposes, which is what we have always assumed. But then why did they take so long to admit it? Maybe because the public doesn't pay any attention to them anymore, because President Andrés Pastrana couldn't care less about the whole thing, and at this point they no longer feel the need to hide their intentions.

I despise our president; he is such an unbelievable prick, such a complete imbecile, in the fullest sense of the term. All he knows how to do is rack up miles on the presidential jet. On the radio, they're always talking about some trip he's on. The other day, in fact, a journalist criticized him pretty harshly, saying that President Pastrana is more concerned about appearing at fabulous events around the world than running his country's government. Pastrana's other big objective, he said, was getting himself on the list of the best-dressed men in Colombia, and I believe it—I mean, why else would everybody criticize him so much? He is such a lazy slob. I want to vomit every time I hear his repulsive voice on the radio: it makes me feel powerless, sad, humiliated, fat, and worst of all, robbed of my freedom.

The more I think about it, the more I realize how much my life resembles Tatica's: it's boring as hell, it takes place within a confined space, I eat the same food every day (that is, if spiders eat at all—I have no idea), and my schedule never changes, it's always the same. I swear, even in that sense I'm like a spider—I've pretty much stopped going to bed at night; instead, I sleep during the day. Of course the main difference between me and Tatica is that she defined her own boundaries, whereas mine were imposed by a bunch of sonofabitches I don't even know, and who never bothered to ask my permission—they simply used force to place these limits upon me. If I ever get out of here, I will never, ever allow anyone to place any kind of limit on my life. The only one who will ever be able to do that is me.

I wonder what Tatica's skin is like. What would happen if I were to grab hold of her? At this stage in the game she must know that I do not represent even the slightest threat to her life. I am bored, so very B O R E D.

Today I started vomiting again. I want to hurt myself, I want to feel, I want to scream, I want to sleep, I don't want to live anymore.

Thursday, January 27, 2000

Day 291.

I cried all night to the song *"Pueblo mío"* by Diego Torres.

Yesterday I dreamt about my mother, Carol, Nandor, and Mauri: in the dream we had new furniture in the house, and Danielito was big and beautiful. God, I'm even sick of my dreams these days because in the end I know they're just a bunch of lies.

Around here people could pretty much care less if you wake up happy or sad, good or bad. Nobody makes the least bit of effort to try to make things a little better for anyone else. The opposite is true, in fact: if they see you in a bad mood, they just shut you out. I don't even know what to think anymore, because who knows? Am I the only one who thinks these things? It's like it says in that book: "You have a red glass and you see everything in shades of red." On top of it all I've gained weight: I confirmed this yesterday when I tried on my jeans.

Francisco came by and asked Fer and Diego to play cards. Yesterday and today at breakfast time I had a run-in with them over some crackers. I didn't want to eat them and they thought I'd left them over because I was sore about something. Then Francisco came by for the cards and he asked me if I was angry. I was sleeping. My father taught me how to play a kind of solitaire three days ago. Yesterday we listened to the radio messages in our hut. The same today. My mother spoke.

Friday, January 28, 2000

Day 292.

Last night I dreamt that I was in a swimming pool and something heavy was weighing me down. I got out and all of a sudden I saw two small children playing in the pool. One of the kids dove underwater, and then after a while he came out, but all I could see was his head, which wasn't a real head but a skull. Then they pulled a huge fish out of the water and they killed it very slowly, and I watched the giant fish writhing in agony.

Last night I heard my mother, Judith, Esperanza, Mara Kálli, and Lauren Kálli on the radio. Then I played Continental with Francisco, Lau, and my father.

Sunday, January 30, 2000

At 6:10 today I got up and crawled under my bed to check things out, and Tatica was right there, waiting for me. Then, when I told her that I wanted to touch her, she didn't move an inch. Was she able to hear me? Understand me? Hmm. I think so. I placed my palms side by side, faceup, and rested them on the floor, some 20 centimeters away from her. Holding my hands out, I moved closer and closer, and she stayed totally still, not moving an inch. As my middle finger began to graze one of her legs I swear my heart almost jumped right out of my chest, but I kept on going, inching forward more and more and more. Instead of recoiling, Tatica began to lift her legs and my hands slid underneath her body. Finally, there she was, resting in the palm of my hand. I was trembling. There I was, holding on to Tatica, and she didn't do a thing to me, she was soft as could be, not biting, not attacking, not doing anything. At that moment she was the loveliest spider in the world, and I know she could feel how nervous I was, and she stayed as still as before. As I stood up and studied her carefully, slowly, I wondered what I looked like to her. What a marvelous experience: after that, I curled up and placed my hands on the floor, slowly separating my fingers. Our little reverie was over, and lovely little Tatica returned to her spot on the floor, and there she remained, quiet and pretty. When it was all over, I thanked her for allowing me to pick her up. To think that these people kill spiders!

Monday, January 31, 2000

Yesterday a new guerrilla arrived with his wife. Two new guerrillas, but no news.

I cried all afternoon. At night I played cards with Uriel, Laureano, Francisco, and my father. My father burned three cards when he held them up to the candlelight, and Uriel jumped up, furious. Uriel is very disrespectful with my dad, you can really tell how much he hates him. And he was already in a bad mood because the Colombian soccer team lost to Brazil today, 9–0.

My father was just fixing the cards he burnt last night. They got all crumpled from the heat, but they're all right now.

There is nothing to do here. Yesterday I did twenty abdominals and laid out in the sun for a little while. I think I'll do the same today; it's nice and sunny.

At 5:45 I went over to Fer and Diego's hut. Francisco and Juan were inside, eating some crackers and biscuits. They offered me some, because they very clearly felt bad, but I said no because I'm on a diet. It made me feel so bad. . . . Anyway, I stayed around long enough not to make the situation weird, and then I left. The same thing happened to my father the other day: my father walked in on Diego, Juan, and Fer drinking something alcoholic, and as soon as they saw my dad they quickly hid the bottle. My father didn't care about the drink; he was bothered by the fact that they were hiding things. My father is so generous with them, always offering them whatever he has—he actually gave them a chair he made! I have to say, though, these guys are pretty typical as far as Colombians go: stingy and cheap. Thank God I am neither of those things, because I take after my father, and my father takes after his parents, who were Hungarian. My mother is very generous, too, though, and her family is Colombian. But they're nothing like these people.

Clemencia Suárez died exactly one year ago today.

Tuesday, February 1, 2000

Day 296 in captivity.

So far, today has been even more boring than usual. This camp-site is so tedious. Always the same thing for breakfast. Ditto for lunch and dinner: rice and beans. The desperation is showing on my father's face. He just told me how he dreams about eating breakfast at that restaurant, Tonny. My mother and Carol spoke on UIS today, and in the background we could hear Danielito gurgling and playing. Carol told me that I would have such a good time with him because he loves doing little errands and favors for people. After that I sat around crying all afternoon, and the fat guy and another guerrilla tried to make me feel better. After drinking about a bottle and a half of brandy, my father started talking to me. He told me that talking to me was just like talking to Nandor. Everyone else was drinking, too.

Wednesday, February 2, 2000

The guerrillas called a meeting to talk about how we're all feeling, and to discuss the latest news a bit. The only thing I asked was if we were going to be stuck here forever, or if we would get released once the area was cleared for the ELN. He replied that Gabino had reiter-ated that this kidnapping was economic and not political. I asked permission to leave, and then I walked out. The rest of them are still in there, boring themselves to death with that same old story: we rep-resent the people of Colombia, blah, blah, blah.

Uriel is the same as ever. God, that guy is a nuisance to everyone and everything. I'm still pretty much down in the dumps about everything.

Diego González dreamt that we were liberated on March 16 at 4 in the afternoon.

Thursday, February 3, 2000

Day 298.

One year ago today, if you count by the day, and tomorrow if you count by the date, Diego Plata went to Canada.

Today when I woke up, at around 6 A.M., I started thinking about all the things that were going on in my life a year ago, and I remembered how sad I was when Diego left. Then I turned on the radio and started listening to Julio Sánchez Cristo's show, the topic of which was "How to figure out if your boyfriend or girlfriend is gay." They also talked about Víctor G and the FARC, and the trip they took to Norway and Sweden, to try to learn about and copy their economic model. Given all the violence and all the problems we have here, it sounds like a pretty dumb idea to me, but they say we have to make an investment in society.

Sunday, February 6, 2000

Day 301.

I haven't written for two days. Yesterday, Papi and I went to paint everything white. It was wonderful. Last night I played cards with Pacho.

Mami, Nandor, and Carol sent me a message through Radio Caracol.

Diego, Lau, and Pacho are taking swimming classes with Fernando.

I made a facial mask with sugar and lemon. It's obvious that I've gained weight. Today I made oatmeal tortillas. Everybody loved them.

My Dad and I finished the crossword puzzle that was printed in the *Vanguardia* paper on Monday, January 31, 2000.

Monday, February 7, 2000

Day 302.

Last night we got a delivery of meat, and the smell is overpowering. Today everyone is eating except for me.

I had a really unpleasant run-in with Uriel today: since I don't eat meat, they gave me an egg and two potatoes. When Uriel walked by, he said to the supply man: "Ooh, that looks good. Who's it for?"

The supply man answered, "It's for Leszli. The poor thing hasn't eaten anything because she doesn't eat meat and all we had was meat today."

Then that idiot Uriel replied, "Well, she's going to have to share, because I don't want any more meat."

When I heard that I spun around and exploded: "Oh really? Well, that's too bad, because I haven't had anything to eat in a long while, and I do not intend to share my one meal of the day with you because you don't happen to feel like eating any more meat."

To top it off, when I was taking a bath down by the water, Juan pushed me into the river and I went crashing down onto the rocks. When I got up I said, "Eat shit, Juan! Eat shit." I was furious, really furious at that. But he apologized immediately, saying that he only pushed me for fun, to break the ice a little between us.

Tuesday, February 8, 2000

Day 303.

Today I talked to Lau for a while about movies, and about what I am going to do when I get out of here. I told him how frustrated I feel because nothing seems to be happening, nothing at all.

My mother spoke on UIS today: "Hello, sweetheart. I want you to know that I miss you and I want you back at home as soon as possible. My darling, you have to try to stay positive, you have to try to stay strong. Visualize yourself at home, free. Lina and Diego and all your friends ask me about you all the time. There are thousands of stories I could tell you, and they're all about you, and that's because you are beautiful and important to all of us."

Thursday, February 10, 2000

Day 305.

Last night everyone started talking about their fears, about ghosts, about Mohán, the mythical beast. . . . The guerrillas were very scared and said they had seen lights. They asked us if any of us had been bathing in the river with flashlights or lanterns.

After that, Uriel suddenly appeared with a tragic look on his face and told us he just found out that he'd been fired from his job. Nobody paid him any attention, though, so he sulked for a while playing martyr, and then took off. Now he's going to be completely unbearable—he's going to harp on that nonstop until they finally release him.

Today I woke up early, swept up the hut, and put on some makeup. My father told me that the Russians bombed Chechnya today. After that, I spent some time rooting around in search of the black Parcheesi tile that the monkey tossed out last night. I didn't smoke a single cigarette yesterday; we're all out.

Friday, February 11, 2000

Today they blew up fifteen electricity posts, just as one of the guerrillas said they would.

My mother spoke over the radio yesterday and asked me to play that little telepathy game we used to play when I was a kid, and tell her that I'm okay. Carol talked for a little while, too. Nothing new.

Saturday, February 12, 2000

We've been in captivity for ten months now. Day 307.

Last night my dad said something that made me feel really bad. First off, I can tell he's annoyed by me; it's as if everything I do irritates him. He told me that he would never let me come and live with him in Bogotá, apparently because I am so awful to him. He keeps saying the same thing over and over again; he's like a broken record: once we're out of here, in six months, he's going to stop giving me free plane tickets. I didn't care so much about that; it was the other thing that really bugged me, the thing about me never coming to live with him.

When he was done, I got into bed and started to cry. I was so sad, so distraught. Then I got up as if nothing was wrong and made like I was working on a dress, and I made a mess of the blanket, which made my dad even more hysterical. Lately he has really gotten out of hand.

Oh, I want to get out of here! My heart aches, that's the only way I can describe it. I feel as if my soul has shattered into a thousand little pieces. Mommy, I love you so much. Will we ever see each other again?

There is a mole just under my right ear that's been hurting me a lot, a very sharp shooting pain.

Tonight I played 21 with Fer and Diego. Then we playacted a little scene, pretending what we would do if we walked into a bar. At night I danced with Diego and Fer.

Sunday, February 13, 2000

Day 308.

No messages today on *"Voces del Secuestro."*

Last night I dreamt that I was standing on a bluff overlooking the Mediterranean. I was afraid of falling in, and then I fell, and while I was underneath the water I saw more cliffs. One by one I crawled over all of them, clambering my way up; it was very strange. Then I helped everyone else get out of the water, but nobody bothered to help me. Then, in another scene, I found myself in a very old cemetery, where I saw a lady in sort of an old-fashioned European outfit selling worms, and then I went running out of the place.

I am so tired of listening to *vallenatos* [traditional Colombian music] all day long, of seeing green everywhere, of hearing so many crickets and birds and the sound of the river rushing below. I am sick of listening to the radio, of hanging on to every last word they say on the news, of seeing so much black plastic. I am sick of living in this place, sick of everything here.

This goddamn mosquito net is all clogged up with ants that bite and smell like hell. All of this is so revolting. And on top of it I have my period.

Today I asked my father if he thinks we'll ever get out of here. Of course, of course, he said, but I could tell he wasn't too sure.

Monday, February 14, 2000

Day 309.

Today I woke up early and got busy fixing things with my dad. First we removed the wooden planks, washed them, and then we rearranged things inside our hut. After that I washed the mosquito nets. Yesterday we received the newspapers from February 10 and 11. On the news they've been talking a lot about the ELN: apparently they're proposing that a peace envoy be appointed, because Víctor G. is in Norway with the FARC and he seems to have forgotten that we have to work together to achieve some kind of peace.

Day 310.

Last night I had some very strange dreams. In one of them, everyone told me that since they hadn't heard any news about what had happened to us, they decided to bury us symbolically. But they had split us up, burying the women on one side and the men on the other. My mother cried and cried over my "death," and I stood there looking at the coffins, among them my own. It all felt unbelievably strange.

After that I dreamt that I was in a very big house visiting Alejandra García, who looked very pretty. As she introduced me to her little girl, the man of the house told me that I was very important, and asked me to pose for a photograph with everyone else there, but I came out looking awful in the photo. Then, in another segment of the dream, I was trying to get hold of some ashes that everyone told me were my father's. I kept telling everyone that they couldn't be my father's ashes because he was still alive, but it didn't matter: they gave me the ashes, and then suddenly Diego appeared at my side, acting very sweet with me, telling me how much he had missed me. I was happy but very startled by his reaction.

Today I heard Pablo, Gabino, and Antonio García in an interview on Radionet. Ana María López, Uriel's ex, also spoke on the show and asked what was happening with us, but they said they couldn't discuss specific cases, and reiterated that the objective of our kidnapping was financial. The last question came from a journalist, who asked about the case of the Avianca Fokker 50 and the 15 people still in captivity.

In all honesty, I really feel that our release is still a long way away. I don't even bother thinking about it anymore because I have already spent so much time imagining it that I am going to drive myself crazy if I think about it anymore.

Life has been so unfair to you, Mommy. Boy, were you ever right when you said to me, "Darling, the world is an unfair place, life is unfair. On this earth everything is the reverse of what it should be: bad things always happen to good people, and bad people always seem to make out just fine."

It has been so long, Mommy, that I don't know if we will ever see each other again. I bet you've changed a lot; I know I have. With my entire body and soul I pray that I will be able to experience just one more day like the kind I used to have all the time. I think life brought me here because I have been an ungrateful person. And now that I know what happiness really is, it seems that destiny has decided to make me suffer even more, because I am still being held here, more and more miserable with each passing day. Mommy, please forgive me for everything I've done. I miss you so much. I thank God that back then when we were still together, you knew how much I loved you, because I always told you so. Do you remember when I would say to you, "Mommy, won't you spoil me a little?" or "Mommy, you don't spoil me like you used to," and you would tell me that I was too old to be spoiled like a little girl, but that I was still your girl even though I was all grown up? Mommy, I have had the darkest, ugliest premonitions lately. Somehow it's gotten into my head that I am going to die.

I feel that I am fading away, little by little. . . .

Wednesday, February 16, 2000

Today I told my father that I wanted to talk to him about something, but that first he had to promise me that he wouldn't tell anyone about what I was about to reveal. He opened his eyes and said, "I promise."

First, I reiterated that the reason I was confiding in him was because I was absolutely certain that what I was about to tell him was not at all dangerous to either of us. With fear in his eyes, he looked at me and said, "All right, sweetheart, what's the animal you've been hiding now?"

"As if there's been so many of them . . . I mean, how many have I had?" I said to him.

"Well, I hope it's not a snake," he replied. No, I said, and then I told him the story of how I had found this particular creature back in December but hadn't said anything because I knew that he would only kill her. And then I reminded him that nothing had happened to me since then—not to me, to him, or Piqui, which proved that there was really nothing to be frightened of. . . .

"All right, all right, get to the point," he said. So I led him inside the hut and told him to sit down on the floor next to his bed. It was 5:45. I pointed my flashlight on the little hole, and we sat there for fifteen minutes. My dad smoked a cigarette while we waited and waited, and I could tell he was nervous. Finally, Tatica emerged from her little den, and that was when I saw my father's face transform before my eyes. His head suddenly seemed frozen to his neck, he shrank back, and then all of a sudden he jumped to his feet, as if sprung by a coil.

"No way," he said to me. "No way. I'm sorry."

I told him a promise was a promise, and if he killed Tatica I would die of sadness because she is the only entertainment I have around here. I tried to explain to him that she was completely harmless, and to prove it I tossed a little piece of paper her way. I thought she would react the way she did before, that she would run back into her hole, but to my surprise, Tatica leapt into the air before the piece of paper touched the ground, and actually caught it in midair. I have no idea why that happened—she's not like that. I told my dad that she never did that before and he said, "Oh, no? So what was that, then? Did you think she'd go back into her hole?" And I said yes—maybe she was hungry or something. But my father just looked at me and said, "Listen, Leszli, I am really starting to worry about you. You are risking my life and the monkey's life, not to mention your own, just so you can entertain yourself?"

I didn't say anything. Instead, I just asked him to think it over for a few weeks, so that he could get to know Tatica and see what she was really like. And then I asked him to please not tell anyone about it.

Thursday, February 17, 2000

Last night my father wouldn't let me go to sleep—he was on high alert all night long, pointing his flashlight at Tatica. Then he grilled me about her hours, asking if she kept some kind of schedule, and I told him that her hours were from 6 to 6. After that, I said, she didn't budge from that hole. I told him to just go to sleep already and stop bothering Tatica, and to let me go to sleep, too. Then he asked me if I had ever tried to pick her up, and he made me swear that I wouldn't ever try. If he ever found out he would kill me.

Thursday, March 2, 2000

Today they told us to start writing letters, because they want to send them for us. I have so many things, so many stories to tell that I decided I would write to my mother, Carol, Nandor, Jairo, and Diego. I think this must be my happiest day yet in captivity, and maybe even my life. I got the most wonderful letters from my mother, Nandor, and Carito—although hers was pretty short. They told me about a ton of things, among them that Diego asked my mother if he could marry me! Apparently he had already talked it over with his parents and they gave him their approval. My mother told him what she thought, or what she had understood, which was that he didn't love me anymore and he told her no, no—he loved me very much. Can this be true? Oh, I hope so, because it would make me so happy ... if it were a lie, it would be just awful!

My mother went to Vallecito and spoke with one of the commanders there. She came out of the meeting pretty happy, because she said they seemed like good people. She said that if she had to, she would join them. Apparently, in Bucaramanga they're saying all sorts of crazy things about me: that I've joined the guerrillas, that I run up and down the mountains with a rifle hanging from my shoulder, that I'm going out with one of the guerrillas, and that my father cries all day long over it. It's really pretty hilarious.

My mother, Nandor, and Carol sent me a couple of pairs of paragliding pants; according to my father, they're completely nuts, but Nandor and I love them. They also sent me some beautiful sandals, three T-shirts, two lovely shirts, socks, two towels, plus a Game Boy, deodorant, and batteries. And as a treat they also sent me peanut butter and a cake with *dulce de leche*. And in addition to all that, tons of joy and optimism.

I gave a shirt and my old jeans to one of the guerrilla women, because they don't fit me anymore.

Sunday, March 5, 2000

Today I woke up and went over to Lau's tent to wish him a happy birthday. Yesterday the head guerrilla asked me to organize a little

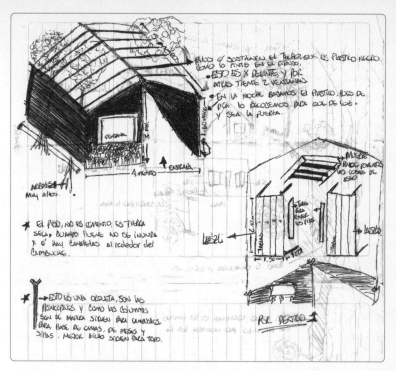

A view of one of the huts where the hostages slept.

party and that's what I'm doing right now. As a gift I gave him some of the candy my family sent me.

My father and I got busy today sealing off the hut with plastic, because after yesterday's thunderstorm the hut sprang a bunch of leaks. The river rose up pretty high, and now the water is totally dark.

Right now I am wearing the outfit I plan to wear the day they release us: jeans, blue shirt, sandals, and a little scarf. I feel good today.

Yesterday I started writing a little story for my mother in the notebook she sent me, and then I painted the wooden planks black and white. Right now I'm reading the book *Nosotros decimos no* [We Say No], by Eduardo Galeano. It's amazing.

Tuesday, March 7, 2000

On the radio messages they said that my mother is in the south of Bolívar gathering letters. That news made me so happy that I started to cry.

Wednesday, March 8, 2000

My mother spoke today; she sounded happy, thrilled in fact. I am so happy. It is absolutely wonderful to hear her sound so calm, so serene.

Thursday, March 9, 2000

Nandor spoke on the radio today. He sounded really good— what a difference! He talked about the *clase pendeja,* or "idiot class," meaning the traditional middle class, and then he said that we have nothing to feel guilty about, that he knows we are hostages and not on vacation. It was really sweet of him. Then Carol spoke for a while. She told me that Diego, Jairo, Lina, and Jito came over to our house on Monday because they thought that my mother might have received some kind of proof of life from us, and then they told her that they were worried that when I came home I would think they were a bunch of morons. Nandor is working at Colmena, an insurance company, or something like that. What a disaster! I really screwed up his education this past year—because of our kidnapping I don't think he was able to do much. I just hope that we get out of here soon so that he can start studying again and so that my mom can really work, because with all this going on, how much mental space have they had for working or studying? I really screwed up everyone's plans.

Saturday, March 11, 2000

Day 335.

Last night I dreamt that I fell into a great big abyss: I was flying in a helicopter but the pilot hadn't strapped me in securely enough so I started to fall. They were able to catch me once, but then they lost me and I started falling again. In the middle of the abyss, right in the very center, there was another abyss, even deeper than the first one. I was petrified because it was filled with garbage, and I said to myself, "This is where I will die." Then I dreamt that María Helena was walking past a jewelry store and asked me to try on a beautiful diamond ring. I was thrilled. Then I dreamt that I was with my father in a really nice restaurant with waterfalls and crocodiles. The place was filled with people I knew, and at one point I turned to my father and suggested we have a coffee in the zoo, but he said no.

Yesterday Juan told me that he doesn't have anything against me, and then he wished me a happy International Women's Day. It was kind of belated, he said, but it was important and he didn't want to let it slip.

On the radio today Carol talked about what it was like for them during the two hours our plane was being hijacked. My mother had gone over to the home of our neighbors, Claudia and José Luis, for a drink. Afterward, they went out for a walk and when they returned the others told them that Lucía had phoned, crying. My mom called her back right away and then turned to Carol and the others and cried, "No! Laszlo and Leszli's plane disappeared. No, Carol, no! I can't take it!" And she broke down crying. They all went into my bedroom to listen to the news on the radio and our story—our tragedy—was the one and only topic discussed that night. Carol said that it was awful, that the phone rang and rang all night, with people calling to ask what was going on. . . .

My mom, so sweet, dedicated another song to me, a song I love: *"Te veo venir, soledad."* Then she said that she was going to spoil me like crazy and that tomorrow she would send me some more things.

What a difference in these messages: these ones are the best!

Sunday, March 12, 2000

11 months. Day 336.

Pretty boring day today. Lately I have been crying out in my sleep, and I can't figure out why. I have a way of dreaming the craziest things, and I guess I just start crying over things that have nothing to do with reality.

Yesterday Nandor told me that our apartment is really different now, because they did some painting and remodeling. I was kind of taken aback by the news. That stinks—I mean, why did they have to go and paint my room when I wasn't there?

Monday, March 13, 2000

Day 337.

No messages today on Luis Carlos's show—and just when I finally got the station to come in loud and clear.

The worst hour of the day around here is 6 P.M., because you can't tell whether it's light or dark out. And the worst day is definitely Sunday. And the two together, even worse. It's so pretty here, but I always end up crying over the silliest little things.

On Saturday night, at around 11 P.M., I went to the supply shack. The fat guy was there—he had brought a snake up from the river and a few fish to eat. He asked me if I was tired, and I told him no.

Today the mule driver came by and we sent him out to buy alcohol and chocolates. Yesterday he gave me some chocolates, Coca-Cola, and biscuits. He's a very nice person. Today he gave me a little sticker commemorating International Women's Day, which I saved.

Somehow we lost the monkey; she went up into the mountains. That was a real shame.

Tuesday, March 14, 2000

Today, a scorpion that was more or less as big as my palm stung me on my right hand. It was completely stupid of me—my fault for not looking before setting my hand down when I went to go to the bathroom. *Bam!* He got me. First I got a rash, then my hand went numb, and I felt this awful burning sensation, but after a while it went away. Now I have a headache, but that's about it.

Today they held a meeting for the relatives of the Avianca hostages, and we found out, through the governor of Santander, that our families have sued the Colombian government.

I didn't eat anything today.

Carol spoke on the radio tonight: Andrea Lagos got married, so did Helga Díaz. Diego is looking very cute these days, she said, and is acting quite differently than before, though that's to be expected.

Angelica came over to our house with her little girl, who's beautiful. She's still going out with César.

Nandor wants me to tell him how we're doing, how we sleep, what the river is like, et cetera. What a bore, that guy . . . He keeps on talking about this letter he's putting together with news and gossip about what's going on there.

Wednesday, March 15, 2000

Day 339.

Big news today: Uriel had an attack of some sort. I don't believe it for a second: I think he's just pulling some kind of stunt, and I have to say we would all be thrilled if they released him already.

Yesterday we got a delivery of newspapers with a picture of my mom receiving our letters. She also talked on the radio and said she was very proud of me because I've done just what she told me to do, and she encouraged me to keep it up. She also said that Pablo, my cat, is as fresh as ever: that he goes out with all the girl cats in the neighborhood and doesn't come back until late at night. When he comes back they scold him, but apparently he always comes back clean after being out for a couple of hours. My friend María took the tests for medical school at the UNAB, but her ICFES score wasn't high enough. She dyed her hair a really nice color, and Mónica did the same. She moved to Medellín and María Fernanda Castillo moved to Bogotá with Lucho. Jairo, Jito, Lina, and Diego are writing a song for me with a band called La Veterana Sexy, or something like that, but they're going to change the name because some of them don't like it.

Thursday, March 16, 2000

My mother, Carol, Nandor, and Lina spoke on the radio today. Lina said that Diego saw some photos of me and said that he'd never realized how pretty I am, and that he's happy to wait for me. Then she said that Jito has practiced their song so many times that he's lost his voice. My mother is overjoyed that I let my eyelashes grow; she says it's the best gift I could have given her this year. Pablo the cat has an ear infection and he's not eating, Nandor said, so he's trying to get him to eat concentrated food. And apparently Danielito has turned out to have a bit of a temper; he sulks over the least little thing.

Friday, March 17, 2000

My father and I woke up in a bad mood today—the entire group, in fact, is very tense because the guerrillas have done absolutely nothing for Uriel. It almost seems as though they just want him to die. And if they want us to be witnesses of something like that, it can only mean that things are going to get very grim for all of us. It just gets worse and worse every day, and I have to wonder how much more of this we are going to be able to take. Just now, at about 9:30 P.M., they took Uriel out of the camp. Apparently he is in very bad shape.

Saturday, March 18, 2000

It's awful out today. I put on my makeup and then I took it all off.

They caught my father reading Uriel's notebook. My father, after hunting around a bit, found a packet of Robaxifen, the pills I needed so badly. What a jerk, that guy. He never gave me a single pill when I needed it.

We're all wasting away from this endless, pointless waiting—none of us can seem to muster energy for anything at all. We just sit around looking at each other, feeling frustrated, distraught, and on the news they don't say a thing about our situation.

Sunday, March 19, 2000

We're all low today. On the news they said that Carlos Castaño sent a letter to the president saying that he's going to add more troops to the group in the south of Bolívar.

Yesterday my father asked me if anything had happened between me and Lau. I said no.

Monday, March 20, 2000

Today we found out that at 9:45 A.M. Uriel was released. They brought him straight to the Carlos Andila Lulle hospital. He is so lucky, and I am so jealous of him right now.

I've been crying a lot lately. I wish they would just release us, all of us, already. What is it with these people? And more to the point, what is it with me? What on earth do they want with me? Conclusion: The ELN must have a massive amount of money, because keeping all of us here is not cheap—come on, it's been a goddamn year already! These people don't know what to do with all the money they've got! God, it would be nice if these COCE people would finally say to us, "Listen, since we've been holding you hostage for such a long time, and you have behaved so superbly, and since after all you are part of the Colombian nation we defend, we've decided to give you a few million." That would be just grand. If they did that, well then, sure, I'd stick around here a little longer. . . . Oh, God, really! How can I even imagine something so stupid? It must be all this time in captivity—it's turned us all into raving idiots.

When I go outside and look around at everything, I can't help it—the tears just start to roll down my cheeks. I wish I could stop crying, but I can't. Lately it's been so hard for me. It must be the depression; it just hits me all of a sudden and sends me spinning around and around until I can't see or think straight anymore. Boy, would I like to know what kind of sonofabitch I was in a previous life to deserve this kind of karma.

Nandor spoke on UIS today about suicide. I know why, too. God only knows what kind of shit Uriel said to them, but now they're all worried about us. The truth is, though, I *have* started thinking about suicide again. This is shit. There is no way out, no light at the end of the tunnel, nothing to cling to, nothing at all. There's nobody around to tell us when all this is going to be over.

Wednesday, March 22, 2000

The head guerrilla came back to the campsite today, but it's just the same old story as always. He read us a letter from Uriel, and told us that another one of the commanders said to say hello. The same old empty words he's said to us before. It's getting pretty old.

My life is over.

During our meeting my father asked them to bring us games and books and good food and some other things. I just stood up and said that I don't want food, or anything else. All I want is my freedom.

Honestly, I fail to understand what those COCE creatures are after. I don't even know who they are. All I know is that our lives, our freedom, and our dreams are in the hands of a bunch of people who lack the decency to even send us a goddamn note. They are like gods on earth: they take people's lives and either spare them or eliminate them—they give freedom and then they take it away, they grant you a bit of happiness and then take it away at will. How fabulous it is to be a member of COCE! What kind of people are they, anyway? I imagine them as tall, fat men with mean, ugly faces, angry all the time and yes, terribly busy up there in the mountains. I bet they don't even show their faces to their own guerrillas. I would really like to know what their lives, their families are like. . . . Or maybe their families have already been killed off? Maybe that's why they are so filled with rage for the rest of us idiots. . . .

Leszli Kálli has put an end to this diary. I will not write another word for the rest of my time in captivity. I will continue this diary when I am free . . . that is, if I ever get out of here. And now, I ask that if something should happen to me, that these words find their way to my mother, Marlene López de Kálli. I leave this diary to her. And if somehow this diary gets lost, please, someone, return it to me one day. This is very important to me, for it contains everything I have thought and felt over the course of the past year, and it is my wish to save it, just as I have saved all the other diaries I have written since I was a little girl.

Thank you.

Sincerely,

Leszli Kálli

My diary came to an end on March 22, 2000, while I was still in captivity, as the last entry indicates. Just as I said, I chose not to write again until I was free. And now I am free. Today is April 30, 2000. It almost doesn't seem possible that I am sitting here in the living room of my home. It is 6:40 A.M., and I didn't sleep at all last night. I stayed up thinking about all the things that have happened to me.

The time has come for me to tell the story of my last days in captivity.

By the end of March, I had lost all hope of ever getting released. The one and only thing that kept me going were the messages my family and some of my friends sent over the airwaves. At that point, I felt certain that I wanted to die. I was completely drained mentally, emotionally. My father and I did the best we could to give each other strength, but it was a lie. He kept telling me that I had to remain calm, but by that point both of us had long since stopped believing the things we kept telling each other.

On April 11 we were listening to "36 Hours for Freedom," a radio program in our honor, a kind of marathon show on behalf of all the people from Santander province who were in captivity, and people called in with messages and comments on the topic. The people of Santander were quite amazing; they really showed the country the meaning of the word *solidarity* that night. Anyway, on that show they announced that on April 12 the ELN would issue a statement about the hostages from the plane hijacking. I didn't think much of it, really, I just figured it was the same old runaround. I wasn't the least bit moved by the news. Never in my life could I have imagined what they had in store for us.

The next day, Commander Antonio García, the number two guy at the ELN Central Command, made the following statement:

"We are going to release seven or eight people from the Avianca Fokker, because we have spoken to the airline, presented our demands, and they have not been met. As such we have decided to release them, because we are not murderers, and we know that they are people who live on salaries, and we have nothing against them.

They are part of the nation of Colombia, and they will be released during Holy Week, before Thursday or Friday, so that they may spend the holidays with their families."

Dumbfounded, I leaped up, jumped around, ran, danced, laughed. I was overjoyed, ecstatic. It was real! It was going to happen! My father looked at me, the emotion in his eyes, as I danced around in my infinite joy imagining all the things I had to pack, the sneakers I had to wash, the mosquito net I wanted to take home with me as a memento, and all the sadness I wanted to leave buried here, and the thousand and one promises I would make good on as soon as I got home. There were so many things to do, and so little time, that I immediately raced back to our hut to start packing my things. It's strange—you arrive at a place like this with nothing at all, but I have a way of finding sentimental value in every stupid little thing, which means that, of course, I end up hoarding a ton of stupid little things. I pulled out my suitcase and brushed the dust off, making a mental list of the things that I had to pack and the things that I would leave behind, and then I realized that I had to talk to my dad to see what he wanted to pack.

So I went back outside to see where he was, but I couldn't find him. I searched all over the campsite, and the others joined me and we looked everywhere for him, until finally the fat guy told me that he was in Iván's hut. So I went over to Iván's tent and I saw my father standing in front of Iván, Aguado, and the guy they called "the nephew." They seemed to be arguing about something, but as I approached them they lowered their voices and once I was inside they stopped talking altogether. My father turned to me and asked me to please go back to our hut and wait for him there; he would be done in a few minutes, he said.

As I walked back, I tried hard to keep the negative thoughts from creeping into my head, but from the way they were acting it definitely seemed that something was not right. Still, I was so completely over-joyed that I just couldn't bear to spoil the moment with the kind of unpleasant, tragic thoughts that always ended up running through my mind at moments like those. So I went back to the hut and pulled out my sneakers, hoping to wash away my fear and trepidation as I cleaned them down by the river. Every so often I looked up to see if my father was on his way back already, but no. No sign of him at all. I finished washing my things and went back to the hut, but my fears had not subsided—they had gotten worse, in fact, and when my father finally returned, his face confirmed my intuition. Something was definitely off.

He sat down on the edge of his bed and right there, right at that moment, I could see how the burden of this experience had taken its toll on him—every one of his years on earth were etched into his face, and then some. His eyes were staring out at nothing in particular, too wrapped up in the anguish he clearly felt to actually see anything in front of him. Without looking at me at all, he asked me for a cigarette, and I gave him one. Then I asked him what had happened, and he said, "Nothing, nothing happened." Come on, I said to him, you don't look like that for nothing, and I begged him to tell me. After about a half hour of pleading, he finally told me, and as the words fell from his lips I felt as if someone had driven a knife through my heart, my life. From that moment on, I was in agony.

"Leszli, these men are telling me that you're going to have to stay, and I have to go because with us, it's different, because you have nothing to do with the deal they made with Avianca. They said that this case is different, it's an economic question, it's . . ."

He kept on talking until finally I interrupted him and said, "Aren't I the daughter of an employee? After everything Antonio García just said, what is it? It's all just talk? How can they do this to us? Why us? Why is God allowing this to happen?"

"Because . . . sweetheart, sweetheart! Listen to me, and listen to me good: never, never, I swear to you, will I let them keep you here without me. I will die before I let them do that to you and they know this now. I will shoot myself if they don't accept a trade."

"What trade? What do you mean?" I asked him, terrified.

"Well, the trade would be for you to go, and for me to stay here in your place."

Just moments earlier, I felt as though a knife had ripped into my heart, and now I felt it hacking its way, back and forth, up and down, through my entire body. My father went on talking: at 9:30 that night, he said, the men were going to radio the Central Command to communicate his adamant refusal to leave without me.

I got up from my bed and walked over to the chair my father had built back in December. As I looked down toward the river, I could see all the others packing their things, washing up, shaving, singing, and laughing. In front of me, I could see the blessing that I had felt for such a miserably short period of time, and behind me I felt a weight bear down upon me, so heavy that I could hardly breathe; I felt as though I was drowning. I sat down in the chair, curled up with my arms wrapped around my legs, hung my head, and began to cry from all the rage I felt—the kind of rage you feel when you are completely, utterly impotent. More than anything in the world I wanted my father to come over, give me a great big hug, and apologize for playing such a terrible joke on me. Of course, that was exactly what my father wanted from me, too, but at that moment neither of us was able to grant the fictional security that, in the middle of the nightmare of this past year, we had alternately given each other whenever one of our moods took an ugly swing. Two hours went by before my father finally found the courage, I don't know where or how, to turn to me and say, "Sweetheart, look at me. Don't cry anymore. Look at me. You're going to leave here. Don't give it a second thought."

"That's not why I'm crying, Daddy. I'm upset because I don't understand how these people can just suddenly decide to do this at the last minute. It's like they've been plotting it, to figure out the best way to be as ruthless as possible with us. It's almost as if someone, I don't know who the hell it could be, said, 'Oh, yeah, let's let them feel good for a few minutes, let's let them enjoy the feeling that they're going to be released, and then we'll really screw them over.' Daddy, how can people be so evil? What are these people made of? They really have no idea how much damage they have done to us. I mean, they could have pulled us aside before announcing the news and said to us, 'Laszlo and Leszli, you can't listen to what García is about to say because you're not part of that deal.' But no! These bastards waited until we could see it up close! After a year here our release was finally right under our noses, so close we could touch it, sense it, and then *bam*! They slapped us across the face."

"Leszli," my father said. "I know none of this makes any sense, it never has. If they had the tiniest little twinge of a conscience we would never have been kidnapped in the first place. But now you have to promise me that you are going to search for the strength you need because I can't bear to see you like this. You have to get it into your head that this is a question of money. This is a negotiation, which means we have to act with that in mind. As for everything you've said, of course you are one hundred percent right, but if you slowed down for a second you'd realize that they've made a mistake here."

When he said that, I opened my eyes wide, dried my tears, and looked him in the eye. "What are you talking about?"

"Listen, these people started off demanding a ridiculous amount of money for our ransom, to secure your release in addition to mine, and as soon as it was out of their mouths I told them that even if I sold everything I owned I would still only be able to come up with half of what they were demanding. Well, without even listening to what I said, without even stopping to confer with any command center, they accepted the amount. Then I told them that you would go and I would stay and only then did they say they had to radio Central Command. Of course, it is possible that Central Command has given them carte blanche to negotiate the ransom with us. That's what we still don't know but don't worry, we're going to find out. Right now they should be talking to Central Command, so please don't cry anymore. Let's just wait."

Wait we did. At a quarter to eleven that evening Iván came by and asked to come into the tent. He said he needed to talk to my father and asked him to step outside. My father followed him out and returned a little while later.

"They said they tried to get through to COCE, but they weren't able to establish communication, so instead they sent our proposal through someone at a radio station who works as a kind of messenger, and if there's any answer we should hear from them sometime in the next four hours. Now, I want you to try to sleep. It's been an exhausting day for you."

"How am I going to sleep?" I retorted. "Give me a cigarette. My heart is pounding like crazy."

My father then got up and started looking through our things for the Ativan pills that Nandor had sent to us, which were to be used only in very extreme circumstances. He took out two and handed me one. The other went into his mouth. Then he lit a cigarette, passed it to me, and lit one for himself.

The flickering candle, along with the wisps of smoke rising up inside those cramped quarters, covered in black plastic, made for a very creepy atmosphere, only adding to the anguish we already felt as we each lay in our respective beds, protected by our mosquito nets. We didn't talk anymore after that, and at 5 on the dot Aguado, one of the three head guerrillas, appeared at the entrance to our hut. He didn't even bother asking to talk to us. With a scornful look in his eyes, which looked out at nothing in particular, aside from his own perversity, he replied: "We just heard from them: the answer is no. She stays and you go."

With that, he turned around and left as icily as he had arrived: without excusing himself, without any warmth or humanity, leaving a trail of bitterness in his wake. I sat up in bed and looked at my father, whose right hand was covering his face. Right then all I wanted to do was run after that disgusting pig, insult him, hit him; given the chance, I would have gladly killed him. It wasn't what he said, it was the way he said it—his attitude, his despotic tone as he said those awful things, leaving my father in a state of pure anguish. As I thought about that, I started to cry again, and my father, who assumed my tears had been prompted by the news and the frustration of having been held captive for so long, turned to me. All of a sudden it seemed as though he had been infused with all the strength in the world, and he said: "Leszli. You don't understand. You're leaving. The person you have to listen to is me, not that guy." Without another word he stood up and went over to the hut where the three head guerrillas were talking, the nephew, Iván, and Aguado.

At 10 A.M. my father came back and said to me, "I fixed everything, you're going and I'm staying." At that moment, I felt as if a part of me had been buried deep in the earth, and I knew that my life would never be the same. I finally understood how insignificant I was, because the fortress that was once Leszli crumbled to the ground in a thousand little pieces right then, and my life disconnected from my body without any warning, because there is no way to accept or resign ourselves to the perverse manner in which people flaunt their callous disregard for their fellow man, as they drag entire families into their conflicts and rip them apart.

By now, my companions in this miserable situation were taking turns consoling us; I cannot judge them for having taken their time to visit us and be with us during this difficult time. After all, they had neither the desire nor the need to spoil the happiest moment of their lives with other people's misfortunes. As they walked off and returned to their respective situations, and the two of us remained behind, left alone in our desperate solitude and silence, we could hear their happy voices, singing off in the distance, reveling in the joy that is the exclusive domain of people who know they will soon be free, people who know they will be reborn after being buried for over a year in the chaos and misery of captivity.

"Leszli," my father said, "I want you to know that this is one more test that life has given you. And I want you to be brave, I want you to prove to me that you can make it. You have to look at this as a negotiation: you are going to get out of here and you are going to have to figure out a way to get the money these people want. I know you can do it. I don't know how, but you will have to find a way. Right now things are very tough for us, because one of us is still in captivity and the government is not going to allow you to sell any property, and our bank accounts will be frozen. According to these people, you have exactly three months to come up with the money, and you will have to bring it somewhere near Barrancabermeja. Later on they will tell you more, and they'll give you an exact time and place. You're going to have to do it yourself, all alone, but not in three months. Even if you get the money before, even if you win the lottery before, or someone gives you all the money, under no circumstances can you give them the money before six months have gone by, because if not, they are going to think that it was very easy for you to get the cash, and then they're going to start in all over again with their games and their nonsense. So I want you to remember that even though it's going to take longer, it's for my own well-being. I will be fine here, and I trust you implicitly. So remember that, sweetheart. Six months . . . not three."

As he talked on and on, all I could think about was how on earth I would explain the situation to my family when I got back to Bucaramanga. I could just picture myself telling them all, "Uh, listen, don't get too excited, because my father didn't make it out and now we have to get our hands on a ton of cash as soon as possible."

"Daddy," I said, "it will be much easier if I stay and you leave. You have more contacts than I do—people will do business with you, but me? A nineteen-year-old girl asking to borrow money because her father has been kidnapped? It's going to be impossible. I'll have to steal it, I guess, or I don't know, and anyway, I can take it—I'm young, and if I made it through a year, I can make it through another six months. Think about your back problems."

"There's nothing to discuss here. You're leaving and that's that."

"Please, let me stay with you. Just like we always said: we came in here together, and we're going to leave together. Don't do this to me, please. . . ."

When I said that, my father came over to me and hugged me tight. Right at that instant I started sobbing uncontrollably. In silence and in tears, we clung to each other for a long time, and I felt that this might very well be the last hug we ever shared. Then I opened my eyes and for some reason I noticed his neck: all of a sudden I wanted to etch in my memory every last spot and beauty mark on his skin, the shape of his ear, the feeling of his arms around mine. I wanted to digest all that information and turn it into a kind of tangible memory for the time when he would no longer be at my side. After a little while the other hostages came by, and they patted us on the back and did their best to console us. Laureano spoke up first, and said that he couldn't believe what a dirty game they were playing with us, and he kept telling me to stay calm. His words were the only ones that had any effect on me, because he has always been so sincere, so kind. Behind them stood Iván, looking at us with his head low and a guilty expression on his face. All he said, though, was,

"People, there's a meeting now in the main hut." My father said he would stay behind in our hut, but Iván insisted that all of us had to be there, and so we all got up. My father and I were the last ones out, at the end of the line of people who were now making their way to the main hut.

As we walked through the campsite, we saw Aguado walking toward the tent, and on his face I could just barely make out a kind of cynical smile that somehow escaped through his eyes rather than his lips. I could tell that he both wanted and didn't want us to see that look on his face. He derived pleasure from my pain, I have no doubt about that. I always knew that about him, and every chance I got I would always flash him the dirtiest look I was capable of mustering. Dirty looks were pretty typical, but on that day and in that situation, the humiliation I felt was so great that it surpassed any other feeling that could have existed between the two of us. At that moment, I actually didn't have the strength to give him a nasty look, to play his game. I already understood that I was an absolute zero as far as he was concerned. And so I just kept on walking, and when we reached the tent I sat down next to my father. His hand was still resting on my back and my head was resting against his neck when Aguado got up and said, "All right, we've gathered you all here to tell you that tomorrow at eight A.M. we're going to start walking for your release, and I don't want anyone to slow things down for any kind of big spectacle or farewell."

Those last words were like dry, hard slaps that reverberated through my head. "Any kind of big spectacle or farewell," I kept saying over and over again. Spectacle or farewell, spectacle or farewell . . . the blood went rushing into my head, jerking me out of my sadness, and it was as if I went deaf right then. Suddenly I felt as if I was drowning, and the one thing I needed to do at that moment was jump to my feet, which I did, and I began to scream at him.

"Why don't you just say it to me straight? The only person here who's going to make any kind of spectacle is me—unless you think there's anyone else here who feels that he's going to die because my father is staying behind! You miserable pig! Look me in the face and say it to me, or don't you have the balls to look me in the eye? Be a man, a real man." As I said this, my father tried in vain to get me to calm down. None of the guerrillas said a word, but I could tell from the expressions on their faces that in some small way they agreed with what I said and did. Aguado kept his mouth shut, though, and walked out of the hut. When it was all over, my father hugged me and as we left for our hut I cried and cried. My father didn't bother to scold me; I knew he hadn't really approved of my little outburst but he didn't say anything. He understood that it was my way of defending myself in the middle of all the pain I felt. The other hostages could only stare at me, dumbfounded by the scene I had made. They were probably scared that I had ruined things with my outburst, or that the release would be delayed on account of me. Back in our hut, my father and I lit cigarettes and sat in silence for a long while, sitting it out until we regained our composure.

"What if we try to escape tonight?" I asked him.

"No," he replied, "There are too many land mines down by the river, where we'd have to walk, and anyway, we could go upriver or downriver and they'd be waiting for us just the same. And if we escape, what do we do if one of the land mines explodes on us, one of those legbreakers? The best thing to do is just follow the plan, but I want you to pay attention. Tomorrow, after you start walking, if they separate you from the group, it will be because they are going to keep you here and then come back to me to tell me they've released you. And then they'll take me out and once I'm free, I'll have to negotiate for you. So listen: I want you to do exactly what I tell you to do.

"After you've been walking for a few hours, I want you to tell them that you're having terrible stomach pains. Once you're alone, going to the bathroom, you're going to take out three Ativan pills but you can't let them see you doing it. We're going to sew a little pocket inside your sweater, and we'll put a bunch of them in there. You're going to take three pills all at once, but don't worry—three pills won't do anything to you, they'll just make you really sleepy. So: you take the pills without them catching on, and then you just keep on walking like normal. But then, when the drugs begin to take effect, start complaining that you have a terrible headache, and keep it up until the pills knock you out completely. Then, when you wake up and remember where you are and what you're doing, I want you to start screaming about how much your head hurts, and then, when you're alone again, I want you to take three more of the same pills. That way, you'll make them think that something is very wrong with you, and all they'll want to do is get you out of there as fast as possible.

"I want you to do this because I saw how fast they handed Uriel over—and it was only because he was sick. And if they did it with him they have even more reason to do it with you, since you're the little girl of the group and if you were to die it would make them look terrible. Remember what happened after Gonzáles died: I don't think they're willing to go through that again. When they handed González back, even the government mourned his death, and the ELN actually sent a letter to the family saying that it was an accident and that they were deeply saddened by what had happened. So I can tell you for sure, they will absolutely never let that happen again, much less with the fuss your mother has made all these months. So there you have it: you're going to have to pull off a hell of an acting job—good enough for two Oscars, all right? And remember, I want you to always remember that this is a business, and that they have a lot to lose if it goes wrong. You have to make sure and that they don't catch you with the drugs, though, because if they do, then we're screwed—both of us."

"All right, Daddy," I said. "Don't worry. I'll do it."

We got to work right away: first we took out the knife, then we sliced into my sweater, and in no time at all we had thirty-two pills divided up in the four little pockets we had sewn. Finally I put the sweater on, to see if the pills could be seen or felt from the outside. But no, we did a perfect job; they were completely undetectable. After that we talked for a little while longer but then he told me I ought to go to bed because I probably had a good two or three days of walking ahead of me.

Day 371.

The next day I woke up at 5:30 A.M. As usual, my father had gotten up at 4:30 and was already at the kitchen tent, starting the fire and preparing coffee for everyone, so that by the time the guerrilla on kitchen duty started his shift, the logs would already be burning, and it wouldn't take so long to make breakfast. Getting up early had its advantages: my dad would usually pop into the pantry shack and take out some *panela* or chocolate bars, which he would then crush into little pieces and save in a little cracker box for when we got hungry and there wasn't anything else to eat. He always said, "The best place for a prisoner is in the kitchen."

That day I didn't bother waiting for him to bring me my breakfast, as he always did. He liked serving me breakfast, most of all because by bringing it to me himself, and early, I got the best and the biggest portion of all. His rationale, whenever anyone complained, was that if they wanted more food, they should just wake up earlier. But of course, everyone else usually just preferred to sleep in.

By the time I got to the kitchen he was washing off in the river. As soon as he saw me he got out and told me the coffee was ready, and he asked me if I'd slept well and if I was ready for my freedom. I felt truly miserable: I had had another night of excruciating nightmares and even though I wasn't the least bit tired, my whole body was wracked with pain, the worst I'd ever felt. Every time I thought about being separated from my father, my stomach twisted in knots from the rage.

Time passed by quickly that morning, and in no time at all everyone was up, finished with breakfast and ready to go except for my father, who was putting things into my suitcase. I was devastated, and all I could feel was bitterness: what kind of freedom was this? Freedom? I was leaving, sure, but with my father staying behind I still felt kidnapped—it was the most frustrating feeling imaginable. What should have been the happiest day of my life was now the most miserable. Some freedom.

The hour arrived. It was time to go. Before leaving, the other hostages came by our hut, one by one, crying a bit as they embraced my father, who wished them a happy return with a thin smile on his lips. Then he asked them to think of him, and to drink their second toast in his name. It took them about five seconds to say their goodbyes, and each farewell was tinged with a heavy, infinite sadness. Then it was my turn: my last few moments. We hugged each other tight and my father told me to relax, that everything was going to be all right. Listen to me, he said, and don't waste any more time. Then he gave me one more hug, and all I wanted to do was hold on to him forever. I clung to him as tightly as I could but finally he extricated himself, pushing me away. I turned around and started to walk, but all I could think of was, *No, no—what am I doing? I can't leave my father alone!* He would never have left me by myself, and as I trudged silently along with the others, I said no. No. I am not leaving him behind. Suddenly I cried out, "I am not leaving without my father!" I tossed my backpack on the ground and ran back to him. He hugged me and followed me back into the tent.

"Sweetheart," he said. "You're fucking everything up. I told you once and I'm telling you again, this is a negotiation, and if you want to be a businesswoman, do yourself a favor and start now. If you don't go, I can promise you that these people are going to make things a hell of a lot worse for us, so please do what I say, for the love of God, just this once."

"No, Daddy," I said, and started to say something else but he stopped me and said, "Go! Go! I want you to have your freedom and I want you to win those two Oscars, just go already—otherwise it's going to be much, much harder on both of us. Don't screw it up now, not after we've fixed everything. Go."

"Oh, really? Oh, really, Daddy? Is that what you think?"

"I swear, sweetheart, go now before it's too late." He walked out of the tent and called out to the guerrillas that everything was all right. Then, after another last hug, he pushed me and whispered to me, "Come on, let's just stick to our plan now. You're slowing things down."

I started walking. After about twenty paces I turned around to look at him but he had already gone back into our hut, so I just kept on walking. With my heart shattered into a million bits, I marched on, swearing to myself that when I got out I would tell this story to the whole world. People need to know that this isn't a question of politics—this is torture, this is slavery. People need to know about it, they need to do something about it, we need to put an end to all this suffering. It just doesn't seem possible that now, in the third millennium after Christ, we can simply sit back and allow this type of thing to happen. How is it possible that people just watch, without offering any help or support, as these perverse acts are committed? I mean, if people are cowards, then fine—they can just express their opinions from inside their homes. That's fine—every little bit helps. But I don't know: maybe people just don't want a better world for their children and their children's children.

These were the things that ran through my mind as I walked on through the woods, where every step I took felt like a curse.

After a couple of hours, from far away, through the darkness, I spotted the shadowy figures of three people slowly approaching us. A few more minutes went by and then they were about fifty meters in front of us. My heart started pounding: it was my father. Instantly I looked up and started screaming, "Daddy! Daddy!" and suddenly one of the three men broke from the group and began running toward me.

"Sweetheart, it's me. I'm here, I'm here," he called out, and a few seconds later I was hugging him tight, and then all of the other hostages were gathering around us, hugging him, too. The joy I felt right then was overwhelming—thank you, God, I cried over and over, thank you, God, now I can feel as happy as everyone else because we are all finally being released. Thank you, thank you, thank you.

Once we were through with the hugs, he and I sat down so he could tell me the story of how and why they had finally released him.

"What did I tell you?" he said. "Yes or no? Look at me, I'm here. But wait a second—how could you tell it was me from so far away?" And I told him that as soon as we separated that second time, our group was met by another group of guerrillas who told me not to worry, that later on in the evening they would be bringing him to us, on orders from COCE.

"That was how I knew you were coming. How did it happen?" I asked. He explained to me that shortly after we left, they took him to see another hostage they had been hiding in the same campsite, where we had been: a Spanish man named Angel Blanco Vázquez (Vázquez, he said, with two "z"s), who was now on a hunger strike.

"The head guerrilla," my dad said, "pulled me aside and told me they wanted to see if I could convince him to eat something, because he was on a hunger strike and the only thing he was ingesting was water."

As soon as they brought my father in, the Spanish man assumed my father was a guerrilla commander, because he had been up in the hut by the entrance to the campsite, a hut that we hostages never had access to. The Spanish man had been able to hear the other hostages play soccer and volleyball, and actually thought that we were a group of urban guerrillas on a training session in the jungle, which is what the guerrillas told him. My father cleared up the confusion and introduced himself properly, as Captain Laszlo Kálli, and told the Spanish man that his daughter and a group of other hostages had been delivered to freedom just an hour earlier.

After hearing this, the Spanish man explained to my father that the guerrillas had forced him out of the home of his parents-in-law at midnight on December 31. Since then he hadn't heard a word from any of his relatives and had decided he wanted to die. In response, my father said to him in no uncertain terms that if he, a Colombian through and through, had been kidnapped by ETA in Spain, he would never have allowed himself to die of hunger in the hands of his captors. If he was going to die, he said, he would die trying to escape. Then he pointed to the east and told the man that Barrancabermeja was less than 30 kilometers away: if he walked from 5 to 7 in the morning, and then from 5 to 6:30 in the afternoon—the times of day when the guerrillas are generally back at their bases—he might be able to get out. With those three and a half hours, he could cover at least two kilometers a day. Of course, he'd have to bring provisions—*panela*, rice, candles, lighters, whatever canned food he could find, beans, plus a mosquito net and a big plastic bag, and medicine. He told the man to start stockpiling these things little by little, and to save everything in a backpack. Then, when he was finally ready, he should leave at night, walking along the banks of the river for about two kilometers. Then, my dad told him, he would have to cross a few more rivers and go up and down a number of hills, and eventually walk along the shore of another river. Right then, they called my father out to lunch, and my father asked the man: "So are you going to keep this up or are you going to prepare yourself to get out of here?" With that, the Spanish man ended his hunger strike and they all went to eat. Afterward, they sat around talking for a while until finally the guerrillas called my dad over and informed him that they were going to release him. My father said farewell to Vázquez, telling him that he had been held for over a year—Vázquez had only been in captivity for four months—and that once he got out he would send him messages over the radio. Vázquez would know it was my father because he would send his messages with the phrase "you can learn about the life of a man in half a day." That way he would know it was my father. With that, the two men embraced, and my father began walking with two guerrillas and a mule. He was scared to death that they were releasing him because something had happened to me, because they had separated me from the rest of the group, or because I had messed up with the little acting job.

"When I heard your voice, though, I knew everything was all right."

We were together again. What a relief.

"In all this time, that is the most unbelievable story I have ever heard, I swear it. Poor guy," I said.

From there, they brought us to a little hut near the edge of the river, and after a little while it started raining buckets. The guerrillas told us we were to sleep there, and that they would alert us when it was time to resume walking.

Day 372

At 3 A.M., we walked down to the river, where a kind of canoe with an outboard motor, just like the ones they had used the day of the hijacking, was waiting for us. As we piled into the boat, which was totally open, the rain kept coming down, and we all huddled together under the two-ply blanket my father had brought along, thinking it would come in handy, and he was right. The rest of us had unloaded most of our things under the mistaken assumption that the release would happen a lot faster than it actually did, and so that blanket, which had always come in handy before, was now more valuable than ever; we used it the entire way back. What with the rain and the wind that the boat whipped up as it motored down the river, the weather had gotten icy cold, and even though the blanket got completely soaked, it did protect our eyes from the rain and made the cold at least a little more bearable.

The city of Barrancabermeja was just to the right of the river. According to my father, this looked like the Cimitarra river, not the Magdalena, as I had thought. Anyway, we sailed down, carried along by the current until we reached a fork in the river and began heading upstream until finally, much later, we reached a kind of hamlet at the foot of a mountain with a cliff as steep and sharp as a knife. There, we stopped and ate some breakfast, and got rid of the rest of our gear because there were no mules to carry everything, and we walked and walked up to the top of a small hill, where they brought us rice and fish wrapped in plantain leaves. It wasn't much but it was enough: we were so starved that we were thrilled to eat anything at all, and after filling our stomachs we waited around until about 3 P.M., at which point a group of guerrillas arrived with two mules. As my father climbed onto one of the mules, a snake appeared underfoot, and the mule reared up in fright, tossing my father onto a bed of rocks in the middle of a dried-up riverbed. Miraculously, my father wasn't hurt—the mule didn't do anything more than give us a good scare, but all the same my dad got down and walked the rest of the way. We walked and walked, and after a while all of us were dying for something to drink, but there wasn't any water anywhere nearby.

"I can't go on," I said to my father. "I'm too tired. Daddy, tell me something to keep me going. . . ."

"Every minute is one minute less," my father said encouragingly. "We're going to be free soon. Very soon. Just a few more minutes, hang on, hang on. . . ."

We kept on walking, exhausted, but we kept on walking. As night fell, four of the others who were walking ahead with one of the other guerrillas got lost. Later on we found out that they almost ended up at an army building, but a farmworker tipped them off and after a little while they found their way back to us. Once we were all together again, we continued onward until we reached a road where more guerrillas were waiting for us with a minivan, which we boarded. After riding for a little while we reached another campsite with even more guerrillas—a ton of them. There we were received by none other than Commander Gallero, also known as Gak, the head of them all. A group of journalists from a number of different newspapers, magazines, and TV stations were waiting for us there.

Commander Gak told us that we would be liberated that afternoon, in a few hours' time. According to him, everything that had happened with my father was a giant misunderstanding. He clarified this after I rather angrily brought it up, following his words of welcome that included the usual speech about how they were people fighting for a cause, and that they had understood it was time to release us. Then, that afternoon, we saw the helicopter. . . .

First we saw the helicopter fly low, just over our heads. Tears came to our eyes; I, at least, was unable to hold them back. For the first time, I had difficulty breathing, not because I was sad but because I was so unbelievably ecstatic to see that helicopter swooping down, and to know that my desperate pleas of "how much longer?" had finally been answered. That helicopter was the vehicle that would bring me back to my family, my friends, my life, my world. Suddenly I felt as if I were about to be reborn, but with all that experience that had given me a newfound capacity to appreciate things in their truest dimension. Life was giving me a second chance. A gift.

The moment had come: it was time to say goodbye to the guerrillas. I would be a liar if I said that I felt sad to leave them behind. The only thing that made me feel at all sad right then was the thought of all the other people who were still in the same hell that I was now leaving behind.

The official act of release happened when the ELN guerrillas turned us over to the members of the International Red Cross. We walked about 50 meters. Just a bit further on I could see Jaime Bernal Cuéllar, the attorney general of Colombia. I started walking, faster now, and the tears rolled down even faster when I saw that he was crying, too. When I reached him, he hugged me tight and said, "Relax. It's all over. Welcome to freedom!"

I thanked him, and then we all climbed into the Red Cross jeeps, which headed out toward the helicopter. As soon as we were settled and strapped in, the rotors began to hum and whir, and I thought my heart would explode. The helicopter left the ground and as it slowly rose up into the air, I looked down at that miserable little hilltop where I had been held against my will for 373 days. Once again, my eyes filled with tears. I looked up at the sky and uttered the only words I could have possibly uttered right then:

"Thank you, God! Finally, You listened!"

After a little while, as the helicopter soared through the sky, I caught sight of Bucaramanga, the city I had dreamed about for so long. Now it was a reality that nobody, nobody would be able to take away from me. After a little while, we touched down at the heliport of the city hospital. The doors opened, and I was the first one out. All I wanted to see was my family. . . . Finally I was standing on the ground where I would see my mother, my sister, my brother, my nephew, and all the people I love.

Suddenly a door opened, and a throng of people spilled out, all of them clapping and shouting, "Welcome! Welcome to freedom!"

I climbed seven little steps and, finally, I saw my mother and ran into her arms. We embraced for a long, long time, and after an endless silence, she finally said to me, "It's over now, honey. You're with me now."

ABOUT THE AUTHOR

Leszli Kálli was born on December 11, 1980. After finishing high school in 1999, she planned to live on a kibbutz in Israel before attending university. But this kidnapping changed her destiny.

Leszli has been keeping a diary since she was nine years old. What she's written is both moving and defiant. She reveals an exceptional teenager, surrounded by the world's problems, who is desperately trying to find her own identity. Her diary is a moving reclamation in the midst of a terrible Colombia, left for its youth to inherit.

ABOUT THE TRANSLATOR

Kristina Cordero is a translator of Spanish-language novels and nonfiction books. Her most recent translations include *Voyage Along the Horizon* by Javier Marías (Believer Books) and *The Eagle's Throne* by Carlos Fuentes (Random House). She is presently at work on a new translation, *The Essential Writings of St. Teresa of Avila*.